Triumph of the Market

Essays on Economics, Politics, and the Media

Edward S. Herman

South End Press

Boston

Cover design by Matt Wuerker
Text design and production by South End Press collective
Printed in the U.S.A.

Library of Congress Cataloging-in-Publication Data
Herman, Edward S.
   Triumph of the market : essays on economics, politics and the media / by Edward S. Herman
   p. cm.
   A majority of the essays were originally published in Z magazine between Dec. 1989 and Dec. 1994.
   Includes bibliographical references and index.
   ISBN 0-89608-522-8 : $40.00 – ISBN 0-89608-521-x (pbk.) : $16.00
   1. Capitalism. 2. Post-communism. 3. Mass media–Political aspects. 4. Political participation. 5. Economic history–1990- I. Title.
HB501.H466   1995
330.12'2–dc20   95-24733
                                                 CIP

South End Press, 116 Saint Botolph Street, Boston MA 02115

01 00 99 98 97 96 95 1 2 3 4 5 6 7 8 9

CONTENTS

Acronyms

AI	Amnesty International
AEI	American Enterprise Institute
CIA	U.S. Central Intelligence Agency
EC	European Community
EPA	Environmental Protection Agency
FCC	Federal Communication Commission
FDA	Food and Drug Administration
FHLBB	Federal Home Loan Bank Board (central bank for savings and loan associations)
GATT	General Agreement on Tariffs and Trade
IADB	Inter-American Development Bank
ICC	Interstate Commerce Commission
IFI	international financial institution
IMF	International Monetary Fund
LDC	less developed country
MIA	soldiers missing in action
NAFTA	North American Free Trade Agreement
NET	National Educational Television
NSS	National Security State
NWO	New World Order
OSHA	Occupational Safety and Health Agency
PAC	political action committee
POW	prisoner-of-war
PR	public relations

S&L   savings and loan association

SEC   Securities and Exchange Commission

TNC   transnational corporation

Preface

The unifying theme of the essays in this volume is the increasing national and global power and reach of the market and its growing impact on all aspects of human life. I use the phrase "the market" to denote both the corporate institutions that are the leading and dominant factors in production, trade, and finance, *and* the arrangements, mechanisms, and practices that permit and facilitate the buying and selling of goods and money. Thus, the "triumph of the market" refers to the sharp increase in power—and hegemonic position—of the dominant market participants *and* to the now almost universal acceptance of market exchanges and private ownership as the exclusive way of organizing economic life. The two senses of the market are intimately related.

As is implicit in the second sense of "the market," its triumph extends, importantly, to ideology and value systems. If, as the power of the market increases, nonmarket institutions and values weaken and options that conflict with market interests cease to be available, this has profound social and cultural implications. If the dominant institutions of the market want, above all else, to sell more goods, and relentlessly stress the importance of acquiring them, the values of material acquisition and individual satisfaction will be encouraged and the values of community, service to others, and human solidarity will be shunted aside. This has potentially grave implications for the ability of human societies to deal with the problems of mass poverty, growing inequality, and the environmental effects of economic growth and technological change, among other matters.

If the other great objective of the market is cost containment and reduction, in the interest of enhanced profit margins and price stability, this also has extremely important implications. Wages, employee benefits, environmental protection, business and investor taxes, and budget deficits are the targets of the attack on costs, which pits the market against labor, the welfare state, and ultimately democracy itself. The forms of democracy allow the majority to mobilize government to serve their interests and protect them from detrimental policies of the powerful, such as business efforts to reduce costs by firing labor organizers, skimping on safety measures, and dumping wastes in rivers. Democracy can be a problem for the market.

It is true that democracy did advance in the West and that the welfare state was constructed over the course of the past century (albeit by bitter struggle). But the market has won, at least for this historical moment, and as "end of history" ideologists have emphasized, we have entered a period of altered conditions and rapid change. Their own Pollyannaish vision of an enlarging sphere of "market democracies" and a new era of international peace and plenty, has already been contradicted by events before the close of the first post-Cold War decade. The market democracies are proving to be not very democratic; ethnic strife has increased markedly; and strong polarization and immiseration tendencies are obvious on a global scale.

It is becoming clearer by the day that the removal of the socialist threat, the globalization and new mobility of capital, and the weakening of organized labor, have created fresh opportunities for market advances and victories at the expense of the underlying population. Old implicit contracts between capital and labor for the sharing of productivity gains, acceptance of social democratic reforms, and live-and-let-live policies between institutional rivals, are being torn up and open class warfare has become more and more widespread.

This one-sided warfare in the United States is reflected in the aggressive bargaining for cuts in wages and benefits, ruthless firings and moves to non-union locales, many open violations of the law (but uncontested by the state),[1] the widespread use of lockouts and replacement workers, and the increasing demand (also in Europe) for "deregulation" of labor markets. It is manifest also in the deterioration of wages and working conditions for the majority of U.S. workers. One recent *Wall Street Journal* examination of job trends states that "While American industry reaps the benefits of a new, high-technology era, it has consigned a large class of workers to a Dickensian time warp, laboring not just for meager wages but under dehumanized and often dangerous conditions...[Many of these workers are] subject to Orwellian control and electronic surveillance, and reduced to limited tasks that are numbingly repetitive, potentially crippling and stripped of any meaningful skills or the chance to develop them."[2] The use of the word "Dickensian" has become commonplace in reports on New World Order conditions.[3]

The resurgent class warfare is also evident in the attempts to dismantle the welfare state in the United States, Great Britain, and increasingly in other European countries.[4] It can also be read in IMF loan conditions, which consistently impose on Third World (and ex-Soviet bloc) countries worker-damaging macro-policies, and attack the institutional power and policies of the welfare state. In short, the power of the market has kept governments across the globe on a short neoliberal leash. Unable to meet the demands of their majority constituents, as the market stigmatizes any moves that are not "market friendly," liberals and social democrats continue to fail, the political spectrum shifts steadily to the right, and the forms of democracy increasingly lack substance.

One of the major instruments of class warfare in the West is the increased ability of capital to use or threaten "delocalization" and "outsourcing"—that is, to move production in whole or part to the Third World to take advantage of low wages, poor working conditions, and minimal environmental regulation. This reduces costs by the move itself, or by the pressure the action or threat puts on wages, working conditions, and environmental regulation at home. While this process has brought jobs to many Third World areas, it has been at the expense of jobs at home; and the ability of the global corporations to move around and bargain, the large pools of underemployed labor, and the repressive conditions of Third World work have kept wages down and working conditions abysmal.[5] Global capital benefits enormously from this system in which it can bargain down all parties, at home and abroad. This is why income inequality, which in the West at least declined for a long period, has been on the upswing globally.

This book elaborates on these themes in various ways. Part One deals with economic trends, economic policy, and economic analysis proper, describing how market forces have extended their sway in the economy, culture, and within the economics profession itself. Part Two addresses the impact of the market on politics, along with reflections on contemporary political and historical issues and perspectives. Parts Three and Four deal with foreign policy and the media, respectively. In both parts the impact of market forces and market-linked interests is front and center.

A majority of the essays in this volume were published in *Z Magazine* between December 1989 and December 1994. I have edited and updated these (and the other essays) only slightly, mainly by footnote additions. A short epilogue brings some of the issues addressed here up to date and offers a final prognosis and policy agenda.

Part One
ECONOMICS

Chapter One

Commodification of Culture

The Deepening Market in the West (1)

While the members of the former Soviet bloc and China have gained accolades in the West for their rapid moves toward market economies, in the West itself the market extends daily into hitherto neglected areas and niches of opportunity. As was stressed by a well-known Old Mole of the last century, capital has a propensity to expand without limit, and nothing is sacred to it except profits and the market itself.

Market Expansion and Commodification

The market can grow by reaching into new geographic territories or by seeking out new customers in already occupied space; by filling in product gaps with new products; and by converting aspects of life that were once outside the market into marketable products (commodification). Commodification and privatization are overlapping categories. Goods that were provided free of charge by public authorities may be commodified by turning their production over to private parties, who will sell them at a price that covers costs and a profit margin.

The development of the computer and new telecommunications technologies has allowed markets to expand more rapidly: spatially, into new product-service areas, and in new applications in traditional sectors. These technological developments have reduced the cost of doing business at a distance and permitted a more detailed knowledge of business expenses, sales, and margins, and consumer behavior and preferences. Companies themselves have been commodified, in the "market for corporate control." In the 1980s, with the aid of junk bonds and a weakened anti-trust policy, ever larger firms were "brought into play" and bought and sold like pork bellies. If we add to this the greater ability of businesses to move around the world in search of a more favorable climate of investment, the vision of the large corporation as a stable institution rooted in the community, concerned with a variety of constituencies and social interests,[1] has become even more fanciful than in earlier years (when it had occasional application in mainly family-owned companies).

Underdeveloped Markets

The cigarette industry, which has run into obstacles and sluggish domestic growth, has targeted the Third World as an "underdeveloped market" and has been pursuing it aggressively for years. The same is true of the soft drink industry, which in recent years has had much higher growth rates abroad than at home. These businesses have also cultivated less developed market niches at home. R. J. Reynolds prepared a new cigarette honed to the African-American market in the 1980s, which it withdrew from test marketing in 1989 after sharp attacks by Black community leaders and the Secretary of Health and Human Services. The industry's attempt to entice women and children into the cigarette habit has been a durable scandal, oft criticized but continued without much impediment by virtue of the financial power, economic importance, and political muscle of the industry.

A 1988 report in the *Wall Street Journal* noted the penetration of soda pop into the Saturday morning children's TV "junk food ghetto, glutted with commercials pitching candy, fast food hamburgers and sugary cereals to children." Seven-Up broke the soft-drink barrier in children's commercials on the straightforward ground that "kids are an underdeveloped market"; children aged 12 and under account for only 15.8 percent of soft-drink consumption. Seven-Up toyed with the idea of a soft-drink specially adapted to children, with a bubble gum flavor, but finally opted for kid-oriented advertising.[2]

Creating Needs

Products are being created to fill any and every "need." In the financial sector, the public is now offered instruments designed to generate tax losses, tax exempt bonds in any state, "high yield" (i.e., junk) bonds, takeover stocks, swaps, options, options on options, and practically anything else you might want to name. In the real product and service markets, there are steady advances. The pet market in Manhattan offers rhinestone-studded T-shirts, leather fur-lined coats, and sequined tuxedos and dresses for dogs. As Erik Barnouw points out in *The Sponsor*, the market has established its own cosmography in which "the work of Creation has been largely a disaster, functionally and aesthetically." Fortunately, "man himself has invented products to correct the errors"—a whole industry, for example, has grown to make "skinny eyelashes" look thicker and longer. "For the unfortunate races on which Nature has bestowed curly hair, man has developed straightening products; for those with the humiliating heritage of straight hair, curling products. Hair is almost always wrongly colored: dark hair must be bleached, white hair darkened; fortunately, products are available for both problems .... Man has been especially inventive about odors; he has identified and named special odors for almost every zone of the body from 'bad breath' to 'foot odor.' All require special products and commercials for them, including vaginal sprays."[3]

A more sinister set of markets has evolved in products and services for which the demand is strong but whose provision runs counter to ethical norms and existing law. For example, prostitution is one of the booming markets in the New World Order—a multi-billion dollar industry, with finders, brokers, syndicate operations, and pimp "managers" at the scene of the action, but increasingly globalized. Transactions in this business have even been carried out on a credit-card basis in a sophisticated country like Great Britain.[4] Typically, poor people and people from distressed countries serve the demands of the rich in these markets. In poverty-stricken Northern Brazil, some 2,000 young women, mainly between the ages of nine and fifteen, serve a sex/tourism industry with a mainly foreign clientele.[5] Russian, Eastern European, and Asian entrepreneurs and syndicates have supplied thousands of women and children to Western European, Middle Eastern and Japanese sex industries. A large fraction of these recruits were induced into service by misrepresentation or coercion; many of the young were literally sold into bondage.[6]

In the development of an "international division of labor," a country like Thailand has evolved from a "rest and recreation" center for GIs during the Vietnam War into a global sexual service station. In one UNESCO estimate, two million Thai females work as prostitutes, 800,000 of them children or adolescents. Some 30,000 Thai women serve the Japanese market in Japan itself, an estimated 60 percent against their will and unable to escape because of the power of their exploiters.[7] The market has been especially strong for children and virgins, who are "safer" for the customers, and many of the eight- to thirteen-year-old children in Manila, Bangkok, Rio de Janeiro and Brussels are hawked by their pimps as "clean." Young Asian girls recruited for service in the West are often trained in advance in places like Cyprus.[8]

There are also local and international markets for exotic birds and research animals, human body parts,[9] babies for adoption,[10] and even hired mercenaries and terrorists. Many of these markets are *sub rosa* and illegal, but are tolerated or attacked only sporadically and selectively. Sometimes they are even encouraged and funded by governments, as in the case of Latin American death squads in the 1970s and 1980s,[11] the contra war against Nicaragua in the 1980s,[12] and the "Strategy of Tension" in Italy in the 1960s.[13] In each of these cases governments encouraged and/or funded and protected terrorists in a system of covert warfare, partially hidden and more or less plausibly denied.

The Commodification of Culture

In fact, every aspect of culture is in a process of commodification and linkage to the sale of goods. Sports events have been seized by commercial interests as vehicles for marketing, and the force of the market has diminished the element of play in sport. Players as well as managers and owners are increasingly becoming businesspersons/celebrities, and the sports page more and more belongs in the business section of the newspaper. Big-name players make as much or more money via endorsements and commercial appearances as in contracts to play.

The games themselves are increasingly dominated by the demands of the market—the National Football League (NFL) has reportedly been considering moving to an eighteen- instead of a sixteen-week schedule to "better position the product," in the words of one NFL official. Pauses in the game are dictated as much by advertising needs as by the demands of the participants, and advertisers' logos steadily increase their presence—extending to the names of the events, the ads shown in the stadiums and on players' attire, as well as in the increasingly frequent ads within the TV programs. Tennis, formerly a gentlemanly amateur sport, has been transformed by television and money into a professional entertainment vehicle, with playing time schedules and venues dictated by market (and especially TV) demands.

The Olympic Games held in Los Angeles in 1984 were a turning point in the commercialization of that traditional international competition. With television and radio audiences for the games now reaching several billion, the aggressive selling of the audience and marketing of events, heroes, teams, logos, and tied-in merchandise has inevitably followed. The winter games have been shifted so that there will be an Olympics every two years, in accord with the demands of television and the Olympic Committee's drive for greater TV revenue and sponsorship. As Stuart F. Cross, marketing vice-president of Coca-Cola, stated recently, "The Olympics is *all* business." Nations and cities bid for the right to host the games, with a 60 percent cut of broadcasting rights proceeds; transnational corporations (TNCs) buy ad time and rights to market logos and merchandise; and thousands of locals who stand in the way are forced out of their homes to make room for temporary facilities and progress.[14]

In movies and television, brand-name products are used, for a price, in program materials. Since 1982, "product placement" has become institutionalized in movies, with the price now averaging about $50,000 per item/incident.[15] By 1994 product placement had entrenched itself in video games, where "the new advertising is being embraced by game makers as a possible cash cow." A report on this development cites critics saying that "the arrival of advertising in computer games is wiping out one of the last havens children have against commercial messages."[16]

In a further advance of the market into TV, in 1994 a weekly program called "Main Floor" "[took] viewers into department stores to show them the latest fashion and beauty trends, while quietly steering them to specific merchandise that sponsors have paid to promote on the show." There were commercial breaks as well, but the body of the show displayed Paloma Picasso talking about "her new men's fragrance" and "a Lee representative [talked] about the problems women have buying jeans that fit, while also pushing its fall line." That Lee (etc.) paid for time on the show is only disclosed when the final credits are displayed.[17] In magazines, also, the distinction between advertising and editorial material has been eroding under the force of competition for ads, and advertisers' pressures for editorial "support" that will "add value" to the space they buy. Beyond "advertorials," in which ads mimic editorials, we now have "funded journalism," in which articles are paid for by advertisers who gear the story's topic and tone toward the needs of their advertisements.

The market has had a significant effect on culture through the broader impact of commercialization and sponsorship on TV programming. Advertisers want large audiences and a congenial environment for selling goods, and owners strive to provide these, with "lethal effects" on noncommercial values.[18] The long-term drift of programming has been away from the thoughtful, profound, and controversial (which would disturb the sales pitch), away from serious public affairs programming (which draws relatively small audiences), and toward light entertainment. Sex and violence, which sell well both at home and abroad, have been given a large place in TV, just as children's programming has steadily eroded in quantity and quality (see Chapter Twenty-Two).

The global market has been enormously receptive to U.S. movies, rock music, and other U.S. expressions and dreams of individual freedom and rebellion, and wealth and power. In some respects these elements of popular culture *have* been liberating, both ideologically and as a release from suffocatingly narrow environments. But these products are mere entertainment in the form of fun, games, and fairy tales; and to a great extent their huge global audience reflects the global decline in family and civil life, and loss of faith in politics. As Barnet and Cavanagh express it,

> Popular culture acts as a sponge to soak up spare time and energy that in earlier times might well have been devoted to nurturing and instructing children or to participating in political, religious, civic, or community activities or in crafts, reading, and continuing self-education. But such pursuits sound a bit old-fashioned today, although political theory still rests on the assumption that these activities are central to the functioning of a democratic society. Yet increasingly, vicarious experience via film, video, and music is a substitute for civic life and community. As it becomes harder for young people in many parts of the world to carve out satisfying roles, the rush of commercial sounds and images offers escape.[19]

The market has moved slowly but steadily into the schools, where the business community has long offered educational aids in the form of printed and video materials on their companies, products, and industries, and on the principles of free enterprise. More recently, companies have entered into "partnership" relationships with schools, some 40 percent of all public schools now receiving modest assistance on this basis. The business community vigorously supports political parties and leaders who defund the schools, and bargains and fights for lower local taxes, but then gallantly offers small change to alleviate the troubling "crisis in the schools"![20]

A notable development of recent years was Whittle Communications' offer of free equipment to schools in exchange for the right to show students a news broadcast containing advertising. This camel's nose under the tent has been accepted by thousands of financially strapped schools,[21] and the advertisement as part of the formal educational package has thus found a home. Schools are also selling advertising space on school buses, sport scoreboard logos, and on acrylic-faced billboards in school restrooms, as well as the right to blare music with commercials into hallways and lunchrooms.[22]

Even more important has been the powerful thrust toward "school choice" via vouchers and an enlargement of the private sector in competition with public schools. Entrepreneurs, including Whittle, have come forward to take over schooling responsibilities on a contract basis. These privatizing developments weaken support for public schools, leaving many of them to service the urban poor without adequate resources, while the more affluent attend better financed suburban public schools or private schools.

Playgrounds have been increasingly commodified, providing "security zones" as well as an array of entertainment and food attractions for children and their anxious parents. In a polarizing society, where crime is an important and rational choice for large numbers at the bottom, and safe community play space is not supplied by the state, those who can afford it simply *buy* it. Private playgrounds are smaller versions of theme parks, which are controlled environments heavily oriented toward selling goods. A major playground provider is Discovery Zone (DZ). Selling under the brand name Discovery Zone Fun Centers, it plans to expand globally in the next five years. DZ is affiliated with Blockbuster Entertainment Corporation, which operates music stores, game stores, movie studios, and home entertainment centers, as well as playgrounds. Its head, Wayne Huizenga, states that "our goal is to drive traffic from one Blockbuster business to another."[23]

Museums and libraries have also been integrated more closely into the market. Debora Silverman's *Selling Culture* featured the coordination of the New York Metropolitan Museum of Art's exhibits on China and pre-revolutionary France with Bloomingdale's featured sales of items of the same genre.[24] Both the department store and the museum were being advised by the late Diane Vreeland, a longtime editor of *Vogue* magazine and consultant to both Bloomingdale's and the museum's exhibitions. The latter lacked historical or social context, and seemed like museum versions of sales campaigns.

More generally, museums have increasingly felt the need to obtain corporate sponsorship for exhibits, and thus to adjust their overall orientation to attract this primary source of funding. Corporate expenditures on the arts rose from under $100 million in 1970 to more than $500 million in the early 1990s. One curator noted that "most corporate sponsors finance exhibitions based on centrist ideals and uncontroversial subject matter." Artist and radical critic of museums, Hans Haacke, has stated that "shows that could promote critical awareness, present products of consciousness dialectically and in relation to the social world, or question relations of power, have a slim chance of being approved ...self-censorship is having a boom."[25]

Commodification of Information

The technological revolution in "informatics" has not only made it possible to use information more extensively and intensively within the business world and for social control, it has made information itself more marketable. The result has been a further commodification of information. Data bases in all kinds of fields have multiplied. This "for sale" information is collected and formatted in accordance with the needs of the parties best able to buy it. Public libraries are increasingly by-passed as repositories of information, and they have had to subscribe to some of the new private information services. The "free" library is thus on its way out, as libraries are compelled to impose charges for access to privately controlled information. They are also suffering from severe financial stringency as a result of servicing a disproportionately non-elite clientele in financially stressed urban areas.

Another important development has been the tendency to reduce and privatize information collected by the government, much of which was traditionally subsidized as valuable to the public and fitting the concept of a "public good." For a public good, one person's use does not interfere with that of another person, so that imposing a price restricts use unnecessarily and the market "fails" when price is used as a rationing device.[26] In the 1980s, government-collected information was increasingly turned over to private users to sell on their own terms (even back to the government at a price). So in this "information age" information has been more and more privatized and commodified, its public good quality ignored, in the interest of serving "the market." This strengthens the position of those able to control and pay for such information (i.e., the business sector, especially its larger units), and weakens the position of the general public.

Internet provides a significant new, partially noncommercial means of communication that has a global reach and potentially links together millions of people. It does, however, require ownership of a computer, technical knowhow, means of access to Internet through a linked provider, and knowledge of other users sharing common interests. It is therefore a system serving relatively isolated and elite individuals and small groups, not large numbers of unorganized and non-elite people. Furthermore, its commercial exploitation is being aggressively explored and experimented with by commercial interests, who are likely to make major inroads (and help inundate the system) over the next decade.[27]

Advertising and Public Relations

While traditional, hard information is being commodified and subject to rationing by price, advertising and public relations (PR) expenditures have been growing at a steady clip. We may crudely generalize: hard data is being reserved for business and the "cognitive elite"; the information sector made increasingly available to the masses as public goods (with no direct charge) is *so* "soft" it is hokum.

Advertising is the subsidized message provided by sellers of goods to facilitate sale. PR is its institutional counterpart. These self-serving and inherently biased forms of communication are dominant in modern market economies and are geared to the demands of the owners/managers of firms that pay for them. They reinforce the values of acquisition, consumption, and accumulation, and marginalize values of noncommercial interest (community, equality, ethical concerns, the sacredness of life and nature) although advertisers regularly make opportunistic use of these values for their own advantage. They have had a profound effect on the broadcasting media and the political process, as will be discussed in later chapters.

—Z, March 1990

Chapter Two

Deregulation

The Deepening Market in the West (2)

Another manifestation of the deepening market in the West is the weakening of regulatory controls over business, sometimes under explicit "deregulation" campaigns. This is not all bad. In the transport industries the old regulatory systems protected vested interests at a high efficiency and consumer cost. The unleashing of competition has brought about shakeouts and rationalization of these industries and, on balance, consumer benefits. On the other hand, competition, plus the virtual abandonment of anti-trust limits on mergers, has resulted in greater concentration in the air transport industry, and monopoly pricing and output results have already appeared. Furthermore, transport is a sector in which the negative externalities[1] of autos, trucks, and airplanes (smog, noise, poor land use) warrant significant taxation of those responsible, along with public investment in rail and urban transit systems. But public transit is undernourished in the West, especially in countries like the United States and Great Britain, where short-term business interests and right-wing ideologies have had a dominant policy influence. In the financial sector, these interests and ideologies, in conjunction with market developments, have been even more costly and threatening.

Old and New Regulation

The classic model of the old, traditional regulation was the railroad industry, placed under commission regulation with the Interstate Commerce Act of 1887. Other important industries subject to this kind of regulation have been electric power, broadcasting, trucking, and airlines (although only the first of these remains under commission regulation with any bite). There has been a long-standing dispute as to whether this kind of regulation has given consumers any substantial protection from monopolistic abuse, and whether this has offset its anti-competitive features. There is little disagreement, however, that over time regulatory bodies like the Interstate Commerce Commission (ICC) have tended to be "captured" by the regulated firms and have often served mainly as their protectors and even protagonists.[2] The net public benefits from such regulation have therefore been exceedingly small, if they have existed at all.

The "new" regulation is not industry-specific, but deals with issues that cross industry lines, like consumer and worker safety, environmental protection, the honesty of claims made by issuers of securities, and food and drug safety. Although regulation in several of these areas goes back a long way, in many it originated or blossomed in recent decades, reflecting the growth and recognition of the costs of the externalities of modern industry. The agencies regulating these sectors are a tad more independent than the old ones, and the business outcries about government being on "our" backs have been addressed more to these new forms of regulation than the old. Interestingly, the new regulation, while costly to business, sometimes provides large net benefits to the public; the old regulation, essentially government-sponsored cartels, was often very costly to the public but produced substantial net benefits to the regulated firms.

The Weakness of Regulation in the United States

Business regulation has always been weak in the United States and subject to periodic debilitation in business-sponsored counter-revolutions. This reflects the power of the business community, its individualistic ethos and hostility to government encroachment on its prerogatives, and its opportunism and short time horizon.[3] These attitudes have helped make government service of low esteem and quality and the word bureaucrat an epithet. The business community uses government for its immediate purposes (e.g., export loans, bargaining for tariff breaks, research subsidies), but seeks to gut it and render it ineffectual when it serves primarily public interests.

These attitudes have also made regulatory bodies more easily and cynically captured or paralyzed by the firms subject to their authority. This is done by getting friends of industry on regulatory commissions, obtaining legislation that immobilizes the agency (e.g., requiring expensive and time-consuming investigations, hearings, and court appeals before any substantial action can be taken against regulated firms), and getting damaging cuts in appropriations imposed on those agencies taking aggressive and effective actions.[4]

The Reagan Regulatory Counter-Revolution

In 1981, the business community expected the newly elected president Ronald Reagan to weaken and reduce the costs of regulation. This was done with alacrity and ideological fervor, illustrating well business's parochialism and truncated time horizon. The business community was willing to see agencies like the Environmental Protection Agency (EPA) gutted, and others like the Occupational Safety and Health Agency (OSHA), Food and Drug Administration (FDA), Securities and Exchange Commission (SEC), and Federal Home Loan Bank Board (FHLBB) seriously weakened in the interest of short-term gain. In pumping large resources into Reagan's campaign, the business community and the "market" simply *bought* the impairment of important sectors of the regulatory system, which were defunded and staffed with ideologues and hacks hostile to the regulatory mission,[5] thereby demoralizing committed and quality bureaucrats and inducing them to leave the public service.

This couldn't have been done without the cooperation of the mass media. With regard to the EPA and environmental issues, for example, the media played down the fact that the public was anxious to protect the environment even during the Reagan era[6]; dealt cursorily with the gross conflicts of interest in regulatory agency appointments and vested interest contributions to the party and officials in power; and virtually ignored the steady damage being inflicted on EPA.[7] Only with the Rita Lavelle scandal and departure of EPA head Anne Gorsuch Burdon did the press give substantial attention to EPA, characteristically focusing on a scandal and personalities while continuing to ignore the real story.[8]

The Savings and Loan Industry:
Deregulation, Reregulation and Bailout

The Reagan-Bush era crisis of the savings and loan (S&L) industry provides an important illustration of the nature of deregulation, the thoughtlessness of its design, and its consequences.[9] The S&L crisis has not run its course, and some of its features apply to the banking and insurance industries. The partially deregulated and globalizing financial sector is the possible locus of even more sensational debacles in the future.

The S&L industry was sponsored and protected by the government for many years, to allow it to make mortgage loans that the banks did not care to provide. In exchange for legal confinement to mortgage lending, and other restrictive regulations, the S&Ls received government deposit insurance and subsidized loans from the S&L central bank, the FHLBB. Their shares, essentially deposits, were eventually made payable on demand, while their assets were largely long-term mortgages. This imbalance in the maturities of their assets and liabilities made the S&Ls vulnerable to sharp increases in interest rates, which would drive up the costs of their liabilities but not affect the rates on their long-term (mortgage) assets. They were thus highly speculative ventures, dependent on continuing low interest rates. When interest rates rose in the late 1970s, the S&Ls were in trouble, and when rates skyrocketed in the Reagan-Volker tight money crunch of 1981, they were in desperate trouble. Deregulation during this period allowed S&Ls to raise rates on their deposits, but not on their mortgage assets, causing severe operating losses.

This "first crisis"—of high interest rates—caused numerous failures and left many of the remaining S&Ls badly damaged, with eroded capital. In the midst of this first phase, moreover, the Reagan administration, Congress, and several key states like California and Texas sanctioned further deregulation. Most critically, they allowed the weakened S&Ls to make more risky investments, such as the purchase of junk bonds, land investment, and construction loans. Meanwhile, they maintained government insurance on deposits and even allowed the development of "brokered deposits," in which S&Ls could raise large sums by selling government-insured deposits through brokers, at a fee, to anybody. This set the stage for a second and larger crisis, as the already weakened S&Ls with low net worth had little to lose in "going for broke" with risky investments funded by government insured deposits. Heads they win, tails the taxpayers lose.

As the final ingredient in the Reagan-era recipe for disaster, the early 1980s witnessed a substantial cutback in the FHLBB examiner force, in line with the general cutbacks in regulatory appropriations. This made it increasingly difficult to monitor and respond to the deteriorating quality of industry assets and the influx of crooks and self-dealing builders eager to take advantage of the new opportunities.

There was strong evidence from at least 1984 that the second crisis of fraud and excessive risk-taking was brewing. The insurance fund of the Federal Savings and Loan Insurance Corporation shriveled quickly, and the authorities had neither the money nor personnel to close down insolvent S&Ls. Knowledge of this regulatory paralysis induced further entry of crooks and additional fraud. Not wanting to divert money from such pet projects as the Salvadoran army, the CIA, Star Wars, and Stealth Bombers, the Reagan administration ignored this growing disaster up to the end of Reagan's term in office. The press remained similarly quiet. Until Bush decided to bite the bullet upon entering office, the media hardly remarked on the second crisis, once again discovering a problem only when officials gave them the word. At no point has the media directed attention to the fact that the Reagan administration allowed the problem to fester for years to avoid a budget entry.

The chairman of the FHLBB from 1984-86, Edwin Gray, fought a lonely battle to reimpose regulatory controls and increase the vigor of regulation as the second thrift crisis grew. But he was frustrated by the industry, the Reagan administration, Congress, and the media. *Re*regulation, as is so common, came too late, and the bill to the taxpayer for bailing out the insured industry is large and still growing. The leaders of the establishment have never suggested that the beneficiaries of the Reagan-era income counter-revolution pay for the Reagan-era debacle; it is taken for granted that ordinary taxpayers will foot this bill. The Resolution Trust, established in 1989 to dispose of the assets of failed institutions, moved slowly in the face of personnel and legal problems and soft real-estate markets.

The Threat of Deregulation

Regulatory systems everywhere have been challenged and weakened by the growth of international competition, which has pressed individual firms to reduce costs, including wages, social benefits, and regulatory expenses. Governments at all levels have been put in a poor bargaining position by the greater mobility of capital, and their revenue bases have been eroded by competition, threats to move, and the actual movement of facilities to places offering the best regulatory deals (so-called "regulatory arbitrage"). Regulatory systems are weaker just as their problems have become more complex and urgent.

Deregulation poses a major threat to overall economic stability. Financial markets, under the impetus of the profit-motive and competition, and in environments of prosperity and euphoria, have always tended to take on more and more risk, until the bubble bursts.[10] Weakened regulation, the internationalization of financial markets, and competition on a global basis have encouraged even greater risk taking. This has been helped along further by the continuation of deposit insurance in the United States and virtual government guarantees that the largest financial institutions will not be permitted to fail.

The world's financial institutions have moved from one area of high risk and speculative investment to another in their search for fat profit margins, and they have vast holdings of risky debt. The enormous development of the derivatives market in the past decade is the latest new product yet to be tested in a crisis where such instruments might "require selling in a falling market."[11] The deregulation of financial systems has put more responsibility on central banks and governments to prevent large-scale disaster. But there is no international central bank or lender of last resort to support a highly interdependent global financial system in serious crises. While the small shocks thus far encountered have been dealt with effectively, the world financial system is vulnerable as never before and has yet to be subjected to a major test. Our first global crash may well be a historic landmark of the turn of the century.

—Z, June 1990

Chapter Three

Privatization

The Deepening Market in the West (3)

Like "reform," which the mainstream media and intellectuals equate with moves toward an unregulated, private market system, "privatization" is a key word in the lexicon of the New World Order. It means transferring the ownership of public sector properties to the private sector. This would appear to be in full accord with the theory of capitalism, in which private ownership and the quest for profits are seen as the dynamic of the system. The rationales for privatization stress allegedly greater efficiency of privately owned and managed assets and a free and competitive market.

The Principle of Opportunism

In the actual history of capitalism, however, public ownership has played a substantial role, and state intervention in other forms such as subsidization, protection from competition, the underwriting of risk, and the carving out of foreign markets by imperialist wars, has been of enormous importance and integral to the rise of the great capitalist states (for an admirable summary, see Noam Chomsky's *Year 501*, chaps. 1 and 4). The essential principle operative in defining the relation of private capital to the state has been *opportunism*: that is, the state has been mobilized as needed for a vast number of services, funded by the general taxpayer but benefiting important business interests.

Privatization is rediscovered and pressed in periods when business interests see a net advantage in the liquidation of publicly owned assets and *de*-mobilizing state functions. It may also be imposed on client and weak states as part of a strategy of neo-imperial reconquest. It is always explained, however, in terms of improving efficiency.

Efficiency

The greater efficiency of privately owned property is assumed without question in the mainstream press, but has no solid basis in theory or historical practice. The evidence on the relative efficiency of state versus privately owned and managed properties is mixed. Some state owned businesses have done very well on standard efficiency criteria when given substantial autonomy and headed by qualified personnel committed to the public service.[1] Many cases of public enterprise failure can be attributed to the damaging political influence of the private sector, which can affect personnel and rewards, and impose constraints on public-sector operations.

A proof put forward for the inefficiency of public enterprise is the losses that such firms often suffer. But public enterprises often suffer losses because governments limit their activities, force them to produce and maintain work forces even at a loss, and limit their price-setting discretion. In Latin America, public enterprises have been in the forefront of "inflation control," by virtue of government limits on the price increases of these government controlled entities. "Privatizing" often involves ruthless trimming of the work force and freedom to raise prices. But shifting workers from making steel sold at a loss to the dole does not improve social efficiency, nor do price increases, even though both may improve private profit and loss statements and the nominal efficiency of the single firm.

In principle, public enterprises are better positioned to take account of social costs and benefits than private firms. Radio and TV broadcasting provide a dramatic illustration of a social (and externalities related) balance sheet favorable to the public sector (see Chapter Twenty-Two below). As another example, the U.S. drug industry spends more on sales promotion than research, and much of its research is devoted to duplicative and imitative drugs rather than drugs that break new ground. A publicly owned drug industry would have a different priority system. It might also not charge all that the traffic will bear. The wastes and abuses of the private drug industry result in a huge margin of *social* inefficiency that a public agency would not suffer. Given the importance of government sponsored and nonprofit based drug research globally, it is not at all clear that basic drug research would suffer under a regime of public ownership.

Another social advantage of public enterprise, especially important in the Third World, rests on the great importance of firm size and resources for technical efficiency, and on the value of building backward and forward linkages for the development of an overall technological base in a country.[2] Foreign multinationals establish limited function branch plants in dependent economies and do not encourage forward and backward integration, unless compelled to do so. General

Agreement on Tariffs and Trade (GATT) and North American Free Trade Agreement (NAFTA) rules limiting price discrimination in the sale of raw materials (i.e., charging higher prices to foreigners for timber or oil) or the unequal treatment of non-nationals are designed to prevent Third World countries from encouraging forward integration into refining and manufacturing by indigenous firms, and will help keep these countries in their status of "hewers of wood and drawers of water."

A government enterprise like the Mexican national oil company PEMEX was for many years a major source of indigenous capital, an increasingly important refiner of oil, a developer of a domestic petrochemical industry, a promoter of Mexican-produced pipes and other supplies, and it carried out a low-price policy on energy and fertilizers in the perceived interest of national economic development. Largely for these reasons PEMEX was long considered a sinister threat to the "global interest" by the World Bank and international oil companies.[3]

Competition

It is frequently assumed, without evidence, that privatization increases competition. But when the Tennessee Valley Authority (TVA) was organized in the 1930s, it broke up the tacit cartel-like high pricing policy of the private electric utilities in the Tennessee Valley (and beyond), and was hated by private companies because it *increased* competition.[4] As many U.S. and global markets have few sellers (oligopolies), and as private oligopolists often collude, publicly owned firms can disturb cozy and collective private market arrangements. Privatization therefore can easily lead to reduced competition.

Many years ago the U.S. government did weapons research and produced many of its weapons in government arsenals. This was gradually phased out in favor of the "contract state" in which all research and production was farmed out to private sellers. But without an in-house production and research capability the government's bargaining position was reduced. It no longer had the option of producing for itself, and without the expertise of a manufacturing and research operation the government became a less knowledgeable buyer and could be taken advantage of more easily.[5]

Since 1932, under business pressure, Congress has made periodic surveys to see whether government businesses are competing with private enterprise and whether any government activities can be turned over to the private sector. The underlying legislation supporting these surveys and the philosophy involved are strikingly hostile to competition.[6] Furthermore, when the government has built or taken over facilities during wartime, or after bailouts of the private sector, it has always disposed of them quickly, and usually without disturbing the pre-existing patterns of large firm domination. The government's huge World War II production facilities were sold soon after the War's end in such a way as to slightly enhance the power of the dominant firms.[7] Government holdings in the power industry (dating from the 1930s) have not been divested, but their scope has been sharply restricted and they have been forced to avoid any competitive threat to private utilities. In short, the record of privatization in the United States suggests, on balance, a drive to reduce rather than enlarge competition.

Privatization: the Looting Imperative

Privatization has become an important element in Western and International Monetary Fund (IMF) regimens for ailing Third World debtors, as well as for Russia and her former satellites. The nominal reason is to cut losses and improve efficiency. The *real* reasons, however, are to help pay off bills incurred by bailouts, to allow local compradors and transnational corporations (TNCs) to buy up valuable public assets at favorable prices, and to weaken Third World states and lock them more securely into the global market system.

Regarding the bailouts, many Third World governments, including those of Chile, Mexico, and Argentina, under the pressure of Western banks and governments, took over or agreed to guarantee service on private debts held abroad in the early 1980s, exacerbating an already severe fiscal crisis. Economist David Felix estimates that for Latin America as a whole, between 1982 and 1987, government guaranteed loans increased from 40 percent to 85 percent of the total, with the bailout of foreign creditors adding some $44 billion to public debts.[8] Felix also points out that this coerced rewriting of contracts, which shifted part of the debt burden to Third World governments and taxpayers, "was a power play that violated both capitalistic moralizing about the inviolability of contracts and social norms of fairness."[9]

It also violated the principle of accountability that supposedly made private ownership efficient. The IMF, for example, had argued for privatization on the grounds that private owners would have assets at risk and would therefore behave carefully and rationally. Bailouts, however, reduce or eliminate the need to evaluate risks with care. This was one of the arguments against the Mexican bailout of 1995, outweighed by the ability of the investors threatened with losses to mobilize the U.S. government and IMF to socialize their risks, after the fact.[10] Felix notes that in 1982, when the banks demanded government guarantees as a condition for rescheduling Chile's debt, "the IMF offered no public objection and privately urged acceptance of the bank demands. Saving the banks on their terms apparently took precedence for the IMF over doctrinal consistency."[11]

It is not well known in the United States that Latin American governments—especially in countries that had vigorously pushed economic "liberalization" in the 1970s, such as Chile, Argentina, and Uruguay—engaged in massive bailouts of *domestic* banks and other business firms in the 1980s. This involved very large transfers of income and wealth from taxpayers to the bailed out private sector firms; in one estimate, the bailout costs in Chile from 1982 through 1988 amounted to one-third of the gross domestic product.[12] The large financial burdens incurred by Latin governments with the bailout of failing firms *and* the pressured takeover of private foreign debt obligations constituted a major socialization of private losses, clearly incompatible with the principles of private markets.

The rush to privatize government assets in Latin America was in part a money-raising expedient of governments under extreme fiscal pressure. It has also been a sop to local allies of the government and foreign creditors looking for real assets to buy with paper claims that were shrinking in market value. These asset sales reduce future income of the selling governments in order to serve short-run fiscal needs and the demands of privileged local and external financial interests. The loss is compounded by the fact that the assets are often sold at bargain-basement prices. Having renationalized by bailout in 1982-84, the Pinochet government then privatized these assets once again at well below real value in the years 1985-88, using half the proceeds for non-revenue generating uses like tax reductions.[13] This was a double whammy of service to the elite, with fiscal losses in the future to be paid by ordinary taxpayers.

In Mexico, Salinas' bank privatization program alone brought in $12.4 billion by 1992, and this and other sales gave the government a short-term fiscal boost, sufficient to prevent any deluge until after NAFTA was in place. The spectacular rise in number of billionaires in Mexico during the Salinas era, from two to twenty-four, can only be explained by the corruption in the privatization process. Where Latin American privatization has involved the exchange of government assets for government debt, the paper has frequently been accepted at face value, even though available on the market at heavy discounts. Little or no up-front cash has been demanded of the buyers. The "market friendly" Menem government of Argentina sold off its national airline in a paper trade at face value, with no down payment, to Iberia, the Spanish government airline, and then allowed the "privatized" airline to buy up its main Argentinean competitor. Funny privatization (sold to a foreign government); funny route to competition; and funny way to raise money.

The U.S. establishment and press have not looked too closely at the privatization *process*. Even under favorable circumstances, where governments are stable and preserve some autonomy and integrity, fairly priced and non-privileged sales of public assets are exceptional. Where governments are weak, dependent, and corrupt (Argentina, Pinochet's Chile, Brazil, Mexico), and where conditions are also chaotic and unfamiliar (Russia and Poland), massive theft is highly probable. In Russia, the widespread seizure of public property by former Community Party officials, referred to in Moscow as "nomenklatura privatization," has been "quietly sanctioned by liberal reformers... as the only politically feasible means of breaking with Russia's 70-year Communist legacy."[14] According to economist and member of the soviet's presidium, Yurii Marenvich, "Not only is the people's property being given away free of charge, but it is being appropriated by the very individuals entrusted to manage their property....All the members of the soviet's executive committee set up private companies that they themselves headed."[15] But as these developments are in accord with Western establishment interests, the media avert their eyes from "really existing privatization" (the title of the interview with Marenich) and keep repeating that privatization equals "reform."

Establishment interests also call for downplaying the huge Latin American capital flight by the privileged, much of it stolen and/or evading taxes. Felix estimates that for Argentina, Mexico, and Venezuela, the stock of privately owned foreign assets roughly equals the countries' foreign debts.[16] In other words, effective national mobilization of those assets could extricate these countries from the debt crisis. It has been pointed out by Felix and other critical analysts that during World War I and II countries like Great Britain required their citizens to declare ownership of foreign assets, forced their exchange for domestic government bonds, and used the proceeds to help fund the Wars. Latin American countries cannot do this, despite their terrible economic conditions and the enormous volume and dubious conditions of accumulation of their flight capital, because they are themselves parts of corruption machines, and because their neo-colonial parents (the United States, IMF, and World Bank) essentially impose on them rules requiring "free markets" and freely repatriated profits, and prohibiting capital controls.[17] In this thoroughgoing system of elite and transnational corporate privilege, the private sectors' foreign liabilities and domestic insolvencies can be (and have been) socialized, but their private assets can not even be effectively subjected to taxes.

–Z, April 1993

Chapter Four

Survival of the Fattest

Jobs Through Improving the Investment Climate at Home and Abroad

Bill Clinton's high-stake commitment to passage of the North American Free Trade Agreement (NAFTA) has to be seen in the context of the new global economic order, the new constraints on economic policy that it entails, and the limited options for encouraging economic growth that it leaves open for an establishment politician. Not only Third World clients of the IMF but the great powers themselves have lost much of their control over domestic economic policy. Using traditional Keynesian policy measures to alleviate large-scale unemployment would elicit damaging capital market repercussions, and the new, more conservative and business-oriented internal power alignments, strengthened by privatization and the weakening of organized labor, have increased the pressure toward a focus on inflation control, budget constraints, and otherwise helping to improve the investment climate.

Jobs

George Bush, Bill Clinton, the business leadership, and media have talked incessantly about "jobs, jobs, jobs." Secretary of State James Baker even asserted that protecting jobs was a goal of the Persian Gulf War. This creates an impression of devotion to the interests of ordinary citizens that is remarkably hypocritical. We are in a period when the "reserve army of labor" is steadily increasing in the "Free World," and wages, working conditions, and employee security are deteriorating. This is all functional in a globalizing capitalist order, which explains why it is allowed to proceed without anything serious being done about it.

In the evolving New World Order (NWO) jobs can only be provided by private, profit-making businesses; government enterprise is being liquidated globally, its legitimacy as a producer of social goods is shrinking, and government responsibility for the unemployed is under wide attack. The government is no longer accepted as the employer of last resort, and its support systems like unemployment compensation are under assault because they interfere with a "free labor market." The phrase "free labor market" is the NWO euphemism for "absence of labor bargaining power and social protection." In a "free labor market" an isolated and unprotected worker bargains one-on-one with General Electric.

The key measure of societal concern with a problem is the directness and magnitude of the effort made to deal with it. The absence of any direct attack on unemployment as it increases steadily, and the reliance on the trickle-down effects of policies serving business to deal with it, tells us clearly that jobs are not a first-order national or global priority, although the establishment leadership may worry about social instability and feedback effects on themselves of massive unemployment. They are not worried enough as yet, however. After the Los Angeles uprising of 1992, the U.S. Conference of Mayors proposed a $35 billion spending program, which identified 7,200 public works projects on hold that, if implemented, would have created an estimated 418,000 jobs. Clinton's proposals for direct grants and tax incentives for enterprise zones over a four-year period totalled $3.5 billion, and another $6 billion was to be allocated to housing expenditures. Even this puny set of proposals was drastically cut after legislative attack and subsequent compromises.

But although the priorities are clear, as a majority of people have a greater stake in jobs than business profitability, it is good public relations for the elite to pretend that jobs are their deepest concern and to make them a proxy for the objective that commands first attention. But when jobs and profitability conflict, and it is not possible to increase jobs within a frame of accepted business and profitability rules, jobs are sacrificed, as we are witnessing globally today.

Business's Non-Responsibility

While business has become the sole acceptable job provider, it has no *responsibility* to protect jobs and workers. Sacred though jobs allegedly are, the institutions that have been eliminating them by the scores of thousands for their own private profit advantage are never condemned for this in mainstream comment; they are even complimented for having taken steps to improve efficiency, productivity, and "competitiveness." There are daily news reports to the effect that "GTE to trim 13% of workers" in a "restructuring" and "Procter to shed 1,800 jobs in planned cutback" looking toward greater "efficiency." One "trims" excess fat off a piece of meat, and a snake "sheds" its obsolete skin as a new one takes its place. The euphemisms, including purr words like restructuring and efficiency, divert attention from the fact that human lives are being shattered; they normalize the pain of those "shed" and enable the principals and their agents to keep their priorities intact in the face of large-scale human misery.

And in the news reports about the trimming and shedding, there is not even ironical reference to the business leaders' frequent earlier pronouncements about "team spirit" and the corporation as a happy cooperative joint venture of labor and capital. The Japanese tradition of lifetime employment is occasionally mentioned, often with some relish at evidence of its erosion, but the issue of whether the primary institutions of society shouldn't be responsible for their workers and not be able to throw them on the scrap heap at will is not discussed. This reflects institutional power.

Crisis of Military Keynesianism

The steady rise of unemployment in the major Western states coincides with the disappearance of the Soviet Union and consequent great difficulty in justifying further enormous waste outlays in an arms race. Many left analysts argued for years that military spending was the heart of post-World War II Keynesianism and the linch-pin of Western capitalist growth and prosperity. Under the regime of Military Keynesianism the government contracted out for expenditures that did not conflict with other private outputs, helped enlarge and protect foreign market opportunities, and provided the rationale for massive subsidization of private corporate research and construction. This was one form of spending that could always be increased without much opposition in times of recessionary tendencies.

Nevertheless, during the Cold War years mainstream liberal economists regularly sneered at the idea that capitalism "needed" the arms race, dismissing it as Marxist ideology that failed to understand that social spending (or tax reductions) could easily compensate for declines in military spending. That military spending was doing so well and treated so lavishly, and social spending neglected, was a result of historical happenstance—James Tobin argued that U.S. military spending could be explained as simple "responses to world events," without any need for bringing in U.S. internal and imperial interests. (Tobin even included the Bay of Tonkin incident of 1964 as an external event and provocation to which the United States was reasonably reacting.[1])

Well, the chickens have come home to roost; military spending is falling, with the result that over the past three years over 400,000 arms-industry workers have been laid off, but like the "peace dividend" of the post-Vietnam War days, somehow the political economy is once again not filling the gap with social spending even though the needs there are huge and pressing. In part, this is a result of the NWO downgrading of the role of government—and failure of the private market system to take up the slack. Arguably, also, the huge national debt and deficits constrain further deficits and government spending. Isn't it interesting, however, that "the market" and political establishment didn't get debt- and deficit-conscious during the Reagan years of growing deficits that were funding an elite Potlatch and a huge burst of military spending, but only focused in on the terrible menace of deficits when they might be serving ordinary people?

Increasing "Competitiveness"—In the Interest of Jobs!

What then was left for Clinton to do in the search for jobs? The answer is that in the NWO only policies of expansion through improving "competitiveness" are favored—which is to say policies that help business to enlarge foreign markets and reduce their costs at home. The latter means keeping unions weak and the social wage low, which tends to keep domestic demand sluggish and reinforces the need to focus on external markets. Of course, if workers are fired in "down-sizing" to become competitive, jobs are lost as well, so the improved competitiveness can be a job killer.

Enlarging foreign markets means getting reductions in trade barriers and obstacles to investment for U.S.-based transnational corporations (TNCs). NAFTA fits the new regimen perfectly: it is a means of opening sales and investment opportunities for U.S. TNCs, partly at the expense of excluded rivals like Japan and the European Community (EC) powers, and partly at the expense of domestic U.S. sales and investment. The actuality or threat of shifts to the more favorable investment climate of Mexico will increase "competitiveness" further by dragging down U.S. wages and working conditions. The GATT talks, and those of the Asia-Pacific Economic Cooperation forum dealing with Asian trade-investment liberalization, in which the Clinton administration has shown a strong and aggressive interest, also serve the "competitiveness" strategy and policy thrust.

So, for a weak and opportunistic president unwilling to challenge corporate power and the main drift, there was No Other Option but to get on board the TNC ship and help steer it through international shoals. Although the supporters of NAFTA have portrayed its opponents as hostile to "internationalism," this is a fraud; genuine internationalism implies a non self-serving and non-exploitative basis for extending relations between peoples. NAFTA, by contrast, is part of a system of carefully controlled market enlargement, with numerous exclusions (product and country) and huge power imbalances among participants that make it "internationalism" in the same way as colonialism was (after all, that also enlarged markets and brought alleged mutual benefits). Within Mexico as well, a tiny class aligned with the expanding foreign power has reaped benefits from the new regime, while real wages have fallen; and since the onset of the Mexican crisis in December 1994, policies have been installed that will further immiserate the majority, while protecting investors.

The New Mercantilism

NAFTA and its cousins are more akin to "mercantilism" than "internationalism." That is, each country is seeking to advance its external position by bargaining for trade and investment access abroad while protecting its own turf as much as it can get away with; each seeks "competitiveness" by keeping down internal labor costs; and the dominant and powerful interests whose prospective gains drive the expansion process have successfully identified theirs as the "national interest" and established that the external-expansion route is the only feasible policy option for system growth.

In 17th- and 18th-century mercantilism there was the same preoccupation with external market expansion; and David Hume himself stated the mercantilist class "truth" that "the English [sic] feel some disadvantage in foreign trade by the high price of labor."[2] It was an elite truism of Hume's era that low wages were essential to the "national interest"; and the national interest was implicitly identified with the interest of very narrow elite groups (foreign traders, manufacturers for export). In his analysis of British mercantilism in *The Position of the Laborer in a System of Nationalism*, E. S. Furniss wrote: "Mercantilism teaches us that in working out a system of public policy based upon nationalistic [sic] purposes the dominant class will attempt to bind the burdens upon the shoulders of those groups whose political power is too slight to defend them from exploitation and will find justification for its policies in the plea of national necessity. Present day nationalism gives evidence of a tendency to repeat this experience."[3] Robert Reich, if not in the Clinton cabinet, couldn't have put it better.

In the neo-mercantilist system today, if workers bargain successfully and wage rates increase, this is read as a troubling development threatening the national interest ("Wall Street scores the new GM contract as a plus for the union and 'cave-in' by the auto maker"). As unemployment grows and ordinary citizens become increasingly insecure, this is perceived as a bit worrisome, but with its positive sides: firms are getting more "lean" and "competitive," and there is a braking effect on wages. (An early 1990s Merrill Lynch analysis explained that "since June 1990, the final month of the previous expansion, the labor force has grown by 4.1 million people but private employment is up by just 700,000. At current rates of job growth it could take six years to absorb that overhang. Consequently, wage pressures should remain minimal.") It is most noteworthy that the growth of unemployment and insecurity doesn't cause a reconsideration of policy; for both developed and Third World countries the answer to worsening conditions for ordinary people is not new policies directed to helping them but rather intensified privatization and tighter budget controls. There is No Other Option to policies that work by inducing businesses to expand.

Fat Cats Get Fatter

The mainstream media lined up in solid phalanx for NAFTA, along with Citicorp, Mobil Oil, the Business Roundtable, and the leading economists and political figures, in opposition to labor and a large body of ordinary citizens, who were subjected to a huge barrage of pro-NAFTA propaganda. Although the imbalance in money deployed for NAFTA propaganda was exceedingly favorable to the TNCs and their appendages, the media featured the sinister and aggressive force of labor. Both the *New York Times* and *Washington Post* included in their editorials tabulations of labor's contributions to various legislators, but not those of business, nor did they list the names of recipients or terms fixed in Clinton's massive buyout of votes.

In a letter to the *New York Times*, entitled "Trade Agreement Means Fat Cats Get Fatter" (October 3, 1993), CUNY business school professor Yoshi Tsurumi pointed out that NAFTA involves "a disturbing class conflict...between the organized money class and the disorganized masses." He noted further that as a macro policy, NAFTA is one-sided and trickle-down in action: "Like those 300 economists who endorsed the trade agreement and chief executives of large corporations and their lobbyists, the loudest endorsers are touting a brighter future prospect for the United States macroeconomy. But real people are saying that they cannot live on a fattened macroeconomic pie eaten by the organized money class. Long gone are the days when improved macroeconomic indexes like gross domestic product, the balance of payments and the Dow Jones stock price index also meant improved job and earning prospects for the working classes to middle classes of the United States."

Tsurumi is evidently what Jim Lehrer calls a "whiner"—he doesn't recognize that the TNCs have spoken, the conventional wisdom has declared that NAFTA is good, and that it is time to move forward—or is it backwards, or upside down?

—Z, January 1994

Chapter Five

The Politicized "Science"

The Economists (1)

Economics has always been a politicized discipline, its most prominent members striving to make policy statements as they propound their theoretical doctrines. Adam Smith's *Wealth of Nations* (1776) was geared to demonstrating the negative impact of mercantilist economic policies. David Ricardo's *Principles of Political Economy* (1817) was merely an elaboration of a policy and propaganda tract he wrote shortly before entitled "An Essay on the Influence of a Low Price of Corn on the Profits of Stock" (1815). His "principles" formalized the case for his policy prescription, that removing tariffs on the import of foodstuffs was essential to economic growth.

In his outstanding history of economic thought, *The Meaning and Validity of Economic Theory* (1956), Leo Rogin found the Smith and Ricardo cases typical and that major theoretical developments have been in the service of policy arguments. Rogin showed that the great economists often spelled out normative models of an ideal or allegedly "natural" economy, as with Smith's "simple system of natural liberty," that displayed how well the economy would work if certain perversions, like the mercantilist restrictions, were removed. Or positive models were constructed that described how a particular strategic factor was causing damaging results (with Malthus, population growth, encouraged by "welfare"; with Ricardo, the corn laws, that raised money wages, reduced profits, and caused stagnation; with Keynes, volatile private investment that called for governmental offsets). For Rogin, while economics was scientific in its appeal to facts and requirement of logical consistency, it was inescapably policy based and policy driven.

An alternative view was spelled out in Joseph Schumpeter's *History of Economic Analysis* (1954), in which economics was portrayed as a progressive science, gradually honing a set of analytical tools and sloughing off its ideological baggage. This view contains a germ of truth, and was given plausibility by the development of mathematical and statistical techniques of model building and testing and by the modest early successes of Keynesian forecasting of macro-economic behavior. It has diminished in plausibility, however, as a result of the failure of forecasting to realize early optimistic hopes of improvement and numerous forecasting debacles. Its claims to be ever more scientific were also contradicted by a resurgence of ideology and market accommodation that even mainstream observers have recognized and commented upon.

The Roots of Politicization

Economics, the supposed science of the market, has itself been increasingly integrated into the market system. With the growth in importance of macro-stabilization theory and policies from the time of the Great Depression, governments and business have sought the services of economists to help them forecast the effects of policy actions and other developments. The growth of government regulation also created a demand for economists to advise and testify on regulatory issues. In *The Regulation Game*, Bruce Owen and Ronald Braeutigam describe as one important business strategy the "coopting of the experts,"[1] meaning getting them on the payroll to advise or neutralizing them by funding their research. AT&T, for example, listed corporate payments to 104 social scientists and 215 small consulting firms, many organized by academics, in a 1978 report to the Federal Communications Commission.

The corporate community went on the offensive in the 1970s, trying to transform the intellectual environment to justify lowering wages and taxes. Business poured money into a "conservative labyrinth" of think tanks, funded scores of "free enterprise" chairs, and sponsored numerous university lecture series and individual scholars' research.[2] In the simile used by Heritage Foundation head Edwin Feulner, the design was, like Procter & Gamble's in selling soap, to saturate the intellectual market with studies and "expert" opinion supporting the proper policy conclusions.[3] This was a powerful and conclusion-specific "demand" for intellectual service.

Competition, financial pressure, the increasing cost of computer-based research, and simple self-interest pushed many economists into the market as private consultants or employees of business, or as grantees of the conservative labyrinth's think tanks. The market has worked: the millions flowing into the American Enterprise Institute

(AEI) and offered by the Olin Foundation (among others) found an ample supply of economists willing to provide the required intellectual services. The 1992 Nobel Prize winner in economics, Gary Becker, spent a lifetime showing that the economic calculus of private advantage extends beyond business, even to human behavior in marital choice, gambling, commission of crime, drug abuse, etc. Amusingly, Becker has never pointed to its highly relevant application to the economics profession. Perhaps the subject was too close to home for Becker to be able to see it.

The Cold War and continued force of nationalism also helped politicize economics, with a goodly fraction of the profession accepting as givens vast military buildups and market enlarging foreign policies (including the "pacification" of large segments of the Third World). Another related factor has been economists' desire to be "practical," which means accepting the institutional status quo and the policy limits fixed by those with political power. Many leading economists attached themselves to political factions and parties as advisers, the advice then being constrained by what political leaders saw as the policy limits. In a world of increasing capital mobility and capital market discipline, policy options have diminished and the "practical" advice of economists has shriveled with it.

The promise of advancing economic techniques has also proven to be a mirage. Techniques rely on models and models depend on premises, which may or may not have a close relation to reality. More rapid product change, technological innovation, and the globalization of markets have made the real world more complex, volatile, and ever changing. Models quickly become obsolete and "surprises" continually render their premises, structural relations, and forecasts off the mark. "Error terms" in forecasting models remain stubbornly large. Also, models are most workable when they can use simple assumptions, like perfect certainty, complete information, and unconstrained competition. Economists still commonly use such assumptions, partly for reasons of manageability, but also because they meet many economists' ideological preconceptions, and, no doubt coincidentally, serve well "the market" (i.e., the sponsors of the Olin Foundation and AEI).

While advances in technique have not done much for large-scale economic forecasting, they have helped economists do small things better, like modeling and programming ways to take advantage of price differences between markets and weighing risk-return differences in complex environments. This has helped them create complex financial instruments that serve the needs of business and speculators in global capital markets. Such services are valuable to banks, brokerage firms, and speculators, and economists' rewards in personal investment and consulting services have been substantial.

Further complicating the development of predictive models is the fact that economists cannot perform replicable experiments, but instead must use the economic record of the past as the raw data to test hypotheses. As William Brainard and Richard Cooper have observed, "Marvelous fits of historic data can be obtained by models with widely different implications," given the range of choice of variables and flexibility in specification of time lags.[4] Unscrupulous practitioners can keep adjusting models and searching for amenable data to arrive at preferred conclusions. This has been a common practice of Milton Friedman and other members of the Chicago School, as described below. It should also be noted that modeling and computer use are expensive, which means that well-funded economists can use these technical advances more lavishly. If their critics are few and poorly funded, they can be ignored or overwhelmed by a flood of biased analyses, as Feulner's Procter & Gamble analogy suggested for business-supportive propaganda.

It should be noted that despite the corruption and integration into the market of a great many economists, a substantial number have remained relatively independent, with critical capacities intact. There even emerged a radical fringe large enough to form their own association (Union of Radical Political Economists) and other dissident groups and journals of institutional and "post-Keynesian" economics. The dominant institutions keep these economists and schools marginalized and undervalued, but they exist and may have a brighter future in a New World Order of growing socioeconomic and environmental problems and the absence of a plausible and sustaining Soviet Threat.

The Chicago School

The conservative Chicago School of Economics, with offshoots at UCLA and the University of Rochester, and outcroppings elsewhere in academia and business, steadily increased in influence up to very recent years. Its monetarist theories partially displaced Keynesian economics in macro analysis and policymaking in Western Europe and the United States. Furthermore, the Chicago School is concerned not only with macroeconomics, but deals also with labor and income distribution, trade, competition and monopoly, and regulatory issues. It is therefore of great importance that the Chicago School has been without a peer in the corrupting influence of ideology and the abuse of traditional scientific method.

The Chicago School intellectual tradition traces back to University of Chicago professors Frank Knight and Henry Simon, who flourished in the 1920s and 1930s. These men were conservative, but principled and iconoclastic. Simon's 1934 pamphlet, "A Positive Program for Laissez Faire," actually called for nationalization of monopolies that were based on incontrovertible economies of scale, on the grounds of the evil of private monopoly and the inefficiency and corruptibility of regulation of monopoly.

The post-World War II Chicago School, led by Milton Friedman and George Stigler, has been more political, right-wing, and intellectually opportunistic. On the monopoly issue, for example, in contrast with Simon's 1932 position, the post-World War II School's preoccupation was to dispute the importance and damaging effects of monopoly and to blame its existence on government policy. The postwar school is also linked to U.S. and IMF policies toward the Third World, in its pioneering service, through the "Chicago boys," as advisers to the Pinochet regime of Chile from 1973 onward. This alliance points up the School's notion of "freedom," which has little or nothing to do with political or economic democracy, but is confined to a special kind of market freedom. As it accepts inequality of initial economic position, and the privilege and political influence built into corrupt states like Pinochet's (or Reagan's), its economic freedom is narrow and class-biased. The Chicago boys have always claimed that economic freedom is a necessary condition of political freedom, but their tolerance of political non-freedom and state terror in the interest of "economic freedom" makes their own priorities all too clear.

The Chicago School's attitude toward labor was displayed in the Chicago boys' complacence over Pinochet's use of state terror to crush the Chilean labor movement. The School's general tolerance of monopoly on the producers' side has never been paralleled by softness toward labor organization and "labor monopoly." Henry Simon himself developed a pathological fear of labor power in his later years, as evidenced in a famous diatribe "Reflections on Syndicalism," which may have contributed to his committing suicide in 1944. Subsequently, the labor specialists of the postwar Chicago School, most notably Albert Rees and H. Gregg Lewis, dedicated lifetimes to showing that wages were determined by marginal productivity and that labor unions' pursuit of higher wages was futile. (Rees, however, did acknowledge the non-economic benefits of labor organization in his class lectures.) Chicago School analyses stressed the wage-employment tradeoff and the employment costs of wage increases based on bargaining power (as opposed to those negotiated individually and reflecting marginal productivity). They linked collective bargaining to inflation, viewing "excessive" wage increases as the pernicious engine of inflationary spirals. Milton Friedman's concept of a "natural rate of unemployment" was a valuable tool in the arsenal of corporate and political warfare against trade unions—a mystical concept, unprovable, but putting the ultimate onus of price level increases on the exercise of labor bargaining power.

Milton Friedman. Friedman was considered an extremist and something of a nut in the early postwar years. As Friedman has not changed, and is now comfortably ensconced at the conservative Hoover Institution, his rise to eminence (including receipt of a Nobel prize in economics), like that of the *Dartmouth Review*'s Dinesh D'Souza, testifies to a major change in the general intellectual-political climate.

Friedman is an ideologue of the right, whose intellectual opportunism in pursuit of his political agenda has often been heavy-handed and sometimes even laughable. The numerous errors and rewritings of history in Friedman's large collection of popular writings are spelled out in admirable detail in Elton Rayack's *Not So Free To Choose*.[5] His "minimal government" ideology has never extended to attacking the military-industrial complex and imperialist policies; in parallel with Reaganism and the demands of the corporate community, his assault on government "pyramid building" was confined to civil functions of government. As with the other Chicago boys, totalitarianism in Chile did not upset Friedman—its triumphs in dismantling the welfare state and disempowering mass organizations, even if by the use of torture and murder, made it a positive achiever for him.

Friedman's reputation as a professional economist rests on his monetarist ideas and historical studies, his analysis of inflation and the "natural rate of unemployment," and his theory of the consumption-income relationship (the so-called "permanent-income" hypothesis). These are modest achievements at best. His monetarist forecasts have proven to be as wrong as forecasts can be, and the popularity of monetarism has ebbed in the wake of its failures. Friedman's claim that freeing exchange rates would ease national balance of payments problems and not destabilize foreign exchange markets has also proven to be wildly off the mark. The "natural rate" of unemployment is an unverifiable ideological weapon rather than a scientific tool. His analyses of inflation and the consumption-income relation are ingenious, but neither very original nor anything but partial and special cases. They all have the conservative policy implications that Friedman's "scientific" writings invariably contain.

Friedman's methodology in attempting to prove his models have set a new standard in opportunism, manipulation, and the abuse of scientific method. Paul Diesing points out in his valuable article "Hypothesis Testing and Data Interpretation: The Case of Milton Friedman,"[6] that Friedman "tests" hypotheses by methods that never allow their refutation. Diesing lists six "tactics" of adjustment employed by Friedman in connection with testing the permanent income (PI) hypothesis: "1. If raw or adjusted data are consistent with PI, he reports them as confirmation of PI ... 2. If the fit with expectations is moderate, he exaggerates the fit ... 3. If particular data points or groups differ from the predicted regression, he invents ad hoc explanations for the divergence ... 4. If a whole set of data disagree with predictions, adjust them until they do agree ... 5. If no plausible adjustment suggests itself, reject the data as unreliable ... 6. If data adjustment or rejection are not feasible, express puzzlement. 'I have not been able to construct any plausible explanation for the discrepancy'..."

In a proposed Op Ed column written in 1990, Elton Rayack pointed out the interesting fact that while Friedman's models did well in retrospective fitting to historic data, where the Friedman testing methods could be employed, they were abysmal in forecasts, where "adjustments" could not be made. Rayack reviewed eleven forecasts of price, interest rate, and output changes made by Friedman during the 1980s, as reported in the press. Only one of the eleven was on the mark, a not-so-great batting average of .092; "not enough to earn a plaque in baseball's Hall of Fame, but evidently quite adequate to qualify [Friedman] as an economic guru." The guru was, however, protected by the mainstream media; Rayack's piece was rejected by both the *New York Times* and *Wall Street Journal*. We may conclude that Friedman's truly pathbreaking innovation as an economist has been in the art of what is called "massaging the data" to arrive at preferred conclusions. This innovation has been extended further by other members of the Chicago School.

George Stigler and anti-regulation methodology. A second major figure of the modern Chicago School, and another Nobel Prize winner in economics, was the late George Stigler, a specialist in economic theory, industrial organization (monopoly and competition), and regulation. His writings on the first two topics tended to show the beauties of competition and the relative unimportance and impermanence of monopoly, absent government intervention.

Perhaps his greatest mark, however, was made in developing and sponsoring analyses of the inefficiency of government regulation. In one of his most famous articles on this subject, "Public Regulation of the Securities Markets," published in the University of Chicago School of Business's *Journal of Business* in April 1964, Stigler used an ingenious model of "before and after" effects of regulation to demonstrate that the Securities and Exchange Commission's (SEC's) requirement of full disclosure in new securities issues was of no value. His method was to compile a sample of new security issues of certain size and other properties for several years in the 1920s and a sample in the late 1930s issued under SEC regulation, and then compute what happened to their prices in the years following issuance. If the SEC was effective, and securities buyers were better informed, one would expect the post-offering prices to be closer to the initial prices and the dispersion of price ratios to be less in the post-SEC period. Stigler claimed that his test showed no improvement in the post-SEC period.

Professor Irwin Friend and this writer did a collaborative analysis of Stigler's study, including a sample review of his original data as well as an examination of his reasoning.[7] In our review of his sample data, we uncovered 25 errors in his reporting of data, 24 of which were in the direction supporting the hypothesis that Stigler was trying to prove, and sufficiently important to affect his significance tests, even though based on only a partial review of his data. With the corrections, the performance under regulation was indisputably superior to the unregulated performance, as measured by average price ratios of the 1920s and in the post-SEC period. In Stigler's own analysis, the dispersion of price ratios was also substantially lower in the post-SEC period, but Stigler "reinterpreted" the test, retrospectively claiming that the lower dispersion meant that regulation had reduced the willingness of risky firms to enter the market (this is Diesing's item 3 in the list given above of Friedman's methods of "testing"). Ironically, Stigler had written an earlier article on "The Economics of Information," whose main theme was that increased information reduces price dispersion, which he implied was beneficial and desirable.

Our showing that Stigler had doctored the data in a very serious way, and misread his own results, was published in the *Journal of Business* in October 1964, with an appendix listing the 25 errors and showing in a table the large effect on the test results. Stigler did not challenge the criticisms in substance, but proposed using different data (Friedman's method 4, in the Diesing list above). This exchange occurred in the very year Stigler was made president of the American Economic Association, but had no noticeable effect on his reputation. In subsequent years, Stigler's Chicago School associates continued to cite his original article as proving the ineffectiveness of SEC regulation and full disclosure, which is comparable to a physical anthropologist in the 1980s continuing to cite the Piltdown Man as a valid member of the evolutionary ladder. But if Piltdowns are a commonplace in the "science" and one operates on principles of a truth above fact, it is all comprehensible.

Stigler himself and many of his followers continued their modeling of regulation and its effects by the same or related methods. The most important Stigler follower in this area was Sam Peltzman, who wrote a Ph.D. thesis under Stigler's direction in 1965 that purported to show that the extension of federal regulation to virtually all banks in 1935 caused the entry of new banks to drop by 40-50 percent. Peltzman's method was to specify several factors that might influence entry rates, most importantly bank profit rates, and then explain any decline in entry after 1935 not attributable to the chosen factors by a "residual" called "government regulation." Although branch banking was growing rapidly in this period, Peltzman never included new branches in his model. Among the many other intellectual crimes committed by Peltzman, the model had the interesting characteristic that the poorer the explanatory variables, the better the result from the Chicago School standpoint (i.e., the larger the residual "government regulation").

This terrible study was cited as authoritative in the years that followed, and was never rebutted, in part because the formulation and testing of a rival model required data collection back into the 1920s and would have been very arduous. Peltzman followed up this success with studies of drug and auto safety regulation, each demonstrating by means of the new Chicago School methodology—using dubious explanatory variables, and leaving government regulation as the residual—that government regulation was ineffective. Several analysts went to the trouble of showing that Peltzman's further studies were fraudulent, but his studies continued to be cited as authoritative demonstrations that the case for drug and auto safety regulation was dubious.[8]

A Chicago School Contribution to the S&L Disaster. Another Chicago School product, Professor George Benston, made a notable contribution to the S&L disaster in his research and consulting on the S&L problem in the 1980s. One of the issues during the surge of S&L deregulation in the years 1981-87 was whether allowing S&Ls greater freedom to make riskier direct investments (in land and for construction) was sound policy. (It was not, given the poor financial condition of many S&Ls, the ease of entry of shady dealers, their ability to take advantage of government insurance of S&L deposits, and the inability of regulation to cope with these problems.) Benston was hired in the mid-1980s by Charles Keating, one of the shady dealers (now in prison), to do a study of the costs and benefits of direct investment. His analysis of 34 S&Ls with relatively high levels of direct and riskier investments found their results favorable, and concluded that tighter regulation of such investments "was unsound conceptually, unsupported by meaningful evidence, and likely to be damaging to both the savings and loan industry and the Federal Savings and Loan Insurance Corporation."[9] Although an expert in accounting, Benston was fooled badly by the accounting tricks of the hot operators and by de facto fraud. By 1989, 32 of the 34 S&Ls in Benston's sample were insolvent, and some of them were among the most dramatic cases of fraud in the lavish S&L fraud record.[10]

Mergers in the Best of All Possible Worlds. The Chicago School was also in the forefront of providing intellectual rationales for the merger and takeover boom of the 1980s. Ironically, Stigler himself had casti-gated the turn-of-the-century economists for their apologetics for the first great merger movement, defended then as based on "efficiency" considerations: "One must regretfully record," said Stigler, "that in this period Ida Tarbell and Henry Demarest Lloyd did more than the American Economic Association to foster the policy of competition." But Stigler's own progeny greatly outdid the earlier apologists.

An amusing feature of the 1980s apologias is that the new wave of mergers, and frequent follow-up "restructuring" by divestment of company divisions, was explained in part as a consequence of the excesses of the conglomerate merger movement of the 1960s, when firms like ITT, Ling-Temco-Vought, Gulf & Western, and Litton Indus-tries had gobbled up numerous unrelated firms. But at that time, Chicago School economists explained *those* mergers as based on efficiency considerations. So efficiency is always the basis of merger movements, even those cleaning up the debris of the last one, where we depend on short memories of our last round of apologetics!

Chicago School analyses of the 1980s merger boom rested on the "agency model," on the theory of takeovers as an efficient market instrument, and on the use (and abuse) of stock-price data to measure efficiency effects. In the agency model, managers, while supposedly agents of stockholders (owners), are often able to serve their own interests rather than those of the owners, because of the large number of owners, proxy voting, and managerial influence over choice of directors. Fortunately, the market has evolved a corrective takeover mechanism, allowing outsiders to bid for control of poorly managed companies over the heads of the managers. (As these were poorly run their stock prices would be low.) Michael Milken was thus a servant of the people in providing the financing to those who wanted to bid for these undervalued resources in order to put them to better use.

For the Chicago School, if this takeover mechanism *could* serve to enhance efficiency, then it is assumed that it did. But why ignore the possibility that the buyers might have other motives than efficiency enhancement? Perhaps they want to get bigger in an empire-building process, or to loot the acquired firm (or its workers and their pension funds). Maybe the market is working poorly and undervaluing the assets of target firms. Maybe the bankers and lawyers are encouraging uneconomic mergers to capitalize on buoyant and speculative stock market conditions and to pull down large fees.[11] If U.S. Steel Corpora-tion paid twice the prior market price for Marathon Oil in 1981, while admitting that it knew nothing about managing an oil company, and raising the salaries of the previous Marathon management to keep them on the job, it is obvious that the Chicago School "more efficient management" model was completely irrelevant to explaining that important merger.

The Chicago School has also pioneered in the use of stock price data to measure the effects of takeovers. The argument is that if mergers enhance efficiency, stock prices will rise in anticipation of higher profits. But this measure is indirect, and it could be influenced by unjustified investor optimism or by investor belief that the merger will increase market power or facilitate union busting or pension looting, rather than increasing efficiency. The measure is in the Friedman "natural rate of unemployment" mold, not only in its obscure relation to that which is supposedly being measured, but in its amenability to manipulation. Do we measure the stock-price effect before the merger, at merger time, or later? From what base? The Chicago School has regularly focused on price effects before, at the moment of, or immediately after a merger transaction, which tells us about what investors expect, not about efficiency effects.

A careful study by Ellen Magenheim and Dennis Mueller demonstrated that price study results vary widely depending on timing choices, and that for many recent mergers the longer the time lag the poorer the results.[12] In a Chicago School classic on merger effects by Michael Jensen and Richard Ruback, which finds that mergers enhance efficiency, based on stock-price movements before and at the time of mergers, the authors eventually concede that several years after the merger the results don't look so good—that there are "systematic reductions in the stock price of the bidding firms following the event [merger]."[13] The authors don't incorporate such findings into their conclusions, however; they say it is "unsettling because they are inconsistent with market efficiency and suggest that changes in stock price during takeovers overestimate the future efficiency gains from mergers." In other words, the empirical evidence not conforming to the preconceived hypothesis, the authors resort to the Friedman "test" method number 6: "If data adjustment or rejection are not feasible, express puzzlement," but don't let the incompatible facts interfere with proper conclusions.

Chicago: Nobel Prize Capitol of a Sick Profession

The Chicago School has been an extremely prominent recipient of Nobel Prize awards in economics, increasingly so as its proportion of total awards has increased its leverage in the award process. Friedman, Stigler, Merton Miller, Ronald Coase, Theodore Schultz, and Gary Becker have joined Friedrich von Hayek in a solid, ideological free market phalanx. None of these had better qualifications than Joan Robinson and Nicholas Kaldor, economists of the Left who worked with great distinction within the mainstream traditions of economics.

Their neglect in favor of Chicago School mediocrities like Miller and Becker, and ideologues like Friedman and Von Hayek, testify to a politicization of the Nobel Prize that reflects well the corruption and politicization of the profession as a whole.

In 1992, the Union of Concerned Scientists prepared a World Scientists Warning on global environmental and resource problems calling for action by the world's governments. A majority of living Nobel laureates signed the statement, including a number of economists. No member of the Chicago School appended his name. One of the great accomplishments of 1991 Chicago School Nobel prize winner, Ronald Coase, which helped him win the award, was a 1960 article on "The Problem of Social Costs," the gist of which was that the market could cope even with externalities. In fact, there would appear to be no problem the market cannot solve, at least for those wedded to the proposition in advance and willing to make a few assumptions here and a few adjustments in the data there.

—Z, February 1993

Chapter Six

Liberal Growthmanship and Free Trade

The Economists (2)

Liberal trickle-down theory was reformulated and given a new gloss in the late 1950s and the years of Democratic rule in the 1960s. A number of the leading liberal economists, some drawn from the Brookings Institution, served as advisers and officials in the Kennedy and Johnson administrations. These economists, heirs of and spokespersons for the "new economics" of J. M. Keynes, accommodated well to the demands of the imperial state. Virtually all of them accepted the premises of the Cold War, and eventually treated the Vietnam War as either a noble enterprise or an act of state to be taken as a policy given. The inequality of income and wealth was of little interest to them, and while favoring a vigorous macro-policy oriented to high employment and growth, in the Kennedy years they supported business tax reductions and regressive personal tax cuts as prime instruments for combatting recession.[1]

James Tobin, for example, who later served on Kennedy's Council of Economic Advisers (CEA), denounced the Eisenhower administration's cuts in the military budget in 1958, a time, said Tobin, "when the world situation cried out for accelerating and enlarging our defense effort." The budget cuts were made, Tobin protested, to encourage the production of more consumer goods for "a people who already enjoy the highest and most frivolous standard of living in history."[2] A few years later, Tobin described the new liberal economics of the Kennedy era as follows:

> Redistribution of income and wealth by taxation and government transfer payments was in days gone by another rallying point for liberal political

movements. The fire has gone out of this one too. The current liberal political movement, the New Frontier, is providing incentives for business investment through new tax legislation and new depreciation guidelines. The Kennedy administration is, from all indications, about to be the vehicle for a general reduction in corporate and personal income tax rates, and in particular for substantial lowering of top-bracket rates.[3]

The "Growth Dividend"

In the new liberal analysis, the underlying population was to benefit from the growth-oriented policies through higher employment, increasing productivity and per capita real incomes, and from a "growth dividend" accruing to the public sector. This dividend, a rising tax surplus that would result from the higher incomes and fixed tax rates, would provide "the resources needed to achieve great societies at home and grand designs abroad," in the words of Walter Heller, chairman of Kennedy's CEA. And this dividend would be generated and could be used for benevolent ends without the political struggle that a policy of redistribution would entail. In Heller's words, "When the cost of fulfilling a people's aspirations can be met out of a growing horn of plenty—instead of robbing Peter to pay Paul—ideological roadblocks melt away, and consensus replaces conflict."[4]

This is, of course, straightforward trickle down, the only "liberal" component being the willingness to allow the automatically rising tax revenues to be used for social welfare at home (as well as imperial adventures abroad). There are two problems with this analysis. First, it underplays the extent to which the trickle-down mechanism benefits the wealthy; "conflict" with the business establishment is avoided by giving it all it wants. The majority are asked to wait for the trickling down from the largess to the affluent. A second problem derives from the fact that growth consolidates the power of dominant elites, who may want to command the growth dividend for themselves. If they must be bribed for growth to occur, why assume that they will not be able to direct the allocation of the social dividend later? And, in fact, the Kennedy-Johnson growth dividend was seized by the military-industrial complex to pursue "grand designs abroad" (i.e., the destruction of Indochina), not to create a more equitable society at home.

Growthmanship and Its Enemies (i.e., Environmentalists)

Liberal apologetics and trickle-down theory were advanced by the 1973 publication of Peter Passell's and Leonard Ross's book, *The Retreat from Riches: Affluence and Its Enemies*. The authors were young and trendy liberal academicians, Passell's trendiness displayed later in his 1987 handbook for Reagan-era yuppies, entitled *The Best*. *Retreat From Riches* purported to be concerned with poverty and devoted to finding routes to alleviate it. As in the case of the Kennedy-

Johnson era liberals, however, Passell and Ross quickly dismissed income and wealth redistribution policies as politically unfeasible, and contended that private-sector growth, which made it "more lucrative to wash cars and wait on tables today than it was twenty years ago," was the only practical option. Although growth was their solution to poverty, they made no effort to explain why poverty persisted in the face of the huge growth of the prior several decades.

What made *Retreat From Riches* especially pernicious, however, is that the "enemies of affluence" turned out to be environmentalists like Barry Commoner, modelers of the "limits of growth" like the Club of Rome, and old-style liberal economists like J. K. Galbraith, who were supposedly creating an atmosphere hostile to growth. Passell and Ross portrayed these opponents as "elitists securing their room at the top," while interfering with economic growth benefiting the poor.

This *ad hominem* attack on the environmentalists was eerily similar to that levied a few years later by neo-conservatives like Michael Ledeen, Michael Novak, S. Robert Lichter, and Stanley Rothman against the elitists in the "liberal media," who were allegedly out of touch with the family values of Middle America. In both cases, Mobil Oil Company and Nixon's Vice President Spiro Agnew were also on the side of the poor and against the environmentalist and media elites. Two separate Mobil Oil ads lauded the insights of the "young liberals" Passell and Ross, standing up for the poor, and Mobil also helped sponsor and publicize the neo-con campaign against the media elites. Spiro Agnew lauded Passell and Ross in a speech at the Philadelphia Union League Club; it may be recalled that Agnew was the Nixon administration's hit man in assailing the threat of the Eastern liberal media.

An important component of business's ability to weaken environmental protection is its influence over the intellectual and political environment. Passell and Ross served well business's efforts to undercut environmental controls by disparaging the relatively weak environmentalist forces and downgrading the environmental threat. They never discussed business's power to obstruct environmental controls. While ruling out any institutional changes like income-wealth redistribution, limits on advertising, and control over foreign investment as politically unfeasible, they blithely asserted that pollution control would be effective because it was necessary!

Retreat from Riches had a flattering introduction by the distinguished liberal economist Paul Samuelson and was given favorable reviews by leading New Economists in both the *Washington Post* and *New York Times*. Some of the New Economists were to help carry the business war on the control of externalities one step further from official positions in the Carter administration, where they fought against tighter regulations (e.g., on factory emissions of cotton dust) as "inflationary." Growth without redistribution, and with minimal attention to the negative externalities that make nominal growth an inflated number, had become the "Moses and all the prophets" of the New Economics.

Free Trade Trickle-Down

Peter Passell joined the staff of the *New York Times* during the 1970s, and has fit well into that establishment institution. With the recent retirement of Leonard Silk, Passell became the paper's number one analyst of economic affairs. His bent is still toward finding environmental concerns and fears exaggerated ("Experts Question Staggering Costs of Toxic Cleanups," *New York Times*, September 1, 1991), and he rarely has doubts about the superiority of the price mechanism over regulatory controls in dealing with environmental problems (see his "Cheapest Protection of Nature May Lie in Taxes, Not Laws," *New York Times,* November 24, 1992). Superficiality and a hidden ideological input remain omnipresent in his economic writings.

Both of these characteristics stand out in Passell's account of the issues involved in the free-trade controversy and the Uruguay round of negotiations in 1992 in his front page article, "Although Trade Is Trickier, 'More Is Better' Is Still True" (*New York Times*, November 23, 1992). Clichés and the selective use of evidence barely disguise a blatantly ideological frame, as the following summary and analysis demonstrates.

Trade and market versus government. According to Passell, "Trade has been a great engine of prosperity for the last century," and our choices, "say the experts" (unidentified), are "moving forward" with trade and free markets or "regressing to a world in which politicians rather than markets have the last word on what people buy and sell." This broad-brush economic history (and tendentious statement of the choices we face) yields the preferred conclusion by confusing correlation with causation and neglecting the complexity of historical economic processes.

The growth of trade associated with overall economic growth could mean that trade is generated by and follows growth, rather than the reverse. Furthermore, growth has frequently been associated with substantial government intervention. David Felix and Angus Maddison, for example, have pointed out that Western economic growth rates in the post-World War II years of large-scale government intervention (1950-1979) were substantially higher than those from the 1870 to 1913 years of lesser government, and unemployment rates were lower as well.[5] The rapid growth of Japan and the newly industrializing countries of Asia was clearly fostered by massive government subsidy and protection.[6] It would appear that *government* can be an "engine of prosperity" and that a contraction in the role of government may stifle that "engine." Government also plays a major role in stabilizing the economy and protecting people from the negative effects of industrial practices, such as pollution, an increasingly important private market failure that only government intervention can rectify.

More is better, despite "losers." Passell stresses that the increased division of labor and "comparative advantage" from enlarging trade expands total world output, which is good even if there are "losers." He concedes that there *are* losers, but he says little or nothing about their number, class position, location, and the long-run consequences of their impoverishment.

Instead, in his very brief discussion of losers he mentions a hypothetical banana farmer in Florida and a U.S. worker in a trade-vulnerable sector like textiles. He does not discuss the Canadian experience under a free-trade agreement since 1988. Nor does he discuss the experience of Mexico, Peru, Brazil, and the Philippines (among others) where millions of subsistence and cooperative-linked farmers were pushed off the land in favor of agro-exporters and moved into gigantic shantytowns on the outskirts of large cities. The Canadian Ecumenical Council for Economic Justice has pointed out that under Mexico's structural adjustment policies, "The cost of employing a young woman to assemble products in a *maquiladora* fell from U.S. $1.53 an hour in 1982 to just 60 cents in 1990," and that while Mexico now imports 10 million tons of agricultural products annually, per capita consumption of basic foods has fallen by 30 percent over the past eight years.[7] Passell does not address the actual results of his favored policies; the word *maquiladora* does not appear in his account.

Environmental effects. Free trade allows transnational firms to engage in "regulatory arbitrage," shifting from better to worse regulated environments. This encourages a rapid degradation of the environment in poorly regulated states, and, by competitive pressures, weakens it in better regulated countries. And there is evidence that many firms choose Mexico as a place to do business because of lax environmental regulation. Effective regulation may also increasingly be seen as an "unfair trade practice" under supranational rules. The efficacy of multinational regulation has been tested in the Mexican *maquiladoras* and under the La Paz agreement of 1983 between Mexico and the United States. Mexico essentially does not enforce environmental rules, and the La Paz agreement has been "mere words on paper," as stated by Cuauhtemoc Cardenas, leader of Mexico's Party of Democratic Revolution.

We may recall that for Peter Passell in his *Retreat From Riches,* environmentalism was an enemy of the good (i.e., blind economic growth). That is the view of the transnational corporate market participants also. The word "environment" does not appear in Passell's article on free trade.

Infant industries. Passell does admit that there is a possible case for protectionism in the so-called "infant industries" argument. He says that "economists have...muddied the waters by theorizing that countries might be better off protecting some home markets, like those needed to give local manufacturers a foothold in new products." This is quickly dismissed as "too clever by half," and written off as not important and too readily used by groups merely protecting their turf. Actually, the argument goes back to the 18th century and has never been refuted. It can certainly not be pushed out of the way by rhetorical ploys (too clever by half); the increased importance, cost, and rapid obsolescence of new technology has made the interventionary case for protecting infant industries stronger than ever. Passell fails to mention that all the great late industrializers, the United States, Germany, and Japan, as well as the recently successful newly industrializing countries like Taiwan and South Korea, have used protection and other forms of intervention to nurture their infants—they did not rely on free trade.[8]

Competition and technological diffusion. Passell contends that free trade is of increased importance because it brings competition to the newly opened markets and because technological diffusion makes "open global markets...more than ever the ticket to rapid progress." But if large transnational corporations (TNCs) are free to move about like global sharks, won't the number of sellers tend toward the oligopolistic? Won't the local minnows in Third World markets be destroyed or swallowed up into branch systems? Won't the technological diffusion be increasingly a one-way street from developed countries to less developed countries (LDCs)? And won't technological capability and development be increasingly concentrated in the developed countries, while the LDCs provide low-cost labor to produce and assemble products—as long as suitable wage and working conditions prevail? These considerations that suggest strongly non-competitive tendencies and show the "losers" concentrated in poor countries are not even hinted at by Passell.

Dependency. Free trade in an environment of great inequalities in economic and military power threatens the economic, political, and cultural autonomy and independence of the Third World. Poor countries can be overwhelmed by intensive and sophisticated advertising, foreign domination of the media, the buying up of domestic companies and natural resources (including agricultural land), debt dependency, and intelligence-military-political subversion.[9] To prevent this, poor countries need to be able to maintain a certain distance from their powerful "friends" anxious to "do business" with them. The whole thrust of the current "free trade" push in and out of the General Agreement on Tariffs and Trade (GATT) is to break down these barriers and allow the sharks to feed freely.

In support of this powerful First World thrust, it is essential to pretend that the issue of independence versus domination does not exist and that we are just dealing with nasty trade barriers, not cultures and entire peoples at risk and up for grabs. Peter Passell never once mentions dependency and power differentials as issues, and tells his readers that the newly proposed GATT rules that will strip the last defenses from LDCs will hopefully be enacted "before protectionist coalitions grow too powerful to be stopped." This is imperialist apologetics at its best.

The Uruguay Round of GATT. It follows that Passell regards the GATT negotiations and Western proposals on the table there as part of a progressive struggle to free trade further, to get rid of "all those pesky non-tariff barriers, particularly those that affected trade in services like banking, insurance and construction." Another urgent target is "protection of intellectual property, everything from patents on new drugs to copyrights on rock."

Passell admits that in the early years of GATT, the United States could call the shots, with rules skewed accordingly. But now the "old coalition of exporters" has broken down, so he implies that we are in a democratic era in which "every country will presumably get something from the agreement." This is as plausible as saying that the UN Security Council is now a democratic organization with the decline in relative U.S. power. In fact, the collapse of the Soviet Union and the increased debt dependency and splintering of the Third World have sharply diminished its bargaining power and capabilities, and the GATT agenda and proposed changes reflect the interests of the United States and the other major powers to an exceptional degree.

Passell ignores the drive inside and outside of GATT to open up the poor countries to foreign investment and to restrict their powers to regulate foreign business firms. He does not point out that service provision and the "protection of intellectual property" (as well as the unmentioned rights of foreign investment) are all rights demanded, and capable of being taken advantage of, by developed countries only. Passell fails to point out that the ability to exact higher prices for new drugs in the Third World would be a straightforward income transfer from poorer to richer countries and hardly serves to increase competition or diffuse technological knowhow.

Critical models of the campaign for "free trade." There are a number of alternative ways of looking at the recently reinvigorated moves toward "free trade" that depart radically from Passell's Panglossian laissez-faire approach. One is the "recolonization" model. In this frame, the great powers, urged on by the TNCs, and under the pressure of slackened world economic growth and increased competition, have been seeking to exploit the weakness and fragmentation of the Third World and the collapse of the Soviet bloc, to strengthen Western domination of the Third World. In this model, the new GATT proposals, the IMF and World Bank conditionality rules (including pressures to privatize), and the coercive bilateral agreements forced upon the Third World, are seen as elements of a systematic program of forcing denationalization, economic occupation by TNCs, external policy control, and a loss of sovereignty.[10]

A closely related model, which we may call "mercantilist," emphasizes the Western drive for exports and the class nature of its expansionist aims and exploitative character (see the discussion of classic British mercantilism in Chapter Four, p. 29). The struggle to open foreign markets today is not aiming at "free trade," it merely shifts the balance of protectionism to policies enlarging exports, even designated by economist critics as "export protectionism." The need to contain wages and to get U.S. wages and benefits to more "competitive" levels has been a central thrust of Reaganomics and of corporate policy since the early 1970s. The U.S. establishment's support of NAFTA, which promises some export and investment advantage, but will clearly put downward pressure on U.S. wages, shows the mercantilist model in operation.

A third explanatory approach we may designate the "joint venture" model, as it stresses the alliances between groups of Third World politicians, technocrats, and comprador elements and First World elites to jointly "develop" Third World countries in accord with rules that serve the needs of global corporations.[11] The model has the merit of stressing the political corruption and de facto subversion of the Third World countries involved. This helps explain why leaders like Menem in Argentina and Salinas in Mexico will deliberately sacrifice the bulk of their populations to serve mainly foreign interests. As the Ecumenical Council of Canada puts it, Salinas chose a model that means by the year 2000, "50 million Mexicans would be left to languish as a reserve of cheap labor assuring that wages remain low for years to come."[12] This is part of the deal between the joint venture partners, with Salinas supported by Western power in exchange for his opening Mexico to "free trade." It should be noted that a joint venture model explains well the emergence and subsequent U.S. support of the Marcos dictatorship in the Philippines in 1972 and the surge of National Security States under U.S. sponsorship in Latin America in the 1950s and after. In these cases, peasant and working-class organizations were crushed by state terror, which kept the majority atomized and wages exceedingly low, while conditions for transnational investment in agricultural and mining were improved markedly.

The existence of these alternative models is not even hinted at in Peter Passell's highly ideological apologia for the U.S. establishment's version of "free trade" and its benefits.

Reform as the End of Reform

With the triumph of "freedom" and "the market," the meaning of "reform" has shifted. In the old days, reform meant helping the victims of market failure, and it implied attacking and controlling excess market power and its abuses, remedying the market's inability to deal with external costs and produce enough public goods, and helping the victims of the business cycle and structural maladjustments. In the New World Order (NWO), reform means doing those things that will enlarge the scope of the market and cutting back on impediments to capital, like taxes that fund the production of public goods and aid to market victims.

This extraordinary reversal of meaning is an ideological reflection of the triumph of capital. The IMF has been enforcing the NWO definition of reform for years. At this historical juncture, their meaning becomes *the* meaning of reform. As a newly institutionalized usage, it becomes "non-ideological" in the mainstream vision, but is in fact the truly ideological, fitting Roland Barthes' concept of myth as "depoliticized truth" that "goes without saying."

The new usage has found a happy home in the mainstream press. A nice illustration is Sylvia Nasar's front-page article in the *New York Times* of July 8, 1991, entitled "Third World Embracing Reforms To Encourage Economic Growth." The new "reforms" are actions that privatize and reduce market constraints, and Nasar suggests that they are a pretty sure means of raising the standard of living of the world's poor. She never mentions that the "new pragmatism" is being forced on Third World countries by Western carrot-and-stick policies on aid and loans, and that it is being pressed on these populations by governments of dubious legitimacy. She argues that free-market policies underlie the success of the Newly Industrializing Countries (NICs)—Taiwan, Singapore, and South Korea—as well as Mexico and Chile. As regards the NICs, Nasar fails to cite former World Bank economist Robert Wade's *Governing the Market* and Alice Amsden's *Asia's Next Giant*, both of which stress the great importance of extensive and detailed government intervention as prominent features of NIC successes. Nasar also does not cite the 1991 report of the Inter-American Development Bank, which says in regard to Latin American reform that "drastic fiscal adjustment, inflation and stabilisation programmes have unquestionably exacerbated the problems of poverty existing at the beginning of 1990," with per capita consumption falling and reduced state assistance for health, nutrition, education, and housing.

To report success stories for Mexico and Chile also requires the careful doctoring of evidence: notably, selecting as base year a recent one at the bottom of the early 1980s collapse, plus the downgrading of the consequences of their programs for the majority. For Chile, average gross national product (GNP) growth from 1961-71 was 4.6 percent; from 1974-89 it was 2.6 percent, and on a per capita basis it was negative (and of course there was a large upward redistribution of income that Nasar fails to mention). Mexico has been a disaster area under Salinas for the vast majority, and its growth rates of the past 15 years do not match those of earlier years of state-led expansion.[13] But the U.S. leadership and IMF appreciated Salinas's devotion to "reform," and this is reflected in press appraisals.

—Z, January 1993

Chapter Seven
_____

Hostility to Democracy

The Economists (3)

Economics has always been a "handmaiden of inspired truth,"[1] a class-based and politicized discipline servicing demands emanating from the centers of power. It was no coincidence that the leading British economists were free traders during the age of British industrial supremacy, while major continental and U.S. economists made a case for protectionism; or that the competitive private-enterprise model has been the core paradigm of mainstream economics for two centuries; or that the problems of underemployment and underdevelopment were not major theoretical concerns of economists until the Great Depression of the 1930s. Given the new global capitalist regime, and the continued accommodation of the profession to the demands of the powerful, perhaps we should speak of economics now as the "handmaiden of transnational corporate (TNC) truth."

The 1960s and 1970s witnessed the rapid spread of military dictatorships and National Security States (NSSs) in Latin America and elsewhere in the U.S. sphere of influence (most notably, Indonesia and the Philippines). Although the regimes in question, which regularly installed more "open" economic systems, were based on force, dismantled popular organizations, and killed thousands, these political-economic developments were given minimal attention by the profession. *The Age of Imperialism* was written by Harry Magdoff,[2] not by an academy-based professional, and though imperial intervention was of great importance in the "restructuring" of Third World economies, Magdoff's views were derided or ignored. For the professional mainstream, free markets were assumed to be growing naturally; the political, imperial, and terror processes were taken as given. This is entirely understandable, as the "totalitarian free enterprise" systems of the

NSSs, and their organized terror, were quietly supported by the TNCs, U.S. officials, and the international financial institutions (IFIs, including: the IMF, World Bank, and Inter-American Development Bank). These were supporting "reform" in Argentina, Brazil, Chile, and the Philippines, and the mainstream economists were hardly going to get agitated at the seamy side of something the dominant powers call "reform."

Economists for NAFTA

In this context it is not surprising that all the Nobel laureates in economics signed a petition in support of the North American Free Trade Agreement (NAFTA). NAFTA was strongly backed by the dominant TNCs, and was defended as an enlargement of free trade and an application of the principle of comparative advantage. The leading economists are affluent members of the Western elite, with ties to business and government as advisers, consultants, and recipients of data and awards. The Nobel prize in economics has not gone to outsiders and leftists who have challenged the status quo, even when they have performed outstandingly on traditional academic criteria. A woman like the late Joan Robinson, superior in originality and performance to three-fourths of the laureates, asserted in one of her last books (*Aspects of Development and Underdevelopment*, 1978), "It is not easy to see how the Third World can mount the attack [on mass poverty and unemployment] while preserving private property in the means of production and respecting the rules of the free-market economy." Obviously Robinson would not have signed a pro-NAFTA petition, and just as obviously she could never qualify for Nobel laureate in economics.

For the actual laureates, the pressure to sign a pro-NAFTA petition would be severe not only because of class loyalty and affiliations, but because of the centrality of the free-trade/comparative advantage argument in mainstream economic thought. Saying no to NAFTA would be like refusing to approve virtue or motherhood. (Robinson, by contrast, devoted substantial space in *Aspects of Development* to explaining that the theory of free trade "has no relevance to the question which it purports to discuss" given the static assumptions, the premise of full employment, and the different levels of development and "unequal exchange.")

One problem with the theory of comparative advantage is that it assumes relatively fixed quantities of the factors of production within each country, whereas in the real world capital can move around easily but labor cannot. This gives capital a huge advantage in the search for enhanced income and undermines the argument for trade supposedly based on different national factor endowments. The theory also assumes full employment, so that if U.S. workers are thrown out of work as capital relocates to Mexico, they will soon be rehired in skilled high-tech jobs characteristic of the U.S. economy. This assumption is clearly not met in the United States or Western Europe, where the pool of unemployed and parttime workers is growing steadily and those reemployed over the past decade have moved to less skilled and lower wage jobs. At the September 1993 annual meeting of the IMF and World Bank, IMF head Michel Camdessus estimated the unemployed in the industrialized states to be nearing 32 million, declaring this to be "intolerable" but offering no remedy.

Economists also revert to the "long run," in which the victims of change will be reemployed in comparatively advantageous occupations. This is a cop-out. Long-run effects are very uncertain. It is possible, for example, that capital's increased mobility and the prevalent policy paralysis may make large reserve armies of unemployed permanent in the United States and Western Europe. Furthermore, the argument for long- run benefits neglects the consideration that the path to a new equilibrium affects its final values, so that lengthy high levels of unemployment that erode worker defenses and bargaining power may make "equilibrium" wages lower than otherwise.

Another problem with the comparative-advantage argument is that Mexico does an abysmal job of protecting its working class *and* its physical environment, so that its production costs are artificially low and NAFTA will help drive down environmental standards elsewhere. The pro-NAFTA economists reply that an environmental side-agreement allows complaints about environmental law violations to be referred to a supranational commission, that Mexico has "pledged" environmental reform, and that the gains of trade from NAFTA will provide the resources for improved environmental protection. These arguments are not compelling. There has been a joint U.S.-Mexican agreement since 1983 to protect the *maquiladora* area environment, but it has been totally ineffective. Mexico's new pledge must be evaluated by reference to its record and the interests it serves. In this connection, the dominant economic players who have backed NAFTA favor Mexico precisely *because* of its poorly regulated environment (and low wages), so that enforcement through the Mexican government and the supranational commission is likely to remain as ineffective as it has been in the past. The claim that enlarged revenues from a NAFTA-based economic expansion would allow improved environmental regulation fails on the same ground: NAFTA's success would consolidate the power of those who oppose serious regulation. The design of NAFTA was to open Mexico up to and protect foreign investment, and to harmonize wages and environmental conditions *downward*. The economists' failure to recognize this design, the nominal character of Mexican regulation, and the likelihood that this will continue under a NAFTA regime, is a convenient naïveté that serves the TNC project well.

A third pro-NAFTA argument is that rather than U.S. wages falling, Mexican wages will quickly rise to higher levels based on greater demand and higher productivity. Harley Shaiken points out, however, that between 1980 and 1992, while Mexican manufacturing productivity rose 41 percent, real wages fell by 32 percent.[3] Wages and productivity have been decoupled in Mexico by the flood of unemployed workers flowing from agricultural and industrial "restructuring" and by an institutional system of state-controlled unions and police repression that keeps wages low.

Winners and losers from the enactment of NAFTA can be inferred from its supporters and opponents: the corporate and investment community loves it, labor and most citizens groups opposed it.[4] It was essentially a project of the TNCs, which will gain from investment in a low-wage poorly regulated environment and a consequent downward pressure on wages and environmental regulation in the United States. They will also gain by the fact that NAFTA is another arrangement (like GATT and the IMF) that by treaty wrests control of policy from democratically elected bodies and puts it into the hands of unelected supranational bureaucrats, along with "the market."

Democracy Versus Reform

The TNCs that enthusiastically support NAFTA include many of the same entities that were happy with the rise of the NSS in Latin America, and the rule of Suharto in Indonesia and Marcos in the Philippines. These leaders brought "stability" and "reform," which means that they were unencumbered by democratic pressures or the rule of law and were ready, willing, and able to torture and kill those who stood in the way of "reform." Popular movements were crushed by force, local and foreign elites were able to operate on favorable terms, and income distributions became more unequal and poverty rose markedly. These policies resulted in the now familiar pattern of wonderful "growth" combined with increasing immiseration of large numbers of people—a process which was given its classic expression by Brazilian general and head-of-state in 1971, Emilio Medici: "The economy is doing fine, but the people aren't."

We are now in a new phase of "reform" in the former Soviet bloc and Third World, and as the general drift of the reforms is the same as that supported by the NSS generals, there is the continuing obstacle of democratic forms and the rule of law. Hence the Yeltsin (Russia) and Fujimori (Peru) coups, and the struggle to keep "reformers" like Salinas and Menem in power as they serve their minority and expatriate constituencies. All of these leaders will be given diplomatic, economic, and PR support, and the Western media will always find good reasons for "reformer" coups and excesses; those who obstruct their service to the global corporate system will always be "hardliners" whose subversive actions provoked the suspension of the rule of law.

As the reformers make a travesty of democracy, we can also count on the economists to accommodate. The record of the "Chicago boys" in Chile is well known; less well known is the exceptional degree to which mainstream economists took the Cold War, arms race, security state, and support for repressive regimes abroad as givens. As noted earlier, their main response to the proliferation of NSSs in the U.S. sphere of influence was silence.

In connection with NAFTA, the extremely undemocratic character of the Mexican state, the election rigging, the human-rights abuses, state control and repression of workers, and government corruption don't bother mainstream economists at all. If the mainstream press and government treat Salinas as legitimate and even a great statesman, who are the economists to question this? After all, they are economists, not political scientists. MIT economist Rudiger Dornbusch even sets up Mexico as a model for other countries to emulate, for its "recognizing the need to make peace with the world capital market," its "accountability of officials, continuity, competence, and courage," which "goes far beyond rooting out corruption," "jail sentences for tax fraud becoming part of the culture," and "an incomes policy package used to make the transition to moderate inflation."[5] Does it take "courage" to accommodate to the world capital market and enlist U.S. and IFI support and protection, or would this be the mark of an opportunistic politician? Not a word from Dornbusch about Salinas's populist promises of 1988, election rigging, human-rights abuses, or the trend of income distribution under the courageous leader. The "mask of democracy"[6] satisfies Dornbusch. His remarks on the accountability of officials and new tax integrity are completely off the wall. He advances crude and dishonest apologetics for a profoundly undemocratic system.

The Populist Threat

For the TNCs and their institutional appendages, the primary threat in the Third World is popular movements and governments that foolishly respond to majority needs. The TNC goal is a world of governments responsive to *their* needs—that will keep taxes on business low, national budgets balanced, and social budgets minimal. They want thoroughgoing elite domination of government, preferably with the consent of the masses, but if need be by force. TNC goals were met in the NSSs by terror. They are also enforced by the IMF and World

Bank, whose lending rules enforcing budgetary constraints, privatization, and the opening up of Second and Third World economies, are also geared closely to TNC interests.

Notable under both NSS and IMF systems of control has been the relegation of the interests and welfare of the majority to secondary concern, or worse. With the NSSs, the lower classes were viewed strictly as costs of production to be kept down (Somoza referred to the majority as "oxen"): their welfare was not in the set of objectives pursued by the ruling elite at all. The TNCs and IFIs had no serious complaints about the NSSs, until they suffered virtual economic collapse following the first round of "reform." A 1993 World Bank report *Latin America and the Caribbean: A decade after the debt crisis* does use the word "repression" in reference to Chile—it speaks of the pre-Pinochet situation there as one in which the "capital market was then highly repressed" (p. 105). It never mentions the repression of humans.

In the New World Order, the IFIs sometimes express concern over the massive poverty and unemployment in their domains, but their concern, perhaps genuine, involves them in major intellectual contortions. The crucial fact is that their policy agenda *always* gives primary emphasis to the monetary, budget, and trade policies that meet the demands of the TNCs and global market players; poverty and unemployment are regrettable but unavoidable spinoffs from the primary policies, calling for second-order responses, if affordable. But the primary policies constrain social budgets, and the record under neoliberal regimes shows a consistent savaging of expenditures to alleviate poverty and to serve the majority.

In the extended account on the poverty problem in *Latin America and the Caribbean*, it is revealing how much stress is given to the threat that poverty—if sufficiently extensive and deep—might cause "chaos" and put "the sustainability of the reforms...in jeopardy" (p. 123). The report acknowledges that inequality has grown in recent years, and that it was worse in Latin America than any other part of the Third World. But this is not attributed to World Bank-supported reforms; it is blamed on "government control and regulations." The fact that a great deal of government intervention took place under NSS rule, with at least tacit IFI and TNC approval, is unmentioned. Furthermore, the increase in inequality during the decade of neoliberal reforms remains unexplained by the World Bank economists. In the past, while inequality rose in prosperity it fell in recessions, whereas in the 1980s period of recession-with-"reform" that tradition was broken and inequality continued to increase. Economists cited by the Bank find that Latin America's income inequality is related to inequalities in education, inadequate rates of growth, and populist policies that caused inflation. This is once again modeling to a purpose, with the underlying structure of ownership and control of Third World economies and the policy limits imposed by the global market and IFIs not included as potential causal variables. (The index of this book contains no citation to David Felix's, Susan George's or Arthur MacEwan's critical volumes on Third World debt problems.)

Rudiger Dornbusch, the enthusiast for Mexican-style reform, co-edited a book with Sebastian Edwards entitled *The Macroeconomics of Populism in Latin America* (University of Chicago, 1991) which is repeatedly cited by the World Bank in *Latin America and the Caribbean*, as its themes fit the TNC project admirably. "Populist" economic policies aimed at maintaining full employment and redistributing income have regularly produced budgetary and balance of payments deficits, an excessive money supply, capital flight, high-interest rates, inflation, and eventually economic breakdown. This *could* be blamed on the institutional arrangements that allow corruption, tax evasion, capital flight, the bailing out by government of failing private banks and other institutions (protecting foreign banks and other investors), and foreign bank and IFI policies that discriminate against governments not serving the TNC project. This Dornbusch and company never consider: the existing arrangements and policies are taken as givens, and Dornbusch and friends never suggest alternative policies that might allow populist ends to be met. Ultimately, this reflects a rejection of the populist goals, as anyone giving them any concern would obviously examine alternatives. But for the handmaidens of TNC truth, there is No Other Option to the TNC project and trickle-down-forever.

The Basic Needs/Independence Option

There *is* an alternative to trickle-down-forever, which may be called the "basic needs/independence option." The majority of people in the Third World are poor and work in agriculture, although in some countries the displaced agriculturists who have moved into the shanty-towns of Third World metropoli have made urban populations larger than the rural. These small agriculturists and shanty-town occupants are the uncared for majority whose welfare is far down the TNC agenda and would be of no concern at all if it did not pose the threat of "chaos."

For many years a number of liberal and left development analysts, some lodged in the UN or even in minority positions in the World Bank, have urged that the needs of the majority should be given *first* consideration in policy-making; that poor countries should follow a basic-needs strategy in which the first order of business would be to ensure adequate food, health care, housing, and education for the entire population. This would entail a stress on growing food for home consumption (rather than encouraging an export-oriented agriculture), and enlarging government services in housing, education, and health care. This schema is, of course, entirely incompatible with IMF rules and the interests of the TNCs, which seek to minimize social budgets serving ordinary citizens and to bring all Third World countries into the global system where they can produce coffee, cattle, winter fruit and vegetables, and other raw materials, and provide cheap tourism and low-wage and unprotected labor for export platforms, etc. The wrong interests would be served in a basic-needs/independence strategy. Of course, it is also argued that such a strategy is impractical and will fail, and that even the masses will be better off *in the long run* by following the elite party line of trickle-down-forever. And, of course, because the alternative option is terrifying to Western elites, they will go to great pains to assure that a basic needs/independence program *will* fail. Countries pursuing such a strategy (Cuba, Nicaragua in 1980-89, Guatemala in 1948-53) are immediately ostracized by the civilized world and are subject to economic and even military attack.

But the basic-needs/independence option exists. It requires that Third World (or Second World) countries avoid entrapment in the global network and dependence on the global institutions that will enforce structures and policies serviceable to a global elite-TNC constituency, rather than to the majority of ordinary people. The New World Order has made this option more difficult, with the aid of economists like Dornbusch, but as their policies fail to meet the basic needs of increasing numbers the basic-needs/independence option will become more and more viable. It is important to be aware of this alternative and to be prepared to argue its merits on any suitable occasion. It is also important to recognize the continuity in Western (TNC, IFI, government) policy, from support of the NSSs and Pinochet's freeing the "repressed" capital markets of Chile, to the current campaign for NAFTA and support of neoliberal reformers elsewhere—for the moment under the "mask of democracy."

—Z, December 1993

Chapter Eight

Michael Novak's Promised Land

Unfettered Corporate Capitalism

At one time a liberal theologian and columnist for *Commonweal*, Michael Novak became a neo-conservative in the 1970s, and since 1978 has been a "resident scholar in religion and public policy" at the corporate-funded American Enterprise Institute (AEI). Long the favorite theologian of the corporate community, he has been accommodating to corporate interests on human rights as well as economics issues. Accepting a "call" from President Ronald Reagan and UN Ambassador Jeane Kirkpatrick in 1981 to serve as U.S. representative to the UN Commission on Human Rights, Novak participated in the Reagan-era tilt toward warmer relations with Argentina, Chile, and other states that had institutionalized the use of extreme forms of state terror (such as torture and "disappearances"). He even spoke of "Chile's tradition of respect for the highest values, standards, and institutional aims of human rights" as a prelude to making a case for reduced UN surveillance of the human-rights performance of a government that had destroyed that tradition.[1] As a reward for his services to God, Country, and the Corporate Community, in 1994 Novak was awarded the Templeton Prize for Progress in Religion. Chairing the committee making this award for religious service was that notable exponent of Christian charity, Lady Margaret Thatcher.

The Spirit of Democratic Capitalism

Michael Novak's *The Spirit of Democratic Capitalism*[2] will surely take its rightful place alongside the works of George Gilder, William Simon, and Milton and Rose Friedman as one of the pop classics of the Age of Reagan. It is better written than its rivals, with rhetorical flourishes of some eloquence, but in a long-standing Novak tradition, the style runs to waste on a bedrock of neo-conservative clichés and intellectual opportunism. Novak's book is for the businessman-in-a-hurry, with quotes from theological and economic classics, learned footnotes, and a virtual compendium of short answers to criticisms of the U.S. business system. Not the least of the book's merits is its foundation in Novak's discovery that U.S. capitalism is loaded with "instinctive wisdom," and is possibly the structural end toward which God has striven. In short, this is a work of uplift and propaganda; one from which we can learn something about the author, his sponsors, and the processes of ideological mobilization, but little about reality.

Novak is not an economist. He moves cautiously, surveying the field like a rabbit looking out from its burrow, making forays when the coast seems clear or when some scholar with the preferred message can be mobilized to argue the case. He is especially bold in rebuking church liberals and radicals[3] who have attacked corporate behavior and the workings of the "development model" in Brazil and Chile without first having studied Ludwig Von Mises and Milton Friedman. These churchpeople thus lack an adequate "general theory"—of which the only valid one turns out to be Adam Smith's "invisible hand," still sure to bring net advantages everywhere. If this were understood by Brazilian Archbishop Dom Helder Camara he would presumably eschew "socialism" and raise no objections to the forcible dispossession of peasants who stand in the way of progress. At this level of discourse the argument gets understandably murky. Novak does, of course, concede that things are not perfect here or in Brazil, but instead of addressing these imperfections and defending them directly, he points to the "big picture." In the big picture, we—i.e., Democratic Capitalism, the United States, and especially its larger economic units—are good; our enemies (communism, socialism) are bad. Criticism of the good gives aid to the bad.

This dichotomy between friends and enemies runs through Novak's book and leads him into serious contradiction and hypocrisy. The great merit of Democratic Capitalism in the Novak vision is its pluralism, with economic, political, and cultural-moral spheres that are separate and independent and serve as a system of mutual checks and balances. But Novak's book is a systematic attack on both government and cultural-sphere critics who have raised questions, large and small, about the performance in the economic sphere of the sponsors of the AEI. Thus Novak has his cake and eats it too. He lauds the system in a general way for its marvelous pluralism, while furiously attacking all elements of the pluralism seen as threatening by the corporate community.

Novak works with a simple model. Democratic Capitalism combines a private economy, democratic politics, and an independent cultural system. These nurture and curb one another, preventing monolithic power. Capitalism leads to democracy and the two together aim for and provide wealth and justice. The system is imperfect but better than any other known. The proof lies in the history of the United States. This is the essence of Novak's book, and he adds little to it. The ideas can hardly be described as original, and the brush strokes are broad and lacking in subtlety. Novak asserts that he is looking at the system in order to gain insight into our probable future, but his model is completely static, with no analysis or even acknowledgement of the fact that institutions have changed. Democratic Capitalism sprang fully armed from the minds of the founding fathers, and has proven itself over two centuries of experiment.

Novak reaches heights of spirituality in contemplating the businessman and the large U.S. corporation.[4] The businessman is part of a cooperative enterprise in which he does better "the more his actions are inspired by all the moral virtues" (p. 131). As a community participant and builder he must try to inspire trust in his team and thus "can scarcely be an autocrat." No mention is made of competitive pressures and their possible effect on spiritual values, nor any potential conflict of interest with labor on wages or local communities over tax concessions or waste disposal. This transformation of the modern corporation into a virtual monastic order is done at an abstract level, without supporting evidence or analysis. In this vision of the corporation as a world of morality, trust, and simple creativity, Novak's theological background is compellingly evident. Traditional apologetics made the large corporation a rugged individual; it remained for Michael Novak to make it into a Godly haven. For those tired of the pressures of everyday life, Novak has a spiritual message: "Get thee to a large corporation."

In the real corporate world, the increased size and mobility of business firms have created major problems of "abandonments," structural unemployment, and the systematic "bargaining down" of labor and local government. Other forms of "externalities"[5] arising out of modern technology (hazardous products, workplaces, and wastes) loom large in serious discussions of the problems confronting modern industrial societies. What does Novak say about these matters? He completely evades such issues, except for the following brief reference to abandonments (pp. 180-181):

> In deciding to close an unprofitable plant, managers may recognize political pressures and moral pressures of many sorts, while still determining that economic rationality alone "leaves them no alternative." Some might argue further that reliance on such rationality also repre-

sents, in the larger view, sound political and moral judgment. Their reason is that a policy which subsidizes unprofitable operations penalizes other citizens elsewhere, weakening its own economic future, and, even if in the name of compassion or other noble sentiments, sets in motion pressures for less than moral purposes throughout the society... Some might say, in other words, that economic rationality also ranks among the moral virtues, a form of prudence.

The abandonment of a community leaving many workers stranded imposes real costs on society that can be disregarded by a private firm in a market system. An economist would say that in these cases the market "failed." Only a Michael Novak could convert this private decision, which not only abandons a "community,"[6] but also constitutes a market failure in the technical economic and social productivity sense, into a higher morality.

Notice also that Novak conveys a different tone and moral lesson than in his earlier abstract accolade to the corporate monastic order, where the community spirit prevails. Here coldblooded profit rationality is the key moral virtue; compassion may bring about unwarranted interventions that must be guarded against.

Novak is not subtle in his differential allocation of motives to those favored and disfavored in his ideological system. While the businessman is induced by his position as head of a community to virtuous behavior, the agents of government (excluding the military establishment and police) and the intellectuals (excepting those at the AEI and Hoover Institution) are aggressive, power hungry, self-serving, constantly intrude into other spheres, and do not operate in "communities." Novak also personifies and imputes purpose to entire systems and institutions *ad libitum* and to the convenience of the argument. Thus the "aim" of Democratic Capitalism is a "country of free persons in voluntary association"; and its further "intention" is "to raise the material base of life of every human being on earth." U.S. Democratic Capitalism was created with a "respect for contingency" and a new concept of the family; it "judges corporate size pragmatically"; it "fears the mean pettiness of regimented equality"; it "does not promise to eliminate sin"; it "places its strongest emphasis upon practice."

How does Novak know what "Democratic Capitalism" intends? Quite simply, his alleged distillation of "hidden wisdom" from a complex system is a completely unscientific trick that gives his bias full rein. Novak mentions that the fathers of Democratic Capitalism "were most afraid" of "the tyranny of a majority" (p. 58). The "tyranny of the majority" is arguably a euphemism for effective majority rule. Arguably, the "hidden wisdom" of the "fathers" was their mastery in combining the appearance of majority rule with effective limits and protections of what Madison referred to as the "permanent interests" of society. Novak selects his set of hidden wisdoms for a different purpose.

Although the government is one of the triad of a beneficent Democratic Capitalism, it is a villain and threat. As in other neo-conservative treatments, for Novak it has grown because of bureaucratic and expansionist tendencies and biases of the "new class," not because of legitimate social demands. This is merely asserted, without supporting fact or argument. Thus the drift of Novak's argument is to discredit government in its social (non-military) function. The government is not a social institution that induces community spirit and that represents harmonizing impulses; only profit-seeking business enterprise is so characterized.

Novak is even less forthright when dealing with government-business relations in Third World development. On the multinational role in the development process Novak studiously avoids any suggestion that the U.S. government has ever had anything to do with events in Latin America. The Monroe Doctrine and Guatemala do not appear in the index, and his short chapter on Brazil never so much as hints that U.S. penetration, intervention, and literal subversion were important in the 1964 coup.[7] Given U.S. non-intervention by neo-conservative sleight-of-hand, Novak can proceed with the other formulas, such as the unreasonableness of our sense of guilt. Novak's chutzpah and power of self-deception are so well developed that he can wax indignant over human-rights abuses in *post-Somoza* Nicaragua, where the state terrorists according to Novak actually *murdered someone* (p. 286)—while maintaining absolute silence on the institutionalization of torture, death squads, and disappearances by the thousands in a network of U.S. Latin client states.[8]

On the cultural impact of Democratic Capitalism, Novak has a chapter on "The Family," in which it is shown that a Carter-era White House Conference on Families was run by people who included in the concept of "families" homosexuals and childless and unmarried couples. An indignant Novak cries out, "They did not seem anxious to exclude any arrangement" (p. 158). Novak's account of this sinister event is followed by a long encomium to the nuclear family and its virtues. The businessman-in-a-hurry may find Novak's account so heartwarming that he might fail to realize that it is a demagogic irrelevancy. Instead of addressing the substantive questions of just how the evolution of Democratic Capitalism (individualism, the profit motive, competition, increasing capital mobility) has actually *affected* the family, where the family is going under prevailing conditions, and what we might do about it, Novak takes the easy road of vigorously stating the case for chastity and wedded motherhood.

It is an important part of the neo-conservative credo that in the cultural sphere capitalism has thrown up a "new class" of free-floating intellectuals, full of envy of and hostility toward the socially oriented corporate leaders who are busily guiding their communities toward a better life. These intellectuals are in an unholy alliance with the other baddies, government bureaucrats, who give them money and other support. They exercise extraordinary power in the media as well as in academia and—in tandem with a civil government run amok—their machinations go far toward explaining our problems. Novak has long expounded this doctrine and he reiterates it here. I note again the imputation of ill motives in a childishly asymmetric fashion: in contrast with businessmen, intellectuals and media people are not part of "communities" with internal drives toward the good and generous—they tend to resent their betters "whose methods and life styles differ so much from their own" and lean toward "the left" (undefined). We are left to presume, since Novak is completely silent on this point, that businessmen, unlike the envious and hostile intellectuals, are warm, tolerant and generous toward all, despite lifestyle differences.

Conventional analyses point out that many great humanistic efforts under capitalism—struggles against slavery, child labor, and numerous other traditional and newly emergent abuses—have been given critical leadership and moral support by new class members. This schema of an independent intelligentsia helping curb the excesses of profit-seeking business is not only well grounded in historical experience, it fits Novak's view of a beneficent pluralism with creative checks and balances coming from government and the cultural-moral sphere. But Novak cannot use such an argument, even if grounded in fact, because it implies that the economic sphere, the corporate system, *needs* constraining, and that the new class is playing a necessary function of honest and moral broker. In the corporate and neo-conservative credo, the new class is responsible for the welfare state and unreasonable hostility toward business. The pliable Novak says the same, in violation of the internal logic of his tripartite system, based on no discernible analysis of corporate structure, behavior, or performance, and without any reference to historical evidence.

One curious feature of the neo-conservative theory of the new class is its unduly modest neglect of the rapid growth of the "old class" of spokesmen for the established order. The rise of government, per capita income, and the welfare state, which allegedly created the new dissident elite, also brought with it an increase in the assets of business and of the wealthy elite (e.g., Richard Mellon Scaife), new and well funded business-oriented think tanks, a huge increase in business employment of intellectuals as consultants and experts,[9] and CIA sponsorship of anti-communist journals, books, and intellectuals. The annual incomes of the AEI and Hoover Institution each exceed that of the lonely Institute for Policy Studies by a factor of six or more. The ability of the enlarged old class to get wide publicity for its allegations of insidious power wielded by a much less potent (and partly mythical) new class—while diverting attention from its impressive self—is a testimony to its own enhanced and special powers.

The new class is an extremely fuzzy concept, especially in the hands of a Novak, whose usage extends flexibly from all intellectuals (himself included) to various subsets of "adversaries." An adversary is one who criticizes, whether gently while explicitly praising existing institutions or strongly assailing the institutional arrangements themselves. As Novak uses the concept mainly to attack the mass media I will confine further (brief) remarks to this area only.

A major difficulty faced by the theory of the new class is that the mass media, through which the new class is alleged to do much of its dirty work, is made up entirely of large (and often conglomerate) business entities, controlled by corporate owners and managers, deriving the bulk of their revenues from corporate advertisers. It seems extremely improbable that such a power structure would allow systematic and fundamental attacks on itself and net biases that are hostile to the interests of the corporate system to prevail.

Novak and his neo-conservative colleagues develop their contrary view by several routes. One is to give the cultural sphere more autonomy than it really possesses. Novak supports this by his usual bland assertions without evidence—"The domain of the word—the right to free speech—is specifically protected. Its relative autonomy grants to the moral-cultural system status as a system, on a plane equal to that of the economic system and the political system" (p. 184). Who "grants" relative autonomy to the mass media? This is mystification that dodges any confrontation with the structural fact that the most important segments of the moral-cultural sphere are *parts* of the economic sphere. It even inverts the plausible inferences from the primary facts of ownership and control. Those who *really* oppose the corporate system do not own any large newspapers or TV stations and networks; only large businesses do. We would therefore expect bias to run in exactly the opposite direction from that suggested by Novak, and it does, as is apparent to anyone who asks the right questions.[10]

Novak does not raise or answer any such questions and he does not address the facts of structure. Instead, he asserts that the "culture" of the national mass media is one of artists and entertainers, making no effort to show that the top owners-managers-advertisers fail to direct and manage the "culture." He just implies this, as one might speak of the control of the Soviet mass media by the "culture" of artists, entertainers, and journalists doing their own thing. Some leaders of the mass media, such as Henry Luce, William Randolph Hearst, and Rupert Murdoch, have been aggressively political, and it is clear that their preferences have overwhelmed the "culture" of the "left" supposedly characterizing their relatively autonomous subordinates. These cases not fitting the neo-conservative hypotheses, they are non-facts and can be ignored. But even apart from these cases, there is absolutely no reason to believe that mass-media leaders fail to use their power to enforce fundamental limits that are premises of mass-media employees.[11] It is true that in many important cases subordinates have some autonomy, but it is a neo-conservative fallacy to use *some* autonomy to suggest freedom from basic constraints and limits.

This fallacy is supported by a second, in which Novak and the neo-conservatives claim that the intellectual and media elites are more liberal and critical than their employers and the country at large.[12] This is a half truth: the intellectual and media elites are more liberal than "middle Americans" on social issues, but less so on economic issues like the desirability of more progressive taxes and government regulation of business.[13] The neo-conservatives fail to show empirically that these differences have had any measurable effects on media performance. In Novak's case "liberal and critical" is translated by mere assertion into generalized hostility to the system and unjustified and unfair attacks. This false translation is given credence by evidence showing that the businessman is frequently presented in an unfavorable light on television.[14] The neo-conservative studies never mention the overwhelming volume and bias of commercial advertising messages on television. They also fail to note that even in television programs deemed anti-business the fundamental premises of the system are not attacked, only deviations that the forces of law and order strive to contain. Novak and company also look only at the surface, rarely examining the impact of the TV (or other media) package on viewers' basic attitudes. Studies peering below this surface find that it is largely system-supportive, stressing the importance of the possession and consumption of goods as the source of satisfaction, individual and personal achievement as the route to success, and strengthening the grip of Democratic Capitalism by offering no positive alternatives.[15] The individual viewer in a TV environment heavily dependent on violence and law-and-order solutions is made "socially rigid and mistrustful, and often excessively anxious or repressive"; he or she is depoliticized, homogenized, and deterred from any kind of working-class consciousness.[16]

Analysts of television stress its need as a business to deliver a large block of customers. In order to do that it is necessary to provide excitement and credibility to a mass audience distrustful of the powerful. As George Gerbner expresses it,

The business community has a choice, then, between the delivery of the audience and the flattery of itself. Put in that way, the choice is always clear. The critical, occasionally unflattering portrayal of businessmen on television is a necessary instrument of credibility within an otherwise anxious and insecure lower-middle class milieu.[17]

Novak and his fellow neo-conservatives, and a segment of the business community, are thus objecting to a mass media that not only serves the larger corporate interests on all basic premises, but also adds credibility to the Novak triad by its petty assaults and honest broker exposés. Nevertheless, the mass media upset the sensitive members of the business community. Businessmen are not accustomed to attacks and uncontrolled situations within their organizations, and they often react strongly to criticisms from without. In periods of conservative reaction they frequently attach themselves to irrational causes and demagogues—A. Mitchell Palmer and the Bolshevik scare in 1919-1920; Joe McCarthy and his "205 card-carrying members of the Communist Party" in the State Department, in 1950-1952[18]—which serve their ends by discrediting business's enemies, but at a heavy social cost.

The new-class theory is in the same irrationalist tradition, based on ludicrous and easily refuted claims that are sustained *in the mass media* by the power of Novak's sponsors![19] To this irony add the structuring of the theory to mobilize the masses against a "privileged elite," with Michael Novak and colleagues up front, officials of W.R. Grace, General Electric, Ford, and ITT in the background sponsoring this assault on privilege!

The neo-conservatives have provided comprehensive apologetics for joint business-military rectification of the democratic excesses of pre-1964 Brazil and pre-1973 Chile (among others), and they are energetically preparing the ground for a cleansing at home. Novak castigates the "independent" moral-cultural sector as a "neglected" hotbed of "formidably dangerous" artists and intellectuals, "bewitched by falsehoods and absurdities and unduly empowered to impose them on hapless individuals" (p. 20). This sphere is thus threatening the foundations of the system by criticizing it and playing into the hands of its enemies. In his attacks on government and the moral-cultural sphere Novak shows once again the roots of his moral commitment. Although the complete independence and separation of the three sectors—economic, political, and cultural—he asserted earlier to be the very soul of Democratic Capitalism, the monastic order of large corporations having become restive over "Big Government" and mass media criticisms, Michael Novak provides in *The Spirit of Democratic Capitalism* the intellectual and moral basis for bringing a corrupted cultural-moral-political order under a new and more unified management.

—*Monthly Review, October 1983*

Part Two

CULTURE, SOCIETY, AND POLITICS

Chapter Nine

Privatization of Government

The Deepening Market in the West (4)

Private power and the incessant demands of capital as the main engine of the economy have always dominated the U.S. political system. James Madison foresaw that fragmentation of the population and the great size of the country would always serve to protect its "permanent interests" from confiscation and lesser threats by the majority. Modest change can be effected, however, when things get bad enough and when the interests of the fragmented majority coalesce, usually briefly.[1] These circumstances bring moderate reforms that alleviate pressures from below. But they arouse great anxiety among the dominant elites, who denounce the extremism of "special interests" and their spokespersons in these periods of "democratic excesses" and "crises of democracy" (i.e., movements toward actual democracy).

The processes by which the excesses are contained, although they may make democracy a formal affair without much democratic substance, are institutionalized and are made to seem natural by the established institutions. Their seamier features are glossed over or suppressed. The civics texts in schools and the mainstream media focus on the nominally democratic forms, the wonderful system of checks and balances, and the surface elements of the electoral horse races. As was the case with demonstration elections in El Salvador and other client states, the media stress the positive, while avoiding a critical look at whether the fundamental requirements of free elections are met, such as reasonable equality of funding and access to the mass media by representatives of all major classes and constituencies.

The belief by a considerable proportion of the population that elections in and of themselves represent genuine democracy and give sovereignty and free choice to the public at large is a tremendous achievement of the Western system of governance. It legitimates elite control and weakens criticism against it. The public is rendered quiescent because "it" has spoken, and significant numbers are impressed with the argument that protest is improper because the government represents the popular will, validated by a democratic election. In the classic phrase of William Penn: "Let the People think they Govern and they will be Governed."

A further factor contributing to quiescence is the belief that, given the freedom and opportunity for personal achievement in the United States, failure is a result of individual inadequacies (or bad luck), not defects in institutions. We need more moral fibre, which will only be weakened by coddling the lazy and ne'er-do-wells.

Of course the system must produce some minimal payoff for the underlying population—or at least for a significant fraction of that population—in order to keep the excesses under good control. In the provinces, where this has been more difficult, the U.S. establishment has often actively colluded with and even helped organize National Security States (NSSs) to keep the masses apathetic and passive by means of extreme state terrorism (always called, however, counterinsurgency, pacification, the restoration of stability, or even counterterrorism). While this has not been necessary at home as yet, it is clear from the support of so many terror states abroad that this remains an option if needed. The long history of using Red Squads and police repression to break strikes, prevent and sabotage labor organization, and contain other forms of dissent,[2] and the experience of the post-World War I Palmer raids, the McCarthy-Truman era Red Hunt, the 1960s COINTELPRO program,[3] and the covert war against the Central America movement in the 1980s,[4] demonstrate a system of permanent low-intensity repression that ebbs and flows according to establishment need. If there had been a substantial Left in the United States, and any genuine threat from below, I have no doubt that some variant of the more severe Third World models of pacification with which the U.S. military have been closely linked would have been put into effect.

The Business of Politics

In the early 1990s the mainstream media displayed a surge of interest in and concern over "money in politics" and possible abuses associated with Political Action Committees (PACs) and other anomalies. This was precipitated by a number of developments, including the savings and loan (S&L) scandals and the involvement of five senators with the unsavory Charles Keating, who headed and looted one of the S&Ls, the departure of Democratic Party leaders Tony Coelho and Jim Wright from Congress under a cloud of controversy, the discomfiture of the Democrats as they fell still farther behind in the money quest, and a host of complaints by politicians and critics that money is subverting democracy. A stream of books conveyed the same message: Elizabeth Drew's *Politics and Money*, Philip Stern's *The Best Congress Money Can Buy*, Brooks Jackson's *Honest Graft*, and many others.

The press and liberal critics have discussed the diversion of the attention of politicians from substantive issues to raising money, the growing influence of funders on candidate selection and success, and growing corruption. The last in particular is a dramatic matter that allows a great deal of moralizing and a minimum of serious analysis of the workings of the system. The *New York Times*, for example, had a multipart series on money in politics in March and April 1990 that addressed all of these issues in a superficial way. What it did not do was discuss and examine the class skewing of politics by money and the impact of this on democratic substance.

It did not attempt, for example, to assess the validity of the "investment theory" of politics, spelled out by Thomas Ferguson and Joel Rogers in their book *Right Turn: The Decline of the Democrats and the Future of American Politics*.[5] This theory suggests that the dominant parties and their major candidates shape their programs in accord with the demands of business "investors" in the electoral process, with the result that the non-investing majority of the population is effectively unrepresented and thus disenfranchised in the political process.

The Democrats' Search for Investors

According to "investment theory" analysts, the 1970s and 1980s saw the Democratic Party abandoned by many of its traditional business supporters, who shifted to a party and candidate (Republicans, Reagan) they believed would better serve their changing and urgent interests. The leaders of the Democratic Party responded to this development by abandoning populism and the traditional Democratic appeal to a mass base in favor of a frantic competition for funds from the military-industrial complex, S&L speculators, and other business interests. They chose to go for the money first, the voters as an afterthought. This explains Mondale's suicidal stress on balancing the budget and tax increases (but not tax reform), Dukakis's similarly unappealing program, and the ongoing effort of the Democratic Leadership Council group to slough off the New Deal-populist tradition entirely in favor of "moderation" (i.e., policies that will appeal to monied interests).[6]

In fact, the efforts of the Democratic "moderates" to raise money has provided a textbook case of systematic subversion of politics by money: Brooks Jackson's book *Honest Graft* is largely an account of Tony Coelho's and his fellow moderate Democrats' struggle to increase the Democratic Party's competitiveness by virtually unrestrained pursuit of business money. The book is valuable in showing Coelho's remarkable powers of rationalizing this groveling for money and the policy compromises that ensued. Policy was regularly bent in accordance with the exigencies of money-raising. This pursuit of and accommodation to investors may be read as a more thorough-going integration of politics and government with "the market," meeting the "effective demand" of investors, but removing the interests of the unmonied majority from even the nominal pitches of the contesting dominant parties. It is true that, previously, the populist pitches and promises were often not fulfilled, but at least they were on the agenda to be debated and fought over. In the era of moderation they are no longer even on the agenda.[7]

The abandonment of a populist agenda in favor of investor service should be front-page news on a regular basis. The catch, of course, is that the mainstream media are also dominated by investors, and their proprietors and advertisers don't like populism, progressive taxes, etc. Not surprisingly, the "investment theory" and its devastating implications were not discussed in the previously mentioned *New York Times* articles, and the entire structure of news accommodates to the privatization of politics and government. Robb-Strauss-Nunn-Coelho and company are portrayed as "moderates," and the view disseminated by the media is that the trouble with the Democratic Party is the undue influence of "special interests," not its perversion by the quest for money from "investors" and unwillingness to serve a mass base.

A front-page article by Richard L. Berke in the *New York Times* of July 17, 1989, was entitled "Democrats Trail in Fund Raising, And Many Blame New Chairman." The article did not focus on the effect of fundraising on constituency representation and democratic substance; it framed the issue in terms of the "investors" complaints about Ron Brown's excessive liberalism and ties to Jesse Jackson. The subordination of political party programs and government to investor demands was made a natural background fact not to be questioned, and the problem was seen as the poor service rendered by the "too liberal" party to the investor community.[8]

Capture and Life Cycle Theories of Political Investment

When the business community is under pressure, it mobilizes its forces to alter the political climate drastically. Its command of resources and power is such that when it presents a fairly solid political phalanx, it is often able to put in place a government that will serve its main interests without compromise, and may indulge in genuine class warfare, as the Reagan administration did in the 1980s and the Gingrich Republicans resumed in 1995. In these periods of business-sponsored

counter-revolution, businessmen take over a host of important government positions, conflict of interest becomes blatant, and government
operations are corrupted, dismantled, and manipulated with abandon.
The Teapot Dome scandal of 1922 was easily matched by the operations of James Watt, who was a hero to and excellent fundraiser among
the beneficiaries of Interior Department largess.

When scandals become rampant under a full-fledged business
regime, and substantial segments of the population (including some
sectors of business) are severely damaged, the mainstream press eventually rouses itself, "reform" becomes credible, and an opportunity is
carved out again for the party more moderate in its devotion and
service to the business community. We move perhaps into the reform
phase of the political cycle, although this is no longer certain. The New
Deal came into existence only after an economic collapse in the 1930s.
The Reagan counter-revolution did not result in a collapse, and instead
of a victory for "reform" we had, first, the triumph of a consolidator of
the counter-revolution, and then a victory for a mild reformer incapable
of implementing mild reform (Clinton). This paralyzed (and continuously assailed) reformism lasted only two years, at the conclusion of
which another Republican victory resulted in a further vigorous attack
on governmental impediments to market operations. In October 1994,
the soon-to-be Speaker of the House of Representatives, Newt Gingrich,
urged a private gathering of corporate lobbyists to concentrate their
contributions on Republicans as the best insurance of "future corporate savings."[9] They poured their money in, and got what they considered to be an electoral bargain, "almost too-good-to-be-true" in the
view of corporate CEOs.[10]

At this juncture, it is distinctly possible that the growing power
of the market and importance of large sums of money for electoral
success have made the major parties virtually complete captives of
investors, stalemating reformism, and causing the political spectrum
to ratchet steadily to the right.[11]

−Z, July/August 1990

Chapter Ten

Law and Order

It is a notable fact that the two recent U.S. presidents who most strongly expressed their concern with law and order (L&O), Nixon and Reagan, closed out their terms enmeshed in scandals. Nixon barely avoided impeachment, and Reagan was immune only because of his administration's remarkable success in taming the press and Democrats. Nixon's Attorney-General, John Mitchell, served time in prison. Reagan's Attorney-General, Edwin Meese, left office under a cloud, and there were numerous prosecutions for law violations of other high officials and advisers, although few served jail terms. It is rarely noted in the mainstream media that the present L&O supreme court majority was chosen by officials who went—or should have gone—to jail for blatant disregard of the law. In the Housing and Urban Development (HUD) exposures of massive influence peddling, the Pentagon scandals, the Iran-Contra illegalities and protection given drug dealers willing to support the Contras, are probably only the tip of a large Reagan-era iceberg.[1]

In short, there seems to be an inverse relationship between the trumpeting of a concern for L&O and actual adherence to the rule of law. L&O governments—invariably right-wing—are exceptionally unprincipled in their willingness to ignore the law and manipulate public fears to achieve, maintain, and exercise power. Their aim and role is to serve the governing class, weaken labor and welfare measures, and advance the interests of the national security establishment. These are aims of the dominant class as a whole, although some elements would pursue them less aggressively and in a more compromising spirit, and a minority has a broader vision of the national interest. For the bulk of the dominant class, however, protest marches and strikes in pursuit of lower-class benefits or in opposition to state imperial ventures are readily seen as "disorder" and, if large-scale, a "crisis of democracy." This world view was formalized in Sir Frank Kitson's 1972 book *Low*

Intensity Operations, where "subversion" is identified as any kind of pressure designed to force the governing class "to do things which they would not want to do."[2] The function of L&O is to assure that the majority do not so pressure the governing class.

Class Application of the Law

Law and Order regimes simultaneously weaken the law in its application to the elite and agents of the government, while intensifying its application to the majority. They come into office like an army occupying hostile territory, including in their cadres many crooks who want to take advantage of the new opportunities to loot. Both Reagan and Nixon were fond of distancing themselves from "the government" and "Washington bureaucrats," except when wrapping themselves in the flag to justify an assault on some foreign target. Part of the very design of such regimes has been to bring government into disrepute as well as to weaken and dismantle many of its civil functions. Much of the corruption under Reagan was assured by putting into office administrators who hated the laws under whose authority they served and refused to enforce them (e.g., the Environmental Protection Agency, the Food and Drug Administration, the Occupational Safety and Health Administration, and the civil-rights division of the Department of Justice). Given the intimate relationship of the regime with vested interests, it was inevitable that HUD and Pentagon contracting would attain new levels of corruption.

It is a long Republican tradition, also, to suspend or weaken the anti-trust laws in response to the interests of the party's corporate constituency. As stated by business consultant Charles Stevenson in 1934: "Practically, under the Harding, Coolidge, and Hoover Administrations industry enjoyed, to all intents and purposes, a moratorium from the Sherman Act, and through the more or less effective trade associations which were developed in most of our industries, competition was, to a very considerable extent, controlled. The Department of Justice acted with great restraint and intelligence and only enforced the Sherman Act against those industries who violated the law in a flagrant and unreasonable manner."[3] The anti-trust laws of the 1920s were also weakened by a Supreme Court that interpreted the Section 7 anti-merger provision of the Clayton Act out of existence. In the 1926 decision *Thatcher Manufacturing v. Federal Trade Commission (FTC)*, the court held that if a company illegally acquired controlling stock in another company, but used its control to merge the acquired firm's assets into itself before the FTC could act, the FTC couldn't do anything about it. There is nothing like a well-selected court to adjust the law in accord with the demands of the vested interests!

One of Ronald Reagan's earliest presidential acts was to pardon two FBI agents who had been convicted for illegally burglarizing the office of a legal political organization. In another important symbolic action in 1983, Richard Helms the former CIA head who had been convicted of perjury, was given what Reagan called a "long overdue" National Security Medal. Stealing and lying in the service of the state is not a crime for an L&O regime, even when established as a crime in a court of law. Logically, law violations by state agents should be considered especially serious crimes by true believers in the law, but as noted, L&O regimes are run by individuals for whom the law is merely an instrument for private or ideological service. For them, the end justifies the means, although these same individuals often pontificate that one of the sinister features of communism is the belief of its leaders that the end justifies the means.

How are we to explain the numerous indictments of Reagan officials, the Levine-Boesky prosecutions,[4] and the pursuit of Watergate criminals, if L&O governments and the corporate system are virtually freed of the encumbrance of the law under such regimes? One reason is that the volume of abuses escalates on such a scale that even minimal enforcement must address the more blatant cases, which often enter public consciousness through investigative reporting, court suits, and confessions of disenchanted ex-officials. A second reason is that the elite and government agents who quickly take advantage of the relaxation of legal constraints often get cocky and push too far, threatening other members of the elite and the credibility and viability of major institutions. Boesky, Levine, and their associates were hurting important corporate interests while making their inside-information-based killings, and insider abuses make ordinary investors leery of participating in an unfair game. Nixon and company were attacking the Democratic Party and the prerogatives of Congress. Reagan was also running roughshod over Congress. These aggressors had to be curbed, although not too harshly.

Getting Tough on the Underlying Population

Harsher treatment is meted out to the classes being pacified under an L&O regime. Analyses of trends of law and court decisions under L&O governments show that they gradually increase the rights of the state and the powers of the police, increase the severity of penalties for lower-class crimes, and fill up the prisons.[5] Considerable court discretion exists for many crimes, so that under an L&O judicial system "terrorists" will get long prison terms and brutal treatment—a Japanese radical, apprehended before committing any crime, was recently given 30 years; the radicals Alejandrina Torres, Susan Rosenberg, and Sylvia Baraldini confined in the Female High Security Unit in Lexington,

Kentucky in 1986 were kept in subterranean cells, under constant video surveillance, and were handcuffed and manacled by chains around their waists when requiring a medical visit. Petty drug users and dealers can get probation or long sentences depending on judicial "judgment."

Prison populations grow under L&O regimes partly because of the economic policies that they institute. Planned recessions, union-busting, and a collapse of low-income housing construction and economic support for the poor all increase pressures on the lower classes, pushing them toward anger, protest, and crime. Recognition of government unconcern and even active hostility toward them, lavish displays of wealth, and evidence of blatant favoritism in economic policy and application of the law have similar effects.

As "crime in the streets" increases, middle- and upper-class fears grow and L&O policies are justified in a self-reinforcing system. Increasing crime thus serves the interests of the L&O regime, strengthening its political power and justifying militarization at home and abroad.

Fascist and Third World L&O Regimes

Fascist regimes stress L&O, and their more violent operations have served functions similar to those of L&O governments in countries like the United States and Britain, which have maintained liberal forms. It is understandable therefore that Western elites have tended to be sympathetic to fascism, although occasionally expressing regret over its "excesses." They have become hostile mainly where fascist regimes posed real political challenges to their interests. Thus in the 1920s Mussolini was treated with great warmth by the U.S. elite, Judge Elbert Gary, head of U.S. Steel stating in 1923 that "a master hand has, indeed, strongly grasped the helm of the Italian state," Republican Party statesman Elihu Root remarking before the Council on Foreign Relations in 1926 that "Italy has a revival of prosperity, contentment and happiness..." under the dictator, who was consistently described as a "moderate."[6] Hitler was also a "moderate": the U.S. *chargé d'affaires* in Berlin wrote to the State Department in 1933 that "the more moderate section of the [Nazi] party" was "headed by Hitler himself" and appeals "to all civilized and reasonable people."[7] Spanish fascist dictator Francisco Franco had a steadfast protector and ally in the United States, from the time of Harry Truman onward.

The same of course applies to L&O regimes in the Third World, many of them organized under U.S. sponsorship to contain restive majorities. The need for L&O regimes has always been explained in terms of disorder and a communist threat. The Western mainstream media regularly find that serious instability justifies strong measures in countries being set up for a coup (Brazil in 1964, Chile in 1973), but they have great difficulty locating any Western encouragement of and support for the disorder or local coup agents.[8]

The L&O regimes of Latin America and elsewhere in the U.S. empire are intensified versions of their counterparts in developed countries. Money for the police and army is greatly increased; corruption becomes more systematic and large scale (Chomsky and I have dubbed them "shakedown states"); and economic policies are installed that immiserate the majority and generate "communists," thus justifying an investment in L&O. An excellent case can be made that these are terrorist states, and their Western sponsors are therefore prime supporters of global terrorism, but this is, of course, contrary to Western constructs of terrorism: by definition (and political affiliation) these regimes do not engage in terrorism, they *counter* terror.

A final touch in the hypocrisy in which L&O is imbedded: the goons who run these regimes of terror also frequently attempt to implement traditional moral rules. The mercenary generals installed by the United States in Vietnam imposed regulations against long hair, while running a system of organized prostitution, theft, torture, and murder. The generals in Latin America are also very keen on "morality."

–Z, December 1989

Chapter Eleven

The New Racist Onslaught

The Bell Curve, by Richard Herrnstein and Charles Murray, and the publicity given to it by the mainstream media, is part of a new racist onslaught on the Black poor that, not coincidentally, has gathered steam during a period of austerity for ordinary citizens and pressures for budgetary cutbacks by the corporate community. In his 1974 essay "Racist Arguments and IQ," Stephen J. Gould, writing about an earlier resurgence of "biological determinism," asked, if the new theory "rests on no new facts (actually, no facts at all), then why has it become so popular of late? The answer must be social and political." Furthermore, Gould wondered if impoverishment is a result of either societal and program failure or some inherent character flaw, "which alternative will be chosen by men in power in an age of retrenchment?"[1]

Acceptability of Racist Doctrine

What is most notable and least remarked upon about the reception of *The Bell Curve* is the renewed acceptability and/or tolerance of straightforward racist doctrine. A book that purported to prove, with voluminous statistics, that Italians or Jews were inherently stupid or suffered from other inherited defects, would not be given immediate substantial publicity and serious treatment; mainstream commentators would not assert that such a book was raising reasonable and even urgent questions that we should listen to with open minds. The theme would be seen as invidious and insulting to Italians or Jews, and the book would have to have phenomenal credentials and authentication by experts and notables before it would be taken at all seriously in the mainstream media.

The case of books by "holocaust deniers" is instructive in this regard. Many of their works are large, stuffed with alleged empirical evidence and copious footnotes. But the only books on holocaust denial that are given direct press coverage in this country are those denouncing the deniers; the denier books themselves are ignored and are available only underground. Critics of the denier books are indignant, not only at the falsifications, but also on the grounds that denial of the holocaust is dangerously provocative, is part of a larger anti-semitic package, and is deeply insulting to holocaust survivors and their descendants.

The denier books are, in truth, unworthy of serious media attention, but so are many or all of the racist tomes attacking Blacks that do gain media attention. The fact that racist works such as *The Bell Curve* are deeply insulting to Blacks seems to have no bearing on their treatment in mainstream publications; their authors are even congratulated for their courage in raising touchy, politically incorrect, but important issues. The fact that for 100 years anti-Black racist theories have surfaced, gotten great publicity, and in retrospect can be seen as social prejudice translated into purported "science," doesn't interfere with the next stage of the same process.

With characteristic hypocrisy, the *New York Times* editorialized against the "The 'Bell Curve' Agenda" (October 24, 1994), castigating the publicity given the book, while a week previously the paper had featured it, along with two other similar tomes, on the front page of its Sunday Book Review, with a very long and thoroughly incompetent whitewash by reporter Malcolm Browne (October 16, 1994). Browne's review regurgitated all the old clichés of discredited racist science, including elementary confusions of correlation with causation. The reviewer contended that although the arguments of the book are "unfashionable and unsafe," the issues are really important to society, although the policy conclusions that would follow from *The Bell Curve* argument are left vague. On the one hand, there is the clear implication that we should cut budgets supporting the genetically hopeless. On the other hand, Browne tells his readers that Herrnstein and Murray are deeply worried about the enormous "potential for racial hatred," not in the book and its message but in the facts of genes and race! That their work might actively contribute to racial hatred never occurs to Browne. He even closes his review telling readers that "the most insistent plea of the four authors is for freedom of debate and an end to the shroud of censorship imposed upon scientists and scholars by pressure groups..." In other words, anti-Black theorizing, even if blatant and a rerun of long-repudiated doctrine, is not provocation and bigotry; it is courageous truth-seeking by "scholars."

Racist Tradition and Power

"There is a physical difference between the white and black races which I believe will forever forbid the two races living together on terms of social and political equality." That was Abraham Lincoln, the great emancipator, in 1858. "I experienced pity at the sight of this degraded and degenerate race, and their lot inspired compassion in me in thinking that they were really men." This was Louis Agassiz, the great Harvard scientist, reflecting on Black servants he met at a Philadelphia hotel in 1846, from which he drew large generalizations. Gould points out in his book *The Mismeasure of Man*, "All American culture heroes embraced racial attitudes that would embarrass public-school myth-makers."[2]

Built on Black slavery, with segregation and poverty helping to reinforce stereotypes after 1865, racism has deep and persistent roots in this country. Today, racist Bob Grant has a radio audience of 680,000 in New York City, and racist Rush Limbaugh has a supportive audience of millions (extending to Supreme Court Justice Clarence Thomas). Reagan with his repeated imagery of Black welfare mothers exploiting the taxpayer, Bush with Willie Horton and the menace of "quotas," and a slew of code words bandied about by politicians, show that polarizing racist language and political strategies are acceptable and even integral parts of mainstream culture today. The Republican Party is close to being an openly racist party in the 1990s.

With the culture thus primed, racist theories matching racist stereotypes find a receptive audience, and the marketing strategies of book publishers will feed this same maw of hate, just as anti-semitic works had great marketing potential in Weimar Germany and elsewhere in Europe in the years before World War II.

Racist Fraud and "Science" History

Propaganda that serves the powerful ignores inconvenient history. In the case of weapons "gaps" during the Cold War, each new gap claimed by the military-industrial complex was taken at face value in the mainstream media and treated without any reference to the prior gaps, whose fraudulence had been exposed only after the contracts were let.

Reviewers of *The Bell Curve* don't discuss the Arthur Jensen and Cyril Burt stories (see below), or the longer history of discredited racist theory. Malcolm Browne, in his *New York Times* review, mentions Stephen Gould's *The Mismeasure of Man* in a passing phrase; but he does not tap its contents, which would show *The Bell Curve*'s close family resemblance to earlier doctrine and which would refute argument after argument that Browne reports as if fresh and possibly true.

Gould's *Mismeasure of Man* reviews the evolution of "scientific" racism, which means "any claims apparently backed by copious numbers." Craniometry held the stage for a while, then "recapitulationism," then "neoteny" (literally, holding on to youth), and then IQ testing and theories of a genetic base to IQ. The drollest phase of the evolution of racist theory was the shift from recapitulationism to neoteny, as this involved a reversal of superior-inferior physical characteristics. In recapitulation theory, human embryonic and juvenile development recapitulated earlier evolutionary history, so that Blacks were shown to be inferior by their retention of juvenile traits. By the end of the 1920s this theory had collapsed in favor of the view that the primary feature of human growth was its slowness and long retention of juvenile features and gradual loss of previous adult structures. Under recapitulation, Black adults should be like White children; under neoteny, White adults should be like Black children.

As Gould notes, "For seventy years, under the sway of recapitulation, scientists had collected reams of data all loudly proclaiming the same message: adult blacks, women, and lower-class whites are like white upper-class male children." When neoteny came into vogue, this data should have demonstrated Black superiority. But of course this never happened; supporters of the new theory "simply abandoned their seventy years of hard data and sought new and opposite information to confirm the inferiority of blacks."[3] And they found it.

Gould shows that numerous and eminent scientists throughout the 19th and 20th century subtly, or occasionally with knowing dishonesty, doctored the evidence and classification systems and made seriously unscientific generalizations to support preconceived racist views. The distinguished craniologist Paul Broca collected voluminous data on brain and head size showing conventionally "superior" groups to have larger brains than their inferiors. Gould, after reading Broca's major works, found a "definite pattern in his methods." That is, "Conclusions came first and Broca's conclusions were the shared assumptions of most successful white males during his time....His facts were reliable...but they were gathered selectively and then manipulated unconsciously...Broca did not fudge numbers; he merely selected among them or interpreted his way around them to favored conclusions."

Gould claims that the durable biases and frauds of racist science were mainly "honest," not based on conscious deception. In retrospect, however, it is readily demonstrable that these scientists were embarrassingly wrong, mainly because they were prisoners of racist ideology.

Jensen and Burt

Precursors to *The Bell Curve*, built on the modern focus of racist theory on IQ differences, were Arthur Jensen's publications of 1969 and 1980. His 1969 feature article in the *Harvard Educational Review*, "How much can we boost IQ and scholastic achievement?," contended that intelligence was a genetically transmitted quantity that could be measured by IQ tests, and that the 15-point average difference between Blacks and Whites rested on heredity, not environment. Jensen's political bias and lack of scientific discipline showed itself in his opening-page statement that "compensatory education has been tried, and it apparently has failed." This hint at the possible genetic basis of failure misses two points: environmental effects go beyond education, and compensatory education programs may or may not have been of adequate quantity and quality.

Jensen's main proofs of the dominance of genes rested heavily on studies of identical (White) twins brought up in different households, which provided the basis for a highly dubious estimate that 80 percent of the variability in intelligence could be explained by heredity. He argued that the 15-point difference in Black and White IQ scores was too large to be explained by environment, given the importance of heredity in fixing intelligence. The empirical foundation of this case collapsed when it turned out that the leading scientific source of identical twin studies, Sir Cyril Burt, had concocted data to meet the demands of racist science.

The theoretical fallacies in Jensen's case run deep. Environmental differences could account for substantial variation in IQs within groups, but even more clearly the importance of the genetic factor *within* groups tells us nothing about what determines the differences in mean values *between* groups—environmental differences could easily and fully explain inter-group differences, just as they might explain differences in average weights between groups, one well nourished, the other undernourished. This elementary statistical fallacy was at the heart of Jensen's argument.

Nevertheless, Jensen got a lot of publicity in 1969, and his research, although subject to harsh criticism by people like Gould, Richard Lewontin, Steven Rose, and Leon Kamin, certainly did not cause him to be ostracized as another in the line of racists looking for good reasons to keep Blacks "in their place." In fact, when he came up with another study along the same line in 1980, *Bias in Mental Testing*, he was once again treated respectfully and given space in the mainstream media. Gould points out that Jensen's 1980 book comes to exactly the same conclusion as his 1969 article, but that he had shifted ground from identical twins and genetic theory. "He is simply using a different and more indirect argument to prop up the same old claim. And he has buried the central fallacies of that argument so deeply among the apparent rigor of these 800 pages of lists, figures, and charts that no commentator in the mass media managed to ferret them out."[4] In the new book Jensen argued that IQ tests are "unbiased" in measuring intelligence, using a technical meaning of the word—that is, IQ scores are unbiased in the sense that they do a pretty good job of predicting school grades for both Blacks and Whites. But then he subtly moves to using "unbiased" to mean that the IQ tests are not profoundly affected by environmental factors—that vary greatly between groups—and are measuring genetically based "intelligence."[5] He never even attempts to prove the claim of non-bias between groups, so essentially he arrives at his racist conclusion once again by an intellectual trick. And once again he fooled reviewers in *Time* and *Newsweek*, who are receptive to a racist message and fool easily.

Concluding Note

Racism is *more* American than apple pie. The receptive mass audience is encouraged in its worst prejudices by racist politicians and rightists who see racial polarization as helpful to advancing their power and agenda. Publishers like Basic Books estimate that such an environment will make *The Bell Curve* a bestseller. As the book is advertised heavily and its racist message is approved by large numbers, including many with economic and political clout, it is treated as a serious book. There is criticism in opinion columns, letters and some reviews, but it is taken seriously, and even the criticisms give it valuable publicity. Very few of the reviews frame the book in the history of racist "science," or denounce it as another racist insult that tends toward the encouragement of negative stereotypes and political and social violence against Black people. This is racism *normalized*, made acceptable to an important racist constituency and fitted to serve the political agenda of the powerful, setting the intellectual and moral stage for a new wave of harsh policies toward the descendants of the victims of the slave system.

—Z, December 1994

Chapter Twelve

The "Best Man"

When Barry Goldwater tried to use the "Southern Strategy" in the presidential election of 1964, with barely hidden appeals to White fears of Black advances and crime in the streets, this was viewed in respectable circles as a desperation tactic and not worthy of a major party. With Reagan's diatribes against "welfare mothers," and even more comprehensively with George Bush, the Southern Strategy has become a core aspect of Republican national party politicking. Bush ran against Willie Horton in 1988 and for a while positioned himself to run against "quotas" in 1992 (as well as on his record of masterful management of Middle Eastern and other foreign matters). The *Wall Street Journal's* James Perry, in discussing Bush's abortive selection of William Bennett as Republican national chairman, noted explicitly that Bennett would have been perfect for Bush's running in opposition to "quotas" ("Republicans See 'Racial Quotas' as '92 Weapon and William Bennett as Just the Man to Use It," December 6, 1990).

"Best Man"

In naming Clarence Thomas for the Supreme Court vacancy left by the resignation of Thurgood Marshall in 1991, Bush pronounced Thomas the "best man" for the job. In fact, Thomas was as close to a purely political and ideological appointment as you could get—an extreme right-wing Black man, arguably an anti-Black racist, who participated in the early Reagan administration's gutting of benefits to poor people, with very limited judicial experience and entirely without distinction. He was being rewarded for services rendered to the Republican establishment and, as a Black man, was a clever choice for getting another right-wing ideologue onto the court.

It is not well known that Thomas was a long-time close associate of Jay Parker and William Keyes, two Black men who were registered paid agents of the South African apartheid government. Parker registered as an agent of South Africa's Transkei bantustan in 1977-78, and was the official agent of another South African bantustan, Venda, from 1981 to 1985. Parker also served for many years on the board of the U.S. branch of the far right World Anticommunist League. In 1985, Parker and Keyes incorporated a lobbying firm, International Public Affairs Consultants (IPAC), which registered as a a lobbying agency for the South African government, receiving $360,000 a year plus expenses.

In the years when he first served as a South African agent, 1977-78, Jay Parker organized the Lincoln Institute for Research and Education, which put out a quarterly called *Lincoln Review*. The Institute and *Review* consistently attacked the African National Congress (ANC), sanctions against South Africa, and the leadership and ideas of the U.S. civil rights movement. Parker was also notable for extending the concept of "Black radicals" to Benjamin Hooks and the National Association for the Advancement of Colored People (NAACP), and for his opposition to a national holiday honoring Martin Luther King, who "gave his full support to the North Vietnamese Communists" (Parker's version of opposition to the Vietnam War). In a speech given at California State University on April 25, 1988, Clarence Thomas expressed his warm support for "steadfast dissidents" like Jay Parker (and Thomas Sowell). "I admire them, and only hope I can have a fraction of their courage and strength."

Jay Parker and Clarence Thomas served together on the Reagan-Bush transition team for the Equal Employment Opportunity Commission (EEOC), of which Thomas became commissioner in June 1982. From 1981 Thomas was listed as a member of the Editorial Advisory Board of Parker's *Lincoln Review*. Keyes has been a contributing editor. According to the registration filings of IPAC, under the heading "Political Propaganda," that lobbying organization held a reception for its South African client's Ambassador in 1987. EEOC Chairman Thomas was listed as in attendance, giving a nice lift to the affair and South Africa's efforts to fight sanctions.

In 1984, Keyes organized a "Black PAC (Political Action Committee)," Parker serving as Treasurer. This organization worked hard for the reelection of Jesse Helms in 1984, while strongly opposing the "terrorist outlaw" ANC and "extremists" like Jesse Jackson and members of the Congressional Black Caucus. In June 1987, the conservative weekly, *Human Events*, reported that the Black PAC leaders were holding a strategy meeting that month "to plan for the important political battles being waged in Congress," the attendees including Clarence Pendleton, Reagan's chairman of the U.S. Civil Rights Commission, and Clarence Thomas of the EEOC. That these two top Black officials in the Reagan administration would attend a strategy meeting organized by two paid lobbyists for a foreign government—and a racist government to boot—raises questions of morality and legality that have not been discussed in the mainstream media.

"Self-hating" Blacks?

The notion of a "self-hating Jew" is a common form of name-calling, used freely in the Jewish establishment to castigate Jews critical of Israel. But I have never seen any mainstream reference to "self-hating Blacks" in speaking of Black right-wingers. Consider, however, that a very kind analogue to the Keyes-Parker service to South Africa would be a Jew serving as a paid lobbyist for the Palestinian Liberation Organization (PLO), who not only spent a great deal of time assailing Israel but organized a PLO-PAC as part of his service. This analogy greatly understates the case, as the PLO has not oppressed Jews, it has fought the state of Israel over territory and Palestinian human rights. South Africa has been oppressing and murdering Blacks on a massive scale and systematic basis for many years. Perhaps a closer analogy would be a Jew in Germany or the United States in 1938 who became a paid agent of the Hitler regime.

A similar analogy might also hold for Clarence Thomas, Clarence Pendleton, and the Black conservatives who have attached themselves to the new-look Republican Party. They did this at a time when "the Republican Party has become the 'White Party,' in Texas and in [the] nation as a whole,"[1] and when its leadership was openly employing the Southern Strategy, which polarizes and exacerbates racial hatred and tensions. At the same time, Reagan-Bush policy was a literal assault on the protective mechanisms—both economic and legal—developed since 1954 to partially rectify centuries of racism. Although the Reagan-Bush attack on the poor was partly class-based, there was a significant tie-in with the Southern Strategy, the legal attacks on affirmative action, and "an antipathy toward civil rights that stretches far beyond particular disputes about effective remedies for discrimination" (Robert Plotkin, shortly after his 1981 resignation from heading litigation in the Justice Department's Civil Rights Division).[2]

Super-Affirmative Action: The Black Conservatives

There is no such group as "self-hating Blacks" in mainstream commentary because those who might be so categorized say and do what the White establishment wants Black intellectuals and activists to say and do. Those who will work in support of Reaganite policies stripping benefits from the poor, who will denounce well-meaning White liberals as the cause of Black distress, and who call for reliance on the market, will get *super-affirmative action*: they will get "free enterprise chairs," funding from the American Enterprise Institute and

Hoover Institution, and a stream of generous publicity from and ready access to the mass media as they meet the demands of the market for *really correct*[3] Black thinking.

The contrast between the mainstream media's treatment of the sound Black thinkers and those who don't meet establishment demands is dramatic. The table below shows how the *New York Times*, *Washington Post*, and *Philadelphia Inquirer* dealt with the thoughts of three Black rightists—Thomas Sowell, Shelby Steele, and Walter Williams—and three Black leftists—bell hooks, Manning Marable, and Cornel West—over a dozen-year period. It can be seen that the three rightists were treated munificently, the papers' generosity actually understated in the table, which fails to capture the generally sympathetic quality of the coverage. These men are "scholars," sometimes "distinguished" scholars, even if "controversial"; they are never treated as turncoats, traitors, sell-outs, intellectual mediocrities [which they are], or self-hating Blacks. Richard Cohen had a column in the *Washington Post* (October 13, 1985) on "Louis Farrakhan: a threat to blacks," but the Black rightists never "threaten" or damage Blacks, at least in mainstream media headlines and text.

The Black leftists, on the other hand, were invisible persons. E. J. Dionne, Jr., in the *Washington Post* of July 4, 1991, explains the preeminence of the Black rightists by their "sheer intellectual power and persistence." But hooks, Marable, and West are in no way intellec-

SUPER-AFFIRMATIVE ACTION—FOR BLACK RIGHTISTS

New York Times (NYT), *Washington Post* (WP), and *Philadelphia Inquirer* (PI) coverage of three Black Rightist and three Black Leftist intellectuals, 1980-1991*

	Op Eds / Articles By			Articles About			Works Reviewed		
	NYT	WP	PI	NYT	WP	PI	NYT	WP	PI
Rightists									
T. Sowell	4	2	-	6	4	1	12[1]	4	5
S. Steele	1	1	-	3	-	-	2	2	1
W. Williams	1	-	2	-	-	1	2[2]	1	1
Leftists									
b. hooks	-	-	-	-	-	-	-	-	-
M. Marable	-	-	-	-	-	-	-	-	-
C. West	-	-	-	-	-	-	-	-	-

*Based on a Nexis and Dialog data base search from January 1981 through August 1991.
[1] Does not include three short "Editor's Choice" notices.
[2] Includes a flattering review of Williams' documentary on the Bensonhurst case.

tually inferior, less productive, less "persistent," or less focused on relevant issues than the rightist trio. The difference is two-fold: in the nature of their analyses and solutions, and in the fact that the leftists are not generously funded by what John Saloma called "the conservative labyrinth." (Walter Williams, for example, has an Olin chair and is syndicated through the Heritage Foundation; Thomas Sowell is a Hoover Institution scholar.) E. J. Dionne, Jr. never mentioned these other considerations, whose explanatory value carries well beyond the selective treatment of Black intellectuals. (As an illustration, perhaps the most important book on military spending and its rationales written in the 1980s, Tom Gervasi's superb *The Myth of Soviet Military Supremacy,* was never mentioned or reviewed in the *New York Times,* and received a furiously red-baiting attack in the *Washington Post.* Although extremely well documented and addressing a key issue, it had the wrong message.)

Especially generous benefits will flow from established power centers to Black people who are prepared to help administer the necessary blows and discipline to the dispossessed. This is again in accord with the law of markets. Such individuals are in short supply. They will also have to suffer the psychic costs of the contempt and even hatred of most Blacks, liberals and PC types, who view these market-worthy Blacks as sell-outs. These critics, largely excluded from mainstream discourse, do miss the complexities of human motivation. But it remains true that by this route mediocrities and worse may be the beneficiaries of a perverse and market-based super-affirmative action program.

—Z, October 1991

Chapter Thirteen

The Banality of Evil

The concept of the banality of evil came into prominence following the publication of Hannah Arendt's 1963 book *Eichmann in Jerusalem: A Report on the Banality of Evil*, which was based on the trial of Adolph Eichmann in Jerusalem. Arendt's thesis was that people who carry out unspeakable crimes, like Eichmann, a top administrator in the machinery of the Nazi death camps, may not be crazy fanatics at all, but rather ordinary individuals who simply accept the premises of their state and participate in any ongoing enterprise with the energy of good bureaucrats.

Normalizing the Unthinkable

Doing terrible things in an organized and systematic way rests on "normalization." This is the process whereby ugly, degrading, murderous, and unspeakable acts become routine and are accepted as "the way things are done." There is usually a division of labor in doing and rationalizing the unthinkable, with the direct brutalizing and killing done by one set of individuals; others keeping the machinery of death (sanitation, food supply) in order; still others producing the implements of killing, or working on improving technology (a better crematory gas, a longer burning and more adhesive napalm, bomb fragments that penetrate flesh in hard-to-trace patterns). It is the function of defense intellectuals and other experts, and the mainstream media, to normalize the unthinkable for the general public. The late Herman Kahn spent a lifetime making nuclear war palatable (*On Thermonuclear War*, *Thinking About the Unthinkable*), and this strangelovian phoney got very good press.[1]

In an excellent article entitled "Normalizing the unthinkable," in the *Bulletin of Atomic Scientists* of March 1984, Lisa Peattie described how in the Nazi death camps work was "normalized" for the long-term prisoners as well as regular personnel: "[P]rison plumbers laid the water pipe in the crematorium and prison electricians wired the fences. The camp managers maintained standards and orderly process. The cobblestones which paved the crematorium yard at Auschwitz had to be perfectly scrubbed." Peattie focused on the parallel between routinization in the death camps and the preparations for nuclear war, where the "unthinkable" is organized and prepared for in a division of labor participated in by people at many levels. Distance from execution helps render responsibility hazy. "Adolph Eichmann was a thoroughly responsible person, according to his understanding of responsibility. For him, it was clear that the heads of state set policy. His role was to implement, and fortunately, he felt, it was never part of his job actually to have to kill anyone."

Peattie noted that the head of MIT's main military research lab in the 1960s argued that "their concern was development, not use, of technology." Just as in the death camps, in weapons labs and production facilities, resources are allocated on the basis of effective participation in the larger system, workers derive support from interactions with others in the mutual effort, and complicity is obscured by the routineness of the work, interdependence, and distance from the results.

Peattie also pointed out how, given the unparalleled disaster that would follow nuclear war, "resort is made to rendering the system playfully, via models and games." There is also a vocabulary developed to help render the unthinkable palatable: "incidents," "vulnerability indexes," "weapons impacts," and "resource availability." She doesn't mention it, but our old friend "collateral damage," used in the 1991 Persian Gulf War, came out of the nukespeak tradition.

Slavery and Racism as Routine

When I was a boy, and an ardent baseball fan, I never questioned, or even noticed, that there were no Black baseball players in the big leagues. That was the way it was; racism was so routine that it took years of incidents, movement actions, reading, and real-world traumas to overturn my own deeply imbedded bias. Historically, this was a country in which human slavery was firmly institutionalized and routinized, with abolitionists in the pre-civil war years looked upon as violent extremists by the dominant elites and masses alike in the North.

The rationalizations for slavery were remarkable. A set of intellectuals arose in the South before 1860 that not only defended slavery, but argued its moral superiority on the grounds of its service to the *slaves*, to the disadvantage of the enslaving Whites![2] Stephen Jay Gould's *The Mismeasure of Man*, discussed in Chapter Eleven, is a superb account of how U.S. science at the highest levels constructed and maintained a "scientific" case for racism over many decades by mainly innocent and not consciously contrived scientific charlatanry.[3] The ability to put aside cultural blinders is rare. And it appears that what money and power demand, science and technology will provide, however outrageous the end.

Mainstream history has also successfully put Black slavery and oppression in a tolerable light. A powerful article by the late Nathan I. Huggins, "The Deforming Mirror of Truth: Slavery and the Master Narrative of American History," in the Winter 1991 issue of the *Radical History Review*, shows well how the "master narrative" in historiography has normalized Black slavery and post-1865 racism. Slavery was a "tragic error" (like the Vietnam War), rather than a rational and institutional choice; it has been marginalized as an aside or tangent, rather than recognized as a central and integral feature of U.S. history; and it has been portrayed as an error in process of rectification in a progressive evolution, rather than a terrible permanent scar that helps explain the Southern Strategy, the current attack on affirmative action, and the enlarging Black ghetto disaster of today.

Profits and Jobs in Death

Normalization of the unthinkable comes easily when money, status, power, and jobs are at stake. Companies and workers can always be found to manufacture poison gases, napalm, or instruments of torture, and intellectuals will be dredged up to justify their production and use. The rationalizations are hoary with age: government knows best, ours is a strictly defensive effort, or, if it wasn't me somebody else would do it. There is also the retreat to ignorance, real, cultivated, or feigned. Consumer ignorance of process is important. Dr. Samuel Johnson avowed that we would kill a cow rather than forego eating meat, but visits to slaughterhouses have made quite a few people into vegetarians. A cover story of *Newsweek* some years ago, illustrating U.S. consumption of meat by showing livestock walking into a human mouth, elicited many protests—people don't like to be reminded that steaks are obtained from slaughtered animals; they like to imagine that they are manufactured in factories, possibly out of biomass.

The bureaucratization of the use of animals for human ends is a large and controversial subject, but the potential for abuse is continuously realized as stock raisers, slaughterhouses, trappers, the Pentagon, the Animal Damage Control Agency, chemical, medical and cosmetic researchers, and academic entrepreneurs search for ways to improve the bottom line or fill in niches of "knowledge" that somebody will pay for. At the University of Pennsylvania a few years ago there was a Head Injury Lab, funded by the government, in which baboons were subjected to head injuries in the alleged interest of helping us (i.e., creatures with souls, the culmination of the evolutionary process, and the realization of the purpose of the cosmos). The lab was invaded by People for the Ethical Treatment of Animals (PETA), who among other things took away some records and films. The documentary which PETA made out of these materials, which showed these intelligent creatures having their heads smashed and rendered into zombies, also gave clear evidence that official rules of treatment of lab animals were violated, and, most important, that the participants' attitudes toward the animals were insensitive and ugly. It was not hard to think of death camps watching the documentary of this lab in action. Yet the scientific community at Penn not only defends the use of animals against outside critics with passion and apparent unanimity, but has never to my knowledge admitted in public that the Head Injury Lab got out of hand.

In building weapons, contractors and the Pentagon have become quite sophisticated in spreading business over many states, to reach a critical mass of jobs, profits and legislators/media by congressional district to maximize the lobbying base for funding. Jobs are jobs, whether building schools or Peacekeeper Missiles or cutting down thousand-year-old redwood trees. I was slightly nauseated during the Vietnam War era by Boeing ads soliciting workers for its helicopter plant, touting itself as an "equal opportunity employer (EOE)." Maybe the Dachau camp management was also an EOE, for jobs that needed to be done and for which there was an effective demand.

Normalizing Shooting Human Fish in the Persian Gulf Barrel

In the Persian Gulf War of 1991 Uncle Sam was an EOE, and our boys and girls over there were doing their assigned jobs, repelling naked aggression in another Operation Just Cause. The war was forced upon us by Saddam Hussein's rejection of the UN's and "allies" insistence that he disgorge Kuwait, much as Bush "plainly" did not want war (Anthony Lewis).

Having made it Operation Just Cause No. 17, and a game with winners and losers, we could reasonably root for us—the moral force—to win. We were also defending Kuwait, and if once again the party being "saved" was "destroyed," well, this was not our fault. Besides, there is the "principle," of non-aggression, to which we are utterly devoted.

The media could thus focus on our brave boys, girls, generals, and officials to tell us all about their plans, moves, reactions, and miscellaneous thoughts. We could watch them in action as they took off, landed, ate, joked, and expressed their feelings on the enemy, weather, and folks back home in the Big PX. They were part of an extended family, doing a dirty job, but with clean bombs and with the moral certainty of a just cause.

The point was not often made that the enemy was relatively defenseless,[4] and in somewhat the same position as the "natives" colonized, exterminated, and enslaved by the West in past centuries by virtue of muskets and machine guns (see John Ellis's *The Social History of the Machine Gun*). Our technical superiority reflected our moral superiority. If it all *seemed* like shooting human fish in a barrel, one must keep in mind that we were dealing with lesser creatures (grasshoppers, two-legged animals, cockroaches), people who don't value life as much as we do, who allowed "another Hitler" to rule over them, and who stood in our way.

One of the effects of high-tech warfare, as well as the exclusive focus on "our" casualties, plus censorship (official and self), is that the public is spared the sight of burning flesh. That enemy casualties were given great prominence during the Vietnam War is one of the great, and now institutionalized, myths of that era. Morley Safer's showing a GI applying a cigarette lighter to a Vietnamese thatched hut is used and referred to repeatedly as illustrating media boldness at that time because other cases would be hard to find. It caused CBS and Safer a lot of trouble (and he has been trying to make up for this sin ever since). Enormous government pressure and flak from other sources caused the media to provide grisly photos of enemy victims only with the greatest caution, and very infrequently, especially in light of the grisly reality. Capital intensive warfare in itself makes for distancing the public from the slaughter of mere gooks and Arabs. This is helpful in normalizing the unspeakable and unthinkable.

On February 5, 1991, the *Philadelphia Inquirer* carried an Associated Press dispatch by Alexander Higgins, "Marriage finds new expression in gulf: Honey, pass the bombs." It is a little romance of a newly married couple, located at an airbase in Saudi Arabia—and therefore regrettably obliged to sleep in separate tents—whose function is to load bombs on A-10 attack jets. It is a personal interest story, of two people and their relationship, with a job to do, in an unromantic setting. A fine study in the routinization of violence, of the banality of evil and the ways it is impressed on the public.

—Z, April 1991

Chapter Fourteen

Politically Correct
Holocausts

The concept of "political correctness," as used by the mainstream media and pundits, has wide applicability. It comprises ideas and claims that challenge established ("really correct" [RC]) thought and behavior, and are pressed upon mainstream individuals and institutions by minorities and other outsiders. There is politically correct (PC) language and deportment, but also politically correct history and even politically correct conspiracies. For example, that the assassination of JFK was carried out by more than one person (Oswald) is PC, and thus has been subjected to indignant repudiation by the dominant media. By contrast, that the shooting of Pope John Paul II by Mehmet Ali Agca in 1981 was a plot hatched by the KGB and Bulgarians was an RC conspiracy that *Newsweek*, NBC-TV, and the *New York Times* accepted enthusiastically and uncritically, despite the absence of any credible evidence.[1]

PC and RC Holocausts

There is also a sharp distinction between *holocausts* that the establishment recognizes and finds deserving of attention and indignation, and those that mainstreamers ignore but which are deemed worthy of attention by marginalized people and "extremists." The former, which are RC, may be illustrated by the case of Cambodians murdered by Pol Pot, or the "Final Solution" under Hitler (although only in retrospect, not at the time of the killing, as described below). Those that are of little interest to the establishment, and which can be classed as PC, may be illustrated by the slaughter of over a million Armenians by the Turks in 1915,[2] and the decimation of the East Timorese population by the Indonesian army from 1975 onward.[3]

There is obviously a close correlation between the "worthiness" of the victims as perceived by the Western establishment and the recognition of the holocaust. As the West was built in good part on the destruction and exploitation of colonial peoples and on a slave system, the associated victims are hardly likely to be "worthy" or their holocausts RC for dominant Westerners. Such holocausts are an embarrassment as well as painfully at odds with myth structures of the West.

It also seems likely that the differentiation between PC and RC holocausts will fit the schema of dividing bloodbaths into those that are Constructive, Benign, and Nefarious.[4] In this classification system, Constructive bloodbaths are those associated with political changes seen as advantageous to Western political interests. They may be carried out by ourselves (Vietnam), or by an ally or factions within a foreign state (Indonesia in 1965-69). Benign bloodbaths are those carried out by Western client states that, while not necessarily helpful, are treated with indulgence and understanding (East Timor, invaded and occupied by Indonesia; South Africa beating up everybody in its neighborhood in the 1980s). Nefarious bloodbaths are those carried out by enemy states. The hypothesis is that there will be great indignation and channeled benevolence in the last case, whereas for Constructive or Benign bloodbaths there will be a combination of rationalization and eye aversion. Only the holocausts associated with Nefarious bloodbaths will be RC—the others will be PC.

PC as Myth Deconstruction: The Case of Columbus

One function of PC (and multiculturalism) is clearly myth deconstruction. This is dramatically evident in the new revisionist evaluation of Christopher Columbus. The conventional-traditional view has been that Columbus was a visionary, a brave pioneer who "discovered America" and thus opened up the "New World" to the West, yielding a beneficent influx of precious metals to Europe, emigration to freedom, and progress. In the traditional view the discovery was an uncontaminated triumph. Hans Koning writes in *Columbus: His Enterprise*, that "It may exist somewhere, but I have not found one grade school or high school book that does not treat Columbus as the great hero he was not."[5]

The revisionist and PC view looks at Columbus' enterprise from the standpoint of the victimized non-White populations "being discovered," the greed, ruthlessness and genocidal racism and policies of the erstwhile "heroes," the cooperative role in this enterprise of the Christian churches, and the mass death and degradation that followed. Columbus, who initially described the Arawak Indians of Hispaniola as gentle and friendly, soon wrote to Spain that "From here, in the name of the Blessed Trinity, we can send all the slaves that can be sold...for these people are totally unskilled in arms." He introduced gold quotas for the Indians, and maltreatment and disease reduced the Indian population of the island from 125-500,000 in 1492 to 10,000 in 1515.

The further advance of the Spanish into the "New World" took a similar toll elsewhere. The population of Mexico went from perhaps 25 million in 1519 to 6.3 million in 1548; in Peru the population declined from 7 million in 1519 to 1.8 million in 1580. A large fraction died from disease, but many were killed or died from overwork combined with widespread demoralization that led to alcoholism and suicides.

The North American Indians: A PC Holocaust

The North American Indian population fell from some 12-18 million before "discovery" to 300-400,000 in 1900, a better than 95 percent decline. Official and scholarly estimates up to recent decades maintained that pre-contact Indian numbers were between 500,000 and 1.5 million, in accord with the vision of North America as "unoccupied" and underutilized, until the takeover by the progressive Christian civilization of Europe.[6] A large fraction of North American Indian casualties was from newly imported diseases, but a great many were killed in numerous massacres by the ruthless, merciless, profoundly racist, but technologically advanced, Christian barbarians. (In a characteristic Orwellian inversion by the powerful, the victimized natives were the cruel and "merciless savages," as expressed even in the Declaration of Independence.) If not killed outright, the Indians were removed from their lands, and the basis for their livelihood and way of life deliberately destroyed. (General Phil Sheridan exterminated an estimated 60 million buffalo in the 1870s "in order to deny a basis for subsistence to the Cheyenne, Lakota, and other peoples of the Great Plains."[7]) There were 19th-century acknowledgements of a policy of "complete extermination," and the Republic of Texas offered a cash bounty for Indian scalps.[8] U.S. policy and practice merits well Ward Churchill's comparison with the operations of the German SS.[9]

But this was *us* in action, the bloodbath was constructive, so that this is not an RC holocaust and is treated with brevity and evasiveness in mainstream textbooks, allowing the occupation of the continent by *us* to be a triumph of good people building a new North American order.

PC and the Slave Trade

PC holocausts usually involve the slaughter of people of color, who have regularly been the victims of Western exploitation and violence. Their role makes them victims of constructive or benign bloodbaths, hence unworthy, and hence not RC. The PC-RC dichotomization parallels contemporary usage in the application of the word terrorism. For example, the apartheid government of South Africa was never a "terrorist state" (or naked aggressor) in Western government-expert-media representations in the 1980s although it was responsible for the death of hundreds of thousands, and perhaps more than a million, Black Africans in that decade.[10]

Earlier, the slave trade produced one of the greatest holocausts in human history, but as the West did the victimizing this is only a PC, not an RC, holocaust. With the virtual extermination of the native populations of the New World, and the discovery of the enormous profitability of slave labor in raising sugar, "the market"—in combination with state organized and protected terrorism that seized, transported, and sold slaves—gave new life to human slavery and the slave trade from the 15th century onward. Later, it was found that tobacco and cotton could also be profitably cultivated using slave labor, and the reach of slavery was extended, persisting until the latter part of the 19th century.

Roger Anstey and J. E. Inikori estimate that some 12 million enslaved Africans were successfully shipped to the New World between 1451 and 1870. But the conditions of the trade were so horrendous that the 12 million were the residual of 48 million originally seized, with 36 million dying en route. As L. S. Stavrianos describes it in *Global Rift*:[11]

> The 36 million casualties were sustained in the course of the overland march from the interior to the coast, and then during the dreaded overseas "middle passage" to the New World. Inhuman crowding, stifling heat and poor food resulted in appalling mortality rates during the ocean crossing. Maize and water once every twenty-four hours was the standard diet. If the slaves refused to eat they were lashed and, if that failed, hot irons were used to force them to eat. When epidemics broke out, as they often did under the foul conditions, the sick slaves were drowned in order to prevent infection from spreading. Sometimes the slaves jumped overboard rather than endure the misery. Indeed, this became so common that nets were fixed all around the decks in order to prevent suicides.

This holocaust served dominant Western interests and was institutionalized and participated in by all the great powers of the West. Their commercial elites built fortunes and respectability on the basis of this business, either directly in trading slaves or indirectly in supplying provisions for the slavers or exporting the sugar and molasses, and later the tobacco and cotton. Accounts of the history of the great powers stress the economic importance of the sugar-cotton-tobacco economy to the West, but the human cost is mentioned only in passing if at all. For example, Richard Cobban, a liberal historian of France, notes the great importance of the Caribbean in French trade and prosperity in the 18th century, and he castigates Louis XVI's foreign policy for failing to give sufficient protection to French interests in the

Caribbean, which he says "were worth fighting for."[12] The condition of the slaves and the morality of slavery and the slave trade, so crucial to Caribbean economics, are addressed in a single parenthetical statement: "(its morality [the slave trade] as yet is barely subject of discussion)."[13]

In brief, slavery and the slave trade are normalized, given their importance in Western economy and institutions. And being normalized they can hardly constitute an RC holocaust.

"The Final Solution": From PC to RC

Western attitudes toward specific holocausts may change over time. This can be illustrated by the evolution of Western responses to Hitler's policy of exterminating the European Jews in the 1940s. At the time this policy began, the position of the Jews in the West was tenuous and their leaders were fearful and cautious. Anti-semitism was deeply embedded in Western cultures. As a result, the slaughter of Jews in the Nazi death camps was not given great attention or credence by the mainstream media. As Deborah Lipstadt has shown, it was mainly in the dissident media like *The Nation* and *PM* (a long defunct liberal-left New York newspaper) that the issue was treated as of first-order importance. In the *New York Times* and most of the mainstream media, reports of the killing of hundreds of thousands of Jews were put on the back pages, often next to the comics (see the final chapter of Lipstadt's book, *Beyond Belief*).

It was only after the war that attention to and indignation at the Final Solution became intense. No doubt this was partly because of fresh disclosures, but the lag in disclosure and the treatment of the substantial and horrifying evidence known earlier remain to be explained. The later attention and indignation were associated with the growth in affluence, confidence and power of Jewish communities in the United States and other great Western powers, and the increasing importance of Israel as a U.S. surrogate in the Middle East. In short, Jews became worthy victims in retrospect, and the Final Solution became an RC holocaust after the fact.

The murder by the Nazis of hundreds of thousands of gypsies, who continue to be a marginalized people, remains only a PC holocaust. In *Congress Weekly*, a publication of the American Jewish Congress, the well-known Zionist academic Edward Alexander referred to the charges of a Nazi genocide against homosexuals and gypsies as an "exploded fiction." At a meeting in Jerusalem of the World Congress of Jewish Studies, Professor Henry Guttenberg referred to the "real or *supposed genocide* of Armenians, homosexuals, Gypsies and American Indians." These denials of other and competing holocausts by spokespersons for those that are RC constitute a form a apologetics for the Nazis and other perpetrators of mass murders that are designated "fictions." But as these are PC holocausts, books on "holocaust denial" never include *these* deniers; they are not worthy of attention.

Vietnam War: A PC Holocaust

The U.S. attack on Vietnam was one of the great holocausts of our time, but as it was perpetrated by *us* it is not only not an RC holocaust, we are portrayed as victims of an unappreciative Vietnamese people. In the "beyond chutzpah" category, the moral issue of the war turns on the Vietnamese treatment of our Missing in Action (MIAs) and Prisoners of War (POWs)!

The arrogant bullies who ran the United States after World War II refused the Vietnamese people the right of self-determination for 30 years because this was incompatible with Western control. We and the British supported French recolonization from 1945-54; we then refused to abide by the Geneva Accords of 1954 and allow unification of Vietnam by free elections. It was well known then and later that the great majority of Vietnamese, in the southern as well as northern parts of the country, supported Ho Chi Minh and the Vietnamese communists.[14] The United States therefore simply ignored the Geneva Accords, the rights of the Vietnamese to self-rule, and the UN Charter, and imposed its own imported dictator on South Vietnam.

When this didn't work, in 1962 the Kennedy administration began pouring in helicopters and thousands of "advisers," and managed a vicious counterinsurgency war, which included using chemical warfare to destroy peasant crops as well as concentration camps for peasants (called "strategic hamlets"). When this also didn't work, Lyndon Johnson fabricated a "Bay of Tonkin" attack by the North Vietnamese, and began the systematic bombing of the North and a massive invasion of South Vietnam in 1965. All through the early 1960s, U.S. officials fought strenuously against any political settlement that would terminate complete domination of the South by a U.S.-controlled faction, despite the general acknowledgement that this faction had no substantial political support within the South.

What followed was one of the most vicious and cowardly wars in history. The greatest military power on earth, with the most advanced technological arsenal, deployed its full power against a poor peasant society without aircraft or a modern technological base. It virtually leveled Indochina with millions of tons of bombs, rained napalm and fragmentation bombs on many hundreds of peasant villages in the South that were without medical facilities, and used dioxin-based Agent Orange in a massive program of destruction of forests and crops (Operation Ranch Hand, the planes called Providers, one cute line of our aviators being "Only you can prevent a forest"). Vast areas of South Vietnam—being saved from "aggression"—were made "free fire zones" and many thousands of peasants were shot in the course of military operations and just for fun in "skunk hunts."

The 500,000-man U.S. invasion force was supplemented by mercenaries from within South Vietnam, Thailand, South Korea, and Australia to "pacify" the country. These troops carried out merciless "search and destroy" operations in which domestic animals and crops were destroyed, villages burned down, and large numbers of men, women and children killed or turned into homeless refugees. It was found that the "enemy" had deep roots in the population of South Vietnam, so the people were treated as an enemy population. Prisoners taken in peasant villages were systematically tortured to obtain information (in violation of international law), and were regularly killed, often by the mercenary forces under U.S. tutelage.

The final toll in Indochina will never be known, and it continues to grow as thousands have died since 1975 from the delayed setting off of some of the millions of unexploded bombs still littering the ground. But the number dead may run as high as four million, and numbers injured and traumatized also run into the millions. The number of victims of Agent Orange is large, but of zero interest to the West. The land ravaged in the chemical war of virtual ecocide may never recover.

As a victim of U.S. actions, the Indochinese catastrophe cannot be an RC holocaust (although Pol Pot's lesser killings in Cambodia are). Because of U.S. power, the strength of its anti-communist ideology, and the conformism of its ideological institutions, the murderous U.S. attack has always been treated as, at worst, a "tragic error." In RC thought, the United States was never engaged in aggression in Vietnam (this would be an oxymoron); its *right* to smash a peasant society by the most cruel and vile means was never called into question, nor were the policies ever called by their proper names. Liberals like Anthony Lewis and Stanley Karnow contended that we were overreaching in our efforts to do good. Karnow in 1988 was still writing that we allowed the *Vietnamese people* to depend too much on us.[15]

In saying this, Karnow was equating "Vietnamese" with our puppets and mercenaries—the people who successfully fought against us and the population we attacked were reduced to non-people. And, in fact, the crucial element in U.S. perspectives on Vietnam has always been the "mere gook rule." The "slopes," "dinks," "gooks"—small, poor, non-White peasants—who failed to accept our dictates had and have no moral standing (any more than Iraqi victims). We had a right to determine who ruled that distant country. If the population refused to accede, we had a perfect right to slaughter them. This was the underlying imperialist-racist morality of the Vietnam War, which persists up to today.

MIAs-POWs: Beyond Chutzpah

The great preoccupation of the U.S. media and establishment with MIAs and POWs dates from 1969, when Richard Nixon latched onto this issue to stall settlement of the Vietnam War. He was successful, and even after the War the right-wing found this a useful means of preventing normalization of relations with Vietnam (as described in the excellent account by H. Bruce Franklin, *M.I.A. or Myth-Making In America*[16]).

That this lunatic endeavor should have worked, and that the status of MIAs and POWs (U.S., of course—the status of Vietnamese MIAs has never arisen) has become the great "moral issue" of the post-Vietnam War era, is a product of a racist nut house. As Franklin shows, there never were many POWs and Vietnam returned all of them it could be expected to account for on schedule. Nixon's trick, of course, led to a lot more fighting and the deaths of many more U.S. military personnel than the prior total of MIAs and POWs. The hypocrisy in the pretended concern over the welfare of U.S. military personnel is also shown by the treatment of Vietnam veterans after their return to this country—they became non-persons, the government struggling to prevent their collecting money for Agent Orange damage, and the vastly more numerous veterans "Missing in America" than Missing in Action being of no interest to the leaders of the nut house.

The Indochinese victims, of course, present no moral issue at all. It is not admitted or of any interest that the United States killed and wounded millions of innocent people and virtually destroyed Indochina in an unprovoked, vicious, and cowardly aggression. These are mere gooks, who, in addition, had the temerity to stand in our way and even shoot at our armed forces occupying their country! In the RC model, we were "protecting South Vietnam" from aggression, expending our resources to save the Vietnamese and allow them democracy and self-determination, etc. Thus we are guilty of nothing and have no moral obligation for damages—but this perspective is achieved by a rewriting of history that makes Stalinist accounts of the role of Leon Trotsky look straightforward by comparison, and by moral insensitivity without limit. The spectacle of elevating our few POWs, who were instruments of a cowardly aggression that victimized millions, to the status of martyrs and victims of somebody else's pernicious behavior, all built on a system of lies and hypocrisy, is the final touch that carries us "beyond chutzpah."

—Z, April 1992

Chapter Fifteen

The End of Democracy?

Democracy is under siege throughout the globe, including in the United States. This of course runs exactly counter to the forecasts of the ideologues of Western triumphalism, who predicted a fairly rapid universalization of democracy in the post-Cold War era. But these analysts overrated the importance of elections as the basis (and proof) of democracy, and underrated the ability of dominant market forces to drain elections of democratic substance.

Elections may be occurring more widely, but even more consistently than in the past they now have material consequences only when they serve the dominant interests of the global market. When they fail to do this, there is a policy stalemate, unless the newly elected leaders "see the light" (i.e., sell out), or until a new election brings "realists" to power. When voters reject a treaty supported by the dominant interests, a second vote may be taken. Thus, when the Maastricht agreement was defeated in Denmark in 1992, a further vote was held following an intensive "educational" campaign to bring the Danes around. It is interesting that nobody is suggesting another vote to see whether the Danes, upon further reflection and experience with the European Community's (EC's)[1] failure to cope with the growing crisis of unemployment, might have changed their minds once more. Voting ended when the proper response was forthcoming.

"Realists" find no insurmountable obstacles to getting things done—tax changes advantageous to business and the wealthy can be enacted, public property can be sold off, labor unions can be dismantled or weakened, large-scale unemployment produced and maintained, and treaties can be passed that compromise the national sovereignty—irrespective of public opinion. In the United States and Great Britain, Reagan and Thatcher were able to carry out right-wing and business-supported agendas that involved drastic changes in income distribution, national spending priorities, and the role of central and local governments. Thatcher could "Break the Nation"[2] with electoral minority support (41 percent). Following her rule, labor costs in Great Britain are now 25 percent lower than the EC average and "only just above Spain and Ireland" (*Financial Times*, July 8, 1993). In Canada, Brian Mulroney was able to carry out regressive economic policies and get treaties enacted even when his public approval rating had dipped below 10 percent. The *Wall Street Journal* reported that at the moment the Tory-dominated Canadian Senate voted approval of the North American Free Trade Agreement (NAFTA) in June 1993, by 47 to 30, the public opposed its enactment by 58 to 39. The dominant Canadian media, closely attuned to the preferences of the national financial and business elite, supported the treaty.

By contrast, Bob Rae, head of the liberal-left New Democratic Party (NDP) in Ontario, Canada, failed to implement most of his promised economic and social reforms following his electoral triumph in 1990. This was partly a result of political cowardice and failure to mobilize the social movements that had supported his candidacy to help him carry out reforms opposed by the powerful. But it was also a consequence of the fact that the corporate and media opposition "mounted an incredibly intemperate and even hysterical campaign" against labor and fiscal reforms, steadily assailing the government for "increasing the deficit," and eventually cowing it into focusing on expenditure cuts and deficit control and largely abandoning its social democratic reform program.[3] Bill Clinton, also, entering office in the United States with a painfully inadequate program of renewal, was under immediate business/media attack for fiscal extravagance, and quickly began a retreat toward conservative orthodoxy and dedication to deficit control. Here, as in Ontario, cowardice and a failure to mobilize a supportive popular constituency were conspicuous, but these seemingly regular failures and retreats are grounded in something deeper than personality defects.

When elected or revolutionary leaders in the Third World threaten to serve local majority interests, as in Jamaica in the first Manley term, Guatemala under Arbenz in the early 1950s, Nicaragua under the Sandinistas, and Haiti under Aristide, the governments may be subjected to simple economic warfare (Jamaica), foreign-organized terrorism (Nicaragua), proxy army invasion (Guatemala), or indigenous military coups and brutal repression carried out by U.S. trained security forces (Haiti). These interventions instruct Third World populations that reforms they may want are not permissible, according to higher authority, and that efforts to put them into practice even by democratic elections may be dangerous to their health and welfare (see further the discussion of Nicaragua and Haiti under "Elections in the Provinces," below).

Institutional Weakening of Democracy

Democracy is being weakened on a global scale by the strengthening of market forces and market interests. These have damaged the institutional basis of democracy and made elections and traditional political pressures incapable of meeting the demands of ordinary citizens. Greater size, diversification, and mobility and geographic spread of business firms has drastically altered the balance of power between capital and labor and increased capital's leverage over government. Corporations, now often global entities, can shift production rapidly to the most hospitable investment climes, and they have been able to make union members compete with one another even within a single country.[4] This has been a cumulative and self-reinforcing process—as unions become less powerful they are less attractive to workers; their decline in membership (in the United States, by 25 percent in the 1980s alone) has weakened them in both the market and political arenas. Meanwhile governments, under increasing business influence, have stripped away union defenses against strikebreaking, organizational harassment, and decertification. This decline, rooted in the structural conditions of an evolving global market, represents a serious weakening of pluralism; the primary organized oppositional barrier to capital's complete domination is receding into the shadows and shows no sign of imminent recovery.

The growth of global money and capital markets has also weakened democracy in that money capital "votes" with its movements into and out of countries, based on fears and hopes of being badly or well treated. If there is a threat of higher taxes on capital or increased benefits to poor and middle-class people, money flees and interest rates tend to rise. This "natural" process sustained Reaganism and constrains those trying to serve ordinary citizens.

The slackened rate of economic growth, intensified global competition, and associated "restructuring" (local firings and speedup) and "delocalization" (plant and production relocations) has also had a devastating effect on government budgets. On the one hand, it has pressed governments to keep business and "investor" (i.e., wealthy people) taxes and inflation low to remain "competitive" with those in other areas trying to attract business; on the other hand, the increase in unemployment resulting from anti-inflation policies, business's actions, and unrelenting demands for government services to meet infrastructure needs and cope with environmental damage have enlarged government outlays. The fiscal crunch and deficits have, of course, made it difficult to meet the needs of ordinary citizens. The irony is that business policies, and tax benefits to the elite provided by governments super friendly to business, are major causes of the fiscal crisis, but in accord with market necessities the solution must still come out of the hides of ordinary citizens. Thus throughout the West the pressure is on to reduce outlays for the unemployed and disadvantaged, as there is No Other Option in a market dominated system; "we" must all sacrifice in order that "we" can be "competitive."

One temporary expedient that fits well the market's imperatives is "privatization," which generates sales commissions for the business elite and allows them to acquire public property at bargain prices, while it provides revenue to government without tax increases. It will reduce government income in the future, but that is hardly the concern of private parties striving to increase their net worth right now. Privatization also has the merit of reducing the government's power, simultaneously enhancing the power of the private sector. This is a plus for those who fear the power of government to serve a democratic constituency, although these same "anti-government" forces are not averse to the opportunistic mobilization of government for elite service in military boondoggles, nuclear energy subsidies, forcing open markets abroad, etc.

The market and its government agents have also erected an institutional apparatus of supra-governmental bodies, such as the IMF and World Bank with powers that go beyond and sometimes supersede those of elected governments. By attaching rules and conditions to their loans, these bodies are able to impose policy regimes on the borrowers that conform to the interests of the transnational corporate community. EC, GATT, Maastricht, the Canadian-U.S. trade agreement of 1988, and the NAFTA treaty are high-level arrangements with associated bureaucratic structures that negotiate economic policy over the heads of the voters. These accords permit the overriding of economic and environmental decisions of national and local authorities. These institutions and agreements thus provide a kind of international government representing the interests of the truly elect—namely, the leaders of the global corporations—whose aims they can pursue without having to undergo any electoral test.

Electoral Processes in the Developed Countries

In the economically developed countries, with the increased cost and importance of TV and other mass media, money has assumed overwhelming importance in electoral campaigns. The decline of organized labor has added to the financial dominance of property interests in elections. Parties and candidates must appeal to "investors" for campaign sustenance—mainly business leaders, the wealthy, and political action committees closely related to them—so that deals, promises and commitments to election funders preclude social democratic (let alone socialist) programs. The "left wing" of the property party will make vague promises of service to the majority during the election campaign, and even the purer business party will speak of "bringing us together" in a "kinder, gentler" country. But these promises will not be kept—partly because of the contrary commitments to the funder-investors, but also because the monied interests can make any attempts to serve the majority very costly. They have the power to stalemate programs by mobilizing friendly legislators to obstruct, lobbyists to bargain and threaten, the corporate mass media to denigrate, and the financial markets to punish deviations from their interests.

When elections bring in nominally populist governments, they will be prevented from taking any significant actions; they will be quickly discredited as having "veered to the left" and created an atmosphere discouraging to business. They will have to reassure capital that they are investor friendly and that they understand that, in an age of deficits and austerity, social spending must be constrained and investment encouraged. If a leader decided to resist—to tell capital to go to hell—and to carry out vigorous expansionary and redistributive policies, he or she would run into a firestorm of opposition and would almost surely not be able to implement such policies in the existing political economy. For this reason political leaders not only will not embark on such bold ventures, they even announce in advance policies designed to placate capital—which contradict their promises of renewal and service to their democratic constituencies. Clinton's 1992 deficit reduction-plus-stimulus plan, even if fully enacted, would have had a net deflationary impact on the stagnant U.S. economy;[5] his proposed welfare-workfare approach was little improvement over Reagan-Bush policies; and his tax reforms—his most progressive endeavor—were only a very partial offset to the Reagan-Bush era redistribution upward.

In brief, markets, money, and the media now work in tandem to allow substantial change in institutional arrangements and policies only where this will serve the larger corporate interest (now called the "national interest"), but quickly quash threats to those interests posed by political leaders responsive to popular demands (i.e., the "special interests"). A massive propaganda campaign has successfully inculcated the idea that Big Government is the source of our problems, with spending for social reform a pernicious manifestation of out-of-control government—an ideological/propaganda coup that discredits government actions that benefit ordinary citizens. With reform, let alone necessary radical change, stalemated ideologically and in electoral political processes, ordinary citizens will gradually lose interest in the election game, cynically write off politics and politicians, and withdraw from the political arena.[6] They are disillusioned and angry, but they seem to have lost in a fair electoral fight (at least this is the impression conveyed by the mainstream media). Thus, although ordinary citizens exit because of the absence of real options, this has no political consequence in constructive action. Real options not being mentioned, let alone debated, do not enter public consciousness. And with the elite beneficiaries of the existing system disproportionately finding political participation worthwhile, the power of capital in election processes is further enhanced.

Elections in the Provinces

Third World elections have become even more grotesque parodies of democratic order than those in the technologically advanced states. For one thing, inequalities tend to be greater in the less developed countries, increasing the bias in favor of property interests stemming from differential resources and media control. Second, the great powers and global market forces and institutions have a very potent impact on Third World countries because of their poverty and financial dependence. Caught in the web of the international financial system, the poor countries depend on borrowing from private commercial banks, the IMF and World Bank, and on aid money from the rich countries. They have No Other Option than to comply with their lenders' demands on budget and monetary policy, and their people are not "free to choose."[7] As a recent illustration, Ramiro de Leon Carpio, the former human rights ombudsman of Guatemala, who became president in June 1993 following the failed coup of Serrano, initially promised to give top priority to overcoming the poverty that afflicts 87 percent of the Guatemalan people. Within a month, de Leon had shunted this objective into the background in the face of IMF demands for austerity, stating that Guatemala's macro-economic policy "has complied with IMF demands, and we need to continue that way, otherwise we'll destabilize the country and cause a loss of confidence. But we need to give it a human face wherever possible."

The "market" does not like anything approaching real democracy, which invariably imposes higher taxes on those who can afford to pay and supports worker rights and benefits, and thus threatens profitability (but is euphemistically said to jeopardize "competitiveness," the "climate of investment," or "stability"). The historic record points quite clearly to the market preference for authoritarian government in the Third World,[8] and it is sometimes acknowledged by bankers and the media. Morgan Stanley and Company managing director Madhav Dhar told *Business Week* (April 23, 1993) that "there is a saying on Wall Street that you buy when there is blood on the streets" (the article was about India's instability and its effects on financial market attitudes); and the *Wall Street Journal* ran an article shortly thereafter entitled "Why Global Investors Bet on Autocrats, Not Democrats" (Jan. 12,

1993). But such facts are not allowed to interfere with the ideological truth that the West supports democracy everywhere.

In a number of Third World countries "demonstration elections" have been staged by the United States to put a positive gloss on terror regimes and justify U.S. aid, as in Vietnam in 1966-67 and El Salvador in 1982 and 1984.[9] Although none of the basic conditions of a free election were met in these cases, the U.S. mass media found them legitimating. Salinas's electoral victories in Mexico have been characterized by blatant fraud, serious human rights violations, and attacks on oppositional forces, as well as vast electoral corruption in using state money and business kickbacks to finance electoral campaigns. Salinas even won in 1988 on a semi-populist program, which he immediately abandoned. But because he is the perfect Third World comprador-politician, servant of the global corporate order, and sell-out of his own majority, the U.S. mainstream media have generously overlooked or downplayed his violations of the democratic rules of the game. He is a statesman and leader by rule of comprador service.

In contrast with these approved elections, which ratify rule by those who will pursue policies serviceable to the truly elect, are elections won by governments threatening to provide unnecessary food, medical care, and education to the human "oxen" (Somoza). Nicaragua under the Sandinistas and Aristide's election victory and ouster in Haiti provide instructive examples. Somoza's rule in Nicaragua had been accepted and treated kindly by the United States for decades, despite its rapaciously undemocratic character. Even before the Sandinistas took power, the Carter government was bargaining hard to keep in place the murderous National Guard, which would presumably have served to preserve "Western values" from the Somoza era. U.S. hostility to the new government was immediate, and Nicaragua was under armed attack by the United States from 1981 until the Sandinista ouster in 1990. Their election victory in 1984 did them no good. Only an election that they lost ended subversion and terror designed to overturn them by any available means. They did not meet the U.S. and market standard of legitimacy, which called for subservience and the pursuit of the "logic of the *minority*."

In the case of Haiti, Aristide, like the Sandinistas, represented the majority of unimportant people and threatened to pursue their interests. Although he won a crushing electoral victory in 1991 with 67 percent of the vote, his ouster by the notoriously corrupt and brutal military, followed by a reign of terror unleashed against his supporters, did not cause the United States to view the matter as urgent and calling for decisive action (not even an early freezing of the assets of the government and elite, or imposing a rigorous blockade, let alone sponsoring a proxy army, as with Nicaragua). U.S. officials even expressed concern over *Aristide's* human rights abuses, and they negotiated for Aristide's return with the military establishment still in place (reminiscent of Carter's effort to keep the Nicaraguan National Guard intact). There was also a call for Aristide to "broaden his base" (67 percent did not suffice) and to choose a "moderate" for Prime Minister (i.e., someone who will oppose his reforms that serve ordinary citizens).[10]

The contrast with Nicaragua is enlightening: after Chamorro's 1990 victory the United States pressured her to exclude the Sandinistas entirely from government and to try to undermine their power base by actions that threatened civil war, although the Sandinistas had received 41 percent of the vote (in an election held under U.S. blackmail threat and direct intervention). The United States also pressed the government to dismantle the Sandinista army, although it was not a thoroughly corrupt and murderous one like the Haitian. The lack of respect for democratic processes where they threaten to serve ordinary citizens rather than the elite and market could hardly be more obvious.

In a number of Latin American states, including Chile, Argentina, Brazil, and Uruguay, elections were held after a period of army rule during which many left and social democratic leaders were tortured and murdered, labor and peasant groups destroyed or weakened, and the economy restructured and opened up in ways favored by the IMF and global rulers. The armies that carried out these terrorist operations were built up and trained by the United States to serve larger (i.e., U.S. and market) interests, and they did this with energy during the periods of direct military rule. With the fall of the military regimes, the murderers and torturers were never punished and were allowed to remain in place as enforcers in case social democratic forces pursuing the "logic of the *majority*" get out of hand once again. Although this immunity from the rule of law and the very presence and threat of these armies badly compromises the democratic integrity of the new "democracies," U.S. pressure to demobilize Latin armed forces has been confined to Nicaragua.

The Prospect Before Us

Back in the 1970s, when the Brazilian military was dismantling the protective institutions of the majority, representatives of the Catholic Church repeatedly and bitterly complained that the New Order was deliberately atomizing the population in the service of the transnational corporation (TNC)—one document was entitled "The Marginalization of the People." The Church contended that the National Security State and its use of terror were integral to the new corporate order, as its economic and social policies "in effect provoke a revolution that did not exist."[11] The intensified exploitation would have led to a quick removal of the government under democratic conditions. Only the army could enforce the new economic order, as was openly acknowledged in 1976 by Martínez de Hoz, the top financial administrator of the Argentine military government: "We enjoy the economic stability that the Armed Forces guarantee us. This plan can be fulfilled despite its lack of popular support. It has sufficient political support...that provided by the Armed Forces."[12]

In the New World Order taking shape today we can see the same economic forces described by the Brazilian Bishops at work on a global scale. It is the very purpose and historic role of the TNC to take advantage of its new global mobility to engage in an arbitrage that depresses wages, working conditions, and benefits toward a lowest common global denominator. In the advanced countries, there is a steady migration of firms to jurisdictions that have low wages and benefits and few environmental restrictions. Unions have been weakened and destroyed by market forces and complementary state action in a further atomization process. Structural unemployment and part-time and temporary work have risen steadily and wage and benefit concessions have been exacted from the work force. Social programs that have protected the majority are under increasing pressure, with John Major and "socialist" Felipe González of Spain urging further European moves toward a "deregulated labor market" (i.e., a removal of support for unions and collective bargaining and reduced unemployment benefits).

In short, the rulers of the world, the TNCs and the leaders of the dominant states and new supra-national organizations, have successfully achieved the goal of limiting the organizational and policy options of the world's leaders and peoples to a private enterprise system and actions that serve its interests. To paraphrase the sardonic remark of Canadian economist Mel Watkins: in the West we have "freedom of choice" among 51 lite beers, but only one choice in the way we can organize our economic life. As Bernard Cassen has pointed out, however,[13] the rules of international behavior and policy under EC, GATT, and IMF don't pretend to serve a human *community* (despite the phrase European "Community"); a human community has complex and variable human needs, whereas the new arrangements are confined to mechanical rules for serving an economic model and an ideology of the powerful, a sure recipe for disaster.

–Z, September 1993

Part Three

FOREIGN POLICY

Chapter Sixteen

The Global Empire

Freedom as the Recognition of Necessity

During the years of disintegration of the Soviet bloc, numerous articles in the mainstream media referred to the ongoing collapse of the Soviet "empire." The same media have never applied the word empire to the world of U.S. (or other Western dominated) client states. By ideological premise these are Free, and at most temporarily advised, aided, threatened, and occupied until the natives are ready for self-rule and responsible leaders are in place.

But this self-serving usage is deceptive. The New World Order (NWO) gives daily manifestations that a more sophisticated phase of imperialism has evolved in which trade, aid, loans, debt management, proxy armies, techno-wars, and international "law" are deployed to keep Third World countries in a dependent status. Free World imperialism has been extended to a virtually global regime with the collapse of the former Soviet Union, opening up a vast new area for exploitation, removing a major obstacle to the First World's use of force against the Third World, and making the UN system once again serviceable in the cause of Freedom. In short, a higher stage of "the highest stage" of capitalism has been reached.

The new system is now working very well to quash or prevent the emergence of Third World leaders and movements that might embark on an independent course of development. Michael Manley, recently retired from office in Jamaica, has pointed out that social reform has become impractical, with Jamaica desperate for foreign exchange and "strapped up to its eyeballs, totally dependent on an IMF that's more powerful than ever." His own earlier experiment in reform was undermined by Reagan policies as well as normal market forces, and the more mature Manley, returning to office in 1989, opted to accept the constraints of the NWO and eschew any attempt at progressive politics. He now not only regards these constraints as inescapable, he has surrendered spiritually as well as in practice to the new realism. The new Manley contends that "the market is the guarantee that you will attain the necessary level of competitive efficiency to be able to survive in a world market."[1]

Freedom in the NWO thus has two aspects: economic freedom to invest, sell, and repatriate profits, which is fundamental; and the derivative freedom of leaders of weaker countries to carry out policies within the constraints of imperial reality. The latter freedom harks back to the Spinozan concept of freedom as the recognition of necessity.

Let us review briefly the main elements and bases of the New Freedom of the Manleys, Ortegas, and their ilk.

The Imperialism of Free Trade

A notable article by John Gallagher and Ronald Robinson entitled "The Imperialism of Free Trade" (*Economic History Review*, 1953) stressed the importance of "economic dependence and mutual good-feeling" as the basis for domination of less developed countries (LDCs) by imperial powers. Trade, loans, dependence on ports and markets, and investment in and control over railroads and other forms of communication produced an "informal paramountcy" over LDCs. This was frequently confirmed by a "treaty of free trade and friendship made or imposed upon a weaker state," which was perhaps "the most common political technique of British empire." Technical, marketing, and financial dependency were supplemented by the political influence of local comprador elements. Once the LDC's economy became dependent on foreign trade, "the classes whose prosperity was drawn from the trade normally worked themselves in local politics to preserve the local political conditions needed for it." Gallagher and Robinson emphasized that intervention was only a supplement to a dominant influence that normally flowed from free-market forces. The imperial power would have to use military force only when local polities "fail to provide satisfactory conditions for commercial or strategic integration."

Subsequent analyses have added the consideration that economic penetration and marketing connections have brought LDC elites into a new social nexus, including acculturation to the advanced consumerism of the First World. "Denationalization" of elites in Latin America thus took the twofold form of working for foreigners, and representing their interests, and absorbing their culture and repudiating one's own. The so-called "international demonstration effect" followed from the latter, and was characterized by a gradual shift of elite purchases from local goods to high-style foreign imports.

This weakened domestic industry and, via the increasing imports, made for balance-of-payments difficulties, enlarged debt, and greater dependency. Some analysts have pointed to the contrast between the Latin American and Japanese elites in this respect: for many decades the latter rejected denationalization in both its aspects. This helped preserve Japanese economic and cultural autonomy and contributed to their ability to take off into sustained economic growth.[2]

"Managed" Trade

The United States and other great powers also "manage" trade, via tariffs, quotas, subsidies, harassment and seizures of imports, threats of retaliation, and boycotts. Much of this management is done under the guise of combatting somebody else's "unfair trade." Thus, beyond the power stemming from the dependency relations of normal trade flows, the great powers manipulate the trade environment with "bilateral initiatives based on bullying smaller trading partners."[3]

The Aid System

Government aid has long been deployed to supplement private trade and financing. In the post-World War II era this was improved and given international sanction by the creation of major international lending institutions, including the IMF, World Bank, and Inter-American Development Bank, all dominated by the United States. Given U.S. power, U.S. hostility to a small country has traditionally resulted not only in the cutoff of direct U.S. aid, but defunding on the part of the "international" institutions, and then by private finance. When added to "managed trade" attacks, the pressures on small countries through these economic channels can be very severe.

On the other hand, states meeting U.S.-IMF-World Bank standards are treated generously. The criteria of acceptability are a suitable degree of political subservience, and policy choices that, as Gallagher and Robinson described in connection with imperial policy in general, "provide satisfactory conditions for commercial or strategic integration." Such policies—namely, establishment of an open economy, privatization, a stress on raw materials exports, protection of the rights of foreign investors, cutbacks in social budgets, and devotion to inflation control—are the elements of Structural Adjustment Programs (SAPs) implemented by the IMF enforcers and missionaries. (James Morgan, an economics correspondent for BBC World Services compares SAP to the "word of God" dispensed by missionaries going out from Western Europe to visit the barbarians in the Middle Ages.)

SAPs have often been implemented by terror states that were the ultimate in non-democracy. But aid and bank funding flowed their way. Nicaragua, pursuing the "logic of the majority"[4] in the early 1980s, was quickly defunded and even put on a Free World hit list; Argentina under military rule from 1976 to 1983 murdered thousands, but received lots of Free World money. Marcos, Mobutu, Suharto, Pinochet, and the Brazilian generals after the 1964 coup met the twofold criteria of freedom noted above: economic freedom and adherence to the proper rules of behavior in Third World countries. The needs and demands of the local majority have been irrelevant in this system, and in fact a "courageous" willingness to resist demands for relief in the face of mass suffering is a key characteristic of qualified leaders.

In this framework, we can see that Yeltsin is now the IMF's and the West's "hit man" who inflicts pain on the general population as required by the imposed model—as Pinochet and Marcos did before him—with much of his power now resulting from the fact that the aid is contingent on Yeltsin's retaining authority and thus preserving the West's "confidence" in Russia's pursuit of a SAP. Structural "reform" funded by "aid" can move only in one direction; if any reforms designed to advance social democracy were attempted, confidence would sag, funding would dry up, and the leaders pursuing such outlandish ends would become demagogues and perhaps even qualify for destabilization.[5]

The Subversion System

Subversion is an invidious word that the mainstream media and intelligentsia rarely if ever apply to their own government's actions, and acts by the United States that would be gross subversion if done by others are normalized in the U.S. media. Most notable was the arming, training, and brainwashing of Latin American police and military establishments from the 1950s onward, to reorient them to U.S. needs and provide a counterweight to populist and radical movements at home. This was followed by the rapid proliferation of military dictatorships, death squads, torture, and disappearances on a continent-wide basis in our most closely watched sphere of influence.[6]

Brazil in the early 1960s is a classic case (and the classic exposition is in Jan Black's *United States Penetration of Brazil*), where the United States operated as a quasi-occupying power in this supposedly sovereign country, the largest in Latin America. The U.S. Embassy expected to be consulted on major decisions. The United States subsidized hundreds of politicians, intellectuals and journalists, organized think-tanks, bought space in newspapers, penetrated and tried to disrupt labor and peasant organizations, and established close relations with a significant segment of the military establishment and other security forces. It was a virtual partner in the 1964 coup, wrote the justifying White Paper (unattributed), and the ruling generals expressed their deep appreciation and loyalty to the Godfather in the years that followed.

In lesser client states, U.S. intervention in policymaking and manipulation of the political environment is equally or more blatant, but it is treated with brevity and understanding in the mainstream media. For example, while U.S. law prohibits foreigners from funding and organizing our elections, major U.S. intrusions in the Nicaraguan elections of 1984 and 1990 were taken as perfectly legitimate in the U.S. mainstream media. An imperial double standard was completely internalized. This is plausible—the normalization of our own subversion is obviously necessary to maintain subversion as a viable instrument of imperial policy.

The Proxy Army System

In addition to subversion by the provision of "military aid and training," proxy forces may be organized and funded to attack a target country whose military forces are not easily won over to counter-revolution. This was the case in Nicaragua after July 19, 1979, where the United States had to make do with Somoza National Guard remnants in Honduras, supplemented by mercenary recruitment, just as it used the Chinese Nationalist Army remnants in Burma after 1949 to harass China, and the Khmer Rouge and its allies in Thailand to attack Cambodia (and by this route, Vietnam) after 1979. As is well known, U.S. support automatically makes these proxies "freedom fighters," as opposed to terrorists. It is also clear that any ruling by the World Court declaring the proxy army system illegal in a particular case (now unlikely in the NWO) would render the Court momentarily a "hostile forum" that can be reasonably and safely ignored.[7]

The Techno-War Option

Panama in 1989 and Iraq in 1991 demonstrated the efficacy of a short, capital-intensive assault as a useful imperial option for displacing a disobedient leader (Panama) or returning to the stone age the society of a disobedient and threatening one (Iraq). The option was made more viable by the disappearance of the Soviet Threat (i.e., Soviet constraint), the associated return of the UN system from demagoguery to reasonableness and utility, and mastery of the art of the short war that minimizes U.S. casualties while providing the media and public with a modern version of the Roman circus (with bombs dropped on "mere gooks," Arabs, etc., instead of barbarians or Christians being fed to lions).

The New Legality

A crowning touch to the new imperial system has been its refurbished base and legitimation in imperial law. First, there was the reconquest of the Security Council, with the demise of the Soviet Union eliminating the threat of a veto, and the virtual dependency status of the members assuring a majority vote in favor of proposals by the United States and its eager British Tory ally. Iraq can be devastated and starved by the United States under UN auspices. At the same time the United States can protect its Israeli client from enforcement of a long-standing Security Council resolution (242) condemning Israel's illegal occupation of territory, and can veto or simply ignore a Security Council vote condemning its own invasion and occupation of Panama.

In a further development of imperialist legality, the World Court, which challenged U.S. direct and sponsored terrorism against Nicaragua in 1986 (albeit without effect), dismissed Libya's appeal to international law which, according to the Montreal Convention of 1971, appeared to give Libya certain options in handling the case of its two citizens accused of involvement in the Pan Am 103 bombing. The World Court now declares that a Security Council resolution supersedes international law! This rounds out the legal system of the NWO nicely. The law is what the Godfather decides.

The Imperial Hierarchy

In sum, the global imperial order has been strengthened by the Soviet collapse and Chinese counter-revolution. It has been weakened somewhat by the economic disabilities of the United States and the rise in economic strength of Japan and Germany. But the United States is still far and away the largest and most diversified economy, has the largest aid budget, dominates the international lending institutions, and its huge investment in military power, and the relatively small Japanese and German military establishments[8] continue to give the United States preeminent power and considerable discretion in dealing with Third World countries. The Gulf War displayed the structure of power: Germany and Japan were compelled to support and even help fund U.S. actions damaging to their own interests.

But while the imperial hierarchy has been strengthened vis-à-vis Second and Third World countries, the increased size and mobility of the transnational corporations (TNCs) (including the global private financial institutions) has weakened the power of individual states, including those at the peak of the hierarchy. Their capacity to run independent monetary and fiscal policies has been reduced and their freedom of action in general is to a great extent contingent on their serving the TNC and banker interest. In the age of the triumph of the market the dominant colossi that stand astride the world are the major TNCs and banks; nations are free to serve these rulers of the world.

—*Z, July/August 1992*

Chapter Seventeen

Hate Thine Enemies

A document found in Soviet files in April 1993, in which a Vietnamese official claimed there were more U.S. Prisoners of War (POWs) in Vietnam than previously reported,[1] temporarily reduced the pressure to abandon the 18-year-long boycott and ostracization of a major victim of U.S. aggression, highlighting once more the vindictiveness of the U.S. establishment toward its enemies. U.S. leaders often proclaim that this country's behavior in international affairs is grounded in a Judeo-Christian ethical tradition, and the biblical text on which this tradition rests is larded with words and phrases like "forgiveness," "love thy neighbor," and "turn the other cheek." But this Western religious tradition has been full of contradictions and has displayed a great adaptability and capacity to rationalize class and national interests. There is too much truth in Jonathan Swift's phrase, "We have just enough religion to make us hate, but not enough to make us love one another."

The Judeo-Christian Tradition

Judaism has produced many noble souls and fighters for human betterment, but the Jewish tradition as described in the Old Testament is rampantly ethnocentric and dehumanizes outsiders with a gusto that could hardly be exceeded. Page after page recounts Jewish destruction and extermination of peoples standing in the way of God's chosen: in Chapter Three of Deuteronomy, "And we utterly destroyed them, as we did unto Sihon King of Heshbon, utterly destroying the men, women, and children of every city." My favorite, however, is in Chapter 31 of Numbers, where, after following the Lord's instruction to beat up the Midianites, "they slew all the males...burnt all the cities," and brought back the women and children. But the payoff is that Moses was angry with the leaders of the military expedition for having spared the women and children, and said: "Now therefore kill every male among the little ones, and kill every woman that hath known man by lying with him. But all the women children, that have not known a man by lying with him, keep alive for yourselves." This tradition in treating enemies, starting with Moses, is well preserved in the Gush Emunim, Shamir, Netanyahu, and Rabin (who several years ago as Defense Minister authorized the Israeli forces to enter Palestinian homes and "break bones").[2]

The Christian tradition, while producing saints and inspiring a great number of people to moral lives, has also been notable for adaptability, corruption, and a capacity to rationalize special privilege, exploitation, and mass murder. Its evolution from condemnation of the "sin of usury" and support of "just prices" to accommodation to a full-fledged market system is described in Max Weber's *The Protestant Ethic and the Spirit of Capitalism* and Richard Tawney's *Religion and the Rise of Capitalism*. The history of the inquisition, slave trade, exploitation of the "new world," and colonialism shows the facility with which Christians have been able to maltreat their neighbors while proclaiming a rigorous Christian orthodoxy. The Christian Bible, with its underlying support of slavery and other traditional institutionalized exploitative arrangements, has afforded a religious cover for almost anything. Robert Green Ingersoll, the great U.S. agnostic of the late 19th century, often remarked in his public lectures that when slavery came to Delaware, sales of the Bible soared. The spectacle of the Christian Right in the United States today, with its frenzied pursuit of the rights of the fetus, combined with support of capital punishment, ruthless policies toward the poor, and unlimited violence against foreign infidels, illustrates well the extent to which Christian texts and traditions have been able to give sustenance to irrationality and inhumanity. More subtle and important, however, has been the strong support by the U.S. corporate elite, presumably the mature fruit of the Jewish-Christian tradition, for Reaganite and neoliberal policies at home and abroad that have killed and imposed untold suffering on hundreds of millions of people.

"The Mere Gook Rule"

During the Vietnam War it was reported that U.S. lawyers working in that country had coined the phrase "the mere gook rule," to describe the very lenient treatment given U.S. military personnel who killed Vietnamese civilians.[3] This was one manifestation of a widespread U.S. contempt for the poor, yellow-skinned people we were allegedly "saving." The racist element in that war of salvation added to another extremely important factor influencing U.S. policy; namely, that the Vietnamese were voiceless in the United States, and their pain and material and human losses were politically irrelevant and largely unreported here. The only politically relevant casualties were those of U.S. military personnel.

We can express the foregoing in the terminology of economics as saying that Vietnamese casualties were "externalities" from the perspective of the important players in the U.S. political system. Put otherwise, the marginal cost of dead Vietnamese was zero for the U.S. leadership. This made it feasible, and desirable, to employ capital intensive methods of warfare in Vietnam, with a lavish use of air and artillery firepower, and extremely destructive weaponry, in order to keep *U.S.* casualties down. The rule was, whenever in doubt, bring in the artillery and bombers to level what would automatically be called "a suspected Vietcong base." These would also regularly be described as "surgical strikes."

But the reverse side of the coin of policies to reduce U.S. casualties was enormous casualties and devastation for the Vietnamese civilian population and land. This linkage was never discussed in the main-stream media, and the Vietnamese slaughter and destruction was politically costless to U.S. political and military leaders. They were mere gooks. When the war ended, the United States didn't have to spend a dime to help the Indochinese societies that the napalm, fragmentation bombs, B-52 raids, defoliants, and Rome plows had devastated and shattered.

A major problem with the Vietnam War from the standpoint of leaders of the U.S. national security establishment was that it lasted too long and produced too many U.S. casualties. One remedy for this is to pick on small victims that we can easily overwhelm and to crush them with advanced weaponry that will keep *our* casualties low. From this viewpoint, Grenada was a model triumph. The invasion of Panama was also a notable success, in the same mold. An important aspect of the Panama triumph was the claim of only 23 U.S. dead. In the Persian Gulf War of 1991, U.S. military deaths were kept to a mere 150, while Iraq suffered 150,000 or more military dead (and a shattered society), and the actual fighting lasted only six weeks. The extremely violent high-tech assault against Iraq was a logical development in a serial process of improving capital-intensive warfare to reduce our own casualties, the increased devastation of property and killing of foreigners well understood to be an unimportant side effect. This is the mere gook rule generalized into a policy imperative, as Western values are instilled in the lesser breeds.

U.S. leaders have not treated all enemies and former enemies vindictively. We may distinguish four categories of treatment: (1) malign neglect; (2) inflicting further injury on the former enemy, sometimes treating their entire population as hostages, to be savaged until their leaders are removed or "cry uncle"; (3) positively aiding reconstruction, as with post-World War II Germany and Japan; and (4), in the case of the former Soviet bloc "collapsars," aiding and abetting the dismantling of publicly owned property and the social welfare apparatus as part of a return of these countries to Third World and dependency status within the Free World.

Malign Neglect

Remember Grenada? The mighty military victory of 1983, with 8,000-odd medals of honor given to our brave soldiers, was designed to clean out the remnants of the left-wing government and also post a cheap public relations victory for Ronald Reagan, whose blundering intervention in Lebanon had just cost several hundred Marine lives. Having accomplished this mission, and left Grenada in shambles, but in reliable hands, the Reaganites and media turned their attention elsewhere, and Grenada has been allowed to fester, out of sight of the U.S. public. Its demoralized populace has experienced exceptionally high rates of unemployment and a sharply weakened safety net.[4] But Grenada is "free" and reintegrated into the Free World. The most prominent news item about Grenada in the last five years focused on the island's new status as home to the international financial mafia—money-launderers, tax shelter providers, and asset-free insurance companies—another illustration of the workings of the international division of labor and free market.[5]

Panama was the victim of another U.S. government and press hit-and-run operation. U.S. economic sanctions for several years prior to the December 1989 invasion, plus the highly destructive invasion itself, left Panama economically prostrate, but back in the hands of the traditional elite and a puppet government. U.S. aid has been extremely skimpy—only a small fraction of the economic losses inflicted by U.S. policies. Unemployment remains very high, the populace bitter, and the drug trade reportedly more prosperous than in the Noriega years.[6] But as with Grenada, the tiny victim is in the U.S. backyard, commands little international attention, and the U.S. media find little newsworthy there. Their rule for places like Panama is "never look back," certainly not without a government lead and a rationalizing myth.

Nicaragua affords another case of malign neglect, with a touch of vindictiveness and coercive pressure thrown in. Having inflicted terrible damage on Nicaragua by boycott, the sponsorship of proxy and direct acts of terrorism, the Reagan-Bush gang were deeply disappointed when Chamorro refused to follow up on her electoral victory of 1990 with a thorough "cleansing" of the Sandinistas. The U.S. victory in Nicaragua was only partial, the Sandinistas remaining a powerful social and political force in the country. Chamorro chose to reach a *modus vivendi* with the Sandinistas, instead of carrying out policies that probably would have provoked civil war. The United States therefore withheld aid and applied heavy political pressure on the Chamorro government to penalize it for accommodating the enemy, as well as to force even more drastic neoliberal "reforms," no matter what the social cost.[7]

Enemy Populations as Hostages

A more active malevolence is operative in U.S. policies toward enemies who persist in remaining outside the Free World or who have not yet made proper acknowledgement of their past sins against us and promised to behave properly in the future. As *New York Times* columnist Leslie Gelb pointed out in his ghastly "When to Forgive and Forget: Engaging Hanoi and other Outlaws" (April 15, 1993), these are "outlaw" states, by definition, having crossed and therefore wronged us, and all amends must come from their side. Gelb does not make explicit why we never have to make the amends; it is just an imperial premise—the Godfather does no wrong, by definition. Being the Godfather he is entitled to submission from the small gravitationally bound objects in his backyard, or even beyond if he deigns to intrude into their affairs.

Thus, Vietnam, refusing to submit after World War II, and having resisted our murderous pacification operations, and actually killing U.S. troops who were invading their country, was very bad indeed. As Gelb says, "These guys harmed Americans." And then their failure to turn over their records and devote much time and effort to help locate or determine the fate of each and every U.S. Missing in Action (MIA), was intolerable. The Vietnamese have not understood that each one of these MIAs is more valuable than a thousand Vietnamese MIAs; that, as Gelb suggests, any whim of the Godfather is more important than the aggregate of Vietnamese claims. In short, "power is justice" for our Judeo-Christian spokespersons. So 18 years of imposed hunger for such recalcitrants has been appropriate.

In the case of Iraq, Saddam Hussein crossed us, and the Bush administration decided to "teach Saddam a lesson" by leveling Iraq, with the enthusiastic approval of the media (and the populace as well once the fighting was underway). The destruction of Iraq's infrastructure went vastly beyond any needs of warfare, and the U.S.-British-UN enforced postwar boycott has ensured the death of many thousands of Iraqi children from malnutrition and disease. One would think that the Judeo-Christian tradition would militate against imposing a war and boycott especially damaging to millions of innocent civilians to teach one individual a lesson, but the West has shown little recognition that there is any moral issue involved.

When Iranians took 82 U.S. citizens hostage in 1979, this was treated in the United States as an utterly outrageous act of terrorism. So were the several hostage-taking plane hijackings over the past decade. But is it not a form of hostage-taking and hostage abuse to subject an entire population of 18 million to boycott, deprivation, disease, and starvation to punish or eliminate a foreign leadership? The design is to make the hostage population suffer, causing their disaffection from the leadership, and by this route weaken its hold on the government. Is this not as vicious as threatening a plane-full of hostages to achieve a political end? And is this not on a larger scale, *wholesale* terrorism, in contrast with the *retail* terrorism of the smaller group hostage takers? Once again, we can explain the failure to note the similarity and to treat the wholesale case with indignation because it is standard *Western* policy, and the victims mere Iraqis or mere Vietnamese. In the indignation-arousing cases of retail terrorism, Westerners are the worthy victims, and we then selectively recall that every human being is precious.

Helping Enemies Become Serviceable Allies

After World War II, the United States occupied the defeated Germany and Japan (jointly with Britain and France in West Germany), and provided substantial aid to them as part of a major project of reorganizing the global economy. They were seen by U.S. leaders and planners as potential regional foci of power in a free market system dominated by the United States. The sizable aid to reconstruction was based on its fit to U.S. plans, which anticipated long-term U.S. control, an open door to U.S. sales and direct investment, and their role in fending off the threat of socialism. This program worked very well, even if in the end the aided countries were able to compete with painful effectiveness against the project organizer. A large part of the aid given was tied to the sale of U.S. products;[8] and the aid was tied also to allowing private U.S. sales and investment, especially in Europe, and military subordination to the United States in the North Atlantic Treaty Organization and under treaty conditions with Japan. The aid was therefore far from being a purely charitable enterprise.

Helping Dismantle Collapsars

With the collapse of the Soviet Union and Soviet bloc, and the rise of Lech Walesa, Boris Yeltsin, and other admirers of Reagan and Thatcher, the West used its influence to privatize and dismantle collective enterprises and welfare functions, and to integrate these clients into the global market system. The resulting huge declines in real income and increases in unemployment and social demoralization did not matter to the West except as possible threats to "reform" and the "reformers." The material aid dispensed to the collapsars has been extremely modest, and has hardly affected the declines in process, but indicates Western support for the reformers and helps keep them in a reformist halter. The West has engineered a major bang—in the form of restructuring and acceptance of great social pain and dislocation—for minimal bucks.

—Z, July/August 1993

Chapter Eighteen

The U.S. Versus Human Rights in the Third World

The United States has had a large negative impact on human rights in the Third World, and should be regarded as a primary source of human-rights violations, rather than as a world leader devoted to their elimination. This is an incomprehensible idea for most people and virtual contradiction in the frame of conventional discourse. But the conventional view in every prosperous and relatively stable society is that its external behavior is decent, benevolent to a fault, and while perhaps influenced by interest and security considerations, operates strictly within the bounds of the rule of law and morality. The mainstream press in every such society does not dispute this patriotic and exceptionalist view.[1] Starting from such self-serving premises, however, precludes objective analysis and genuine understanding.

The truth of the U.S. relationship to human rights was dramatically illustrated by the rise of torture in the 1960s and 1970s. In its 1975 *Report on Torture*, Amnesty International (AI) pointed out that human torture, which for several centuries had been largely a historical curiosity, "has suddenly developed a life of its own and become a social cancer."[2] At the same time, AI noted that reports of torture from the Soviet bloc had declined after the death of Stalin in 1953, leaving the cancerous growth a largely Free World phenomenon. In its 1975-76 *Annual Report* (p. 84), AI noted that "over 80 percent" of the "urgent" cases of torture were coming from Latin America. Another 1979 study of human rights found that of 35 countries that used torture on an administrative basis in the early and mid-1970s, 26 were clients of the United States.[3]

This was hardly inadvertent. After World War II, the Third World was a scene of struggle between the remnants of the old colonial regimes and nationalistic masses seeking a better life. The United States did not align itself with the nationalistic masses. On the contrary, its leadership sought (and continues to seek) a certain form of stability, with governments in place that are friendly and even subservient, maintain an open economy, and eschew populist and radical solutions to demands from below. The late 1950s and 1960s also witnessed the U.S. establishment's trauma over Castro's victory in Cuba and the Vietnam War, its ensuing preoccupation with subversion and insurgencies, and its decision to aid and train the military and police within its sphere of influence.

The "trend in Latin America toward nationalistic regimes maintained in large part by appeals to the masses" and "an increasing popular demand for immediate improvement in the low living standards of the masses" is presented in a National Security Council Policy Statement of 1954 as a challenge and threat to U.S. interests.[4] These interests were seen as best served by governments that participate in an "allied defense effort," eliminate "the menace of internal Communist or other anti-U.S. subversion," and "base their economies on a system of private enterprise and, as essential thereto...create a political and economic climate conducive to private investment."[5] The U.S. establishment has long seen Third World nationalism, genuine independence, and economic radicalism or even serious reformism, as threats. The weights given the interests of the local majorities, and human-rights values, appear to have been close to zero.[6]

In fact, human rights have been a distinct obstacle to accomplishing the primary values. Genuine political democracy would pave the way for the election of independent and nationalistic reformers and would allow subversive groups and organizations to develop. The "outstanding lesson" of the Vietnam War, according to General Maxwell Taylor, was the need to identify and counter in advance "an incipient subversive situation."[7] This is difficult under democratic conditions, but feasible and standard practice under the rule of "authoritarian" generals trained on the omnipresence of subversion in the U.S. Army School of the Americas in Panama.[8] This is why the United States distrusted and allowed the quick displacement of the Dominican Republic's Juan Bosch—an annoyingly independent leader who refused to kill or deport communists in the absence of illegal acts or a genuine threat.[9] On the other hand, the Somoza family in Nicaragua, while violating all the nominal human-rights values, was properly subservient to the U.S. leadership, maintained an open economy (although stealing a great deal for themselves and cronies), and avoided providing unnecessary food, medical care, or education to the "oxen" majority.[10] The result was 45 years of friendly relations and U.S. support, and no destabilization in the interest of "democracy" or "human rights."

It was in pursuit of the primary values that the United States invested heavily in the 1950s and later in building up and educating Third World client-state police and military personnel. They were educated to serve U.S. ends, to ensure their "understanding of, and orientation toward, U.S. objectives,"[11] to function as a constabulary and provide what General Robert Porter described as "an insurance policy" to protect U.S. interests.[12] The training of these de facto agents of U.S. power stressed the threat of communist subversion, broadly and vaguely defined but tied in with popular movements and challenges to existing property relationships.[13] As political scientist Frederic Nunn pointed out in reference to Latin America, "subject to U.S. military influence on anti-communism, the professional army officer became hostile to any form of populism."[14]

In a remarkable display of Orwellian misrepresentation and self-deception, U.S. leaders and military spokespersons have regularly claimed that U.S. aid and training programs are designed to foster democratic values.[15] But the intent, design, and effect of such programs have been blatantly undemocratic—they have been to orient the foreign trainees to *U.S.* objectives and priorities, to wean them away from indigenous loyalties and populist or radical tendencies. They have encouraged these military personnel to distrust democratic institutions and to take matters into their own hands.[16] If carried out by an enemy power, such programs would be called blatant subversion.

What is most telling, however, are the results: In the wake of this large new U.S. effort, "Between 1960 and 1969, eighteen regimes in Latin America, of which eleven had held office constitutionally, were overthrown by the military. By 1969, more than two-thirds of the people in Latin America were living under military dictatorships."[17] Some 80 percent of the core group of generals participating in the Brazilian coup of 1964 were U.S.-trained, whereas only 22 percent of those not involved were products of U.S. programs.[18] The United States was an active or behind the scenes participant in many of these transfers of power, and in the aftermaths of the Brazilian and Chilean coups U.S. personnel helped write the White Papers justifying these positive developments.[19]

The United States quickly recognized these coup-based regimes, gave them protection and support, and proclaimed the clearly undemocratic results to be gratifyingly positive yields from our investment in support programs. General Robert Porter stated in 1968 that "dollar for dollar, U.S. military training assistance pays the greatest dividend of any of our assistance programs in Latin America."[20] Defense Secretary Robert McNamara told Congress in 1966 that recent developments in Indonesia, which involved a military takeover and the massacre of somewhere between 500,000 and a million civilians, was one of the "dividends" of our military training programs.[21]

A spectacular development of death squads and disappearances accompanied the installation of these U.S.-sponsored regimes.[22] It has been shown time and again that U.S. aid has flowed *toward* human-rights violators and *away from* democratic states; the correlation between U.S. aid and human-rights abuses and tyranny is positive and significant.[23] This is because human-rights violators quickly improve the climate of investment by crushing trade and peasant unions and opening the door to U.S. investment, and genuflect to the United States in the Somoza manner.[24] In short, the U.S. pursuit of its primary values has led to the systematic support of gross violations of human rights.

The Case of Guatemala

Let me illustrate the U.S. role in the genesis and protection of human-rights violations by a brief account of the U.S. relationship to Guatemalan state terror. The United States supported a dictator, Jorge Ubico, for many years, despite his systematic disregard for human rights.[25] The revolution that ousted Ubico in 1944, and established a democratic order in the years 1945-54, was strictly indigenous and was not aided by any U.S. destabilization of the dictator. The decade of democracy was essentially free of major human-rights violations, pluralism flourished to a degree not seen before 1945 or after 1954, and tentative steps were taken toward economic democracy.[26] These steps, notably legalizing unions in 1947 and proposals for land reform, partly at the expense of the United Fruit Company, aroused intense U.S. hostility,[27] and a search was on for "communists" whose presence would explain these menacing developments and provide a rationale for removing the offending government.

In June 1954, a U.S.-organized, funded, and directly assisted "contra" army ousted the elected government of Guatemala. Although this was done in the name of democracy, as well as to combat the communist menace, the sequel was a decisive and long-term termination of pluralism and political democracy. The crushing of unions, peasant groups, and the ending of any possibility of social reform by peaceable means, which also followed the U.S. intervention, led to the periodic emergence of guerrilla movements.[28] The response of the United States and its political-military progeny was an escalation of force and state terror. With U.S. aid, training, and participation in anti-guerrilla activities, Guatemala became a counterinsurgency state, run by a brutal military establishment under a system of permanent state terror.

In short, Guatemala represents a case of an institutional structure of domination *built to violate human rights* in the interest of protecting an extremely undemocratic status quo. It emerged in the wake of a major intervention that reestablished a dominant U.S. role, along with regular U.S. inputs from 1954 onward that shaped the character of the military, police, and political establishment. The United States participated actively with Green Berets in the pacification effort of 1966 and after, introducing the worst phases of violence against the civilian population. During the Carter years, the United States cut off military aid to Guatemala, but loopholes permitted a continued flow of U.S. arms,[29] and Israel was permitted to take up much of the arms-advisory slack. There was, of course, no destabilization of Guatemala or support of freedom fighters, as there was for the elected government of 1954.

Following the election of Reagan, a major effort was made to reintegrate Guatemala back into the arms and training network. Unconstrained apologetics for Guatemalan state terror, reclassifications of military items making them eligible for sale, secret transfers of military goods and provision of counterinsurgency advisers, vigorous lobbying of Congress—all set the stage for the official renewal of military aid in 1983.[30] The Reagan administration displayed the spirit of its approach to Guatemala in December 1982 when, at the height of a new wave of Guatemalan state terror, and two months after publication of an AI report enumerating the places and character of a slaughter of 2,600 peasants, President Ronald Reagan visited Guatemala and lauded the head-of-state General Rios Montt as "totally committed to democracy" and getting a "bum rap."[31]

Reconciling Support of Terror with Human Rights

How does the U.S. establishment (including the mass media) succeed in portraying the United States as a protector of human rights in the light of the Guatemala record and its wider role of support for regimes of terror?

First, there is the rule of selective attention and indignation. The U.S. mass media focus heavily and intensively on human-rights violations in enemy states. For example, of the 22 human-rights victims given intensive coverage by the *New York Times* in the period January 1, 1976 through June 30, 1980, 21 were victims of enemy states,[32] although this was a period of increasing terror in Guatemala and other U.S. client states. The U.S. mass media prefer to feature Cuba rather than Guatemala, despite the fact that Cuba's human-rights performance is glowing in comparison with that of Guatemala.[33] Official U.S. silence on the large-scale torture, death squads, and disappearances in its local client states is reflected in the mass media in the form of very low key treatment and considerable suppression.[34] A dramatic illustration is the fact that the first Latin American Congress of Relatives of the Disappeared, held in Costa Rica in January 1981, at which it was estimated that the disappeared in Latin America by then totalled 90,000, was unreported in the *New York Times, Washington Post,* or any other U.S. mass circulation newspaper, magazine, or TV broadcast.

The second rule is that the U.S. role in originating, underwriting, and supporting regimes of terror is played down or ignored altogether, and their terroristic proclivities are portrayed as either inexplicable or a product of Latin genes or "cultures of violence."

The third and most interesting means by which the United States is made to appear a devotee of human rights is by allowing its role on human rights to be defined by official statements and actions regretting, opposing, and appearing to penalize state terror in the U.S. provinces. Given the context of ongoing support for the regimes of terror, this focus yields an Orwellian result. Because its protegés in Guatemala, El Salvador, Chile, Argentina, Indonesia, Zaire, South Vietnam, etc. have been guilty of massive terror, there have been periodic spurts of publicity and outcries over U.S. funding and training of the armies and police forces directly responsible. Every administration is therefore obliged to explain how deeply concerned it is with human-rights violations, and to detail its valiant efforts by "quiet diplomacy" to set things right—while stressing the importance of continuing to aid the regime of terror! Very occasionally, an unusual combination of circumstances actually causes the executive authority to criticize human-rights violations fairly seriously, and Congress may force a cutback of aid and training, as in the Carter years.[35]

The emphasis on U.S. efforts to curb human-rights abuses in its client states not only misses the forest for the trees, it even fails to identify the trees properly. When U.S. officials make statements about their deep concern and quiet efforts to curb abuses, several questions immediately suggest themselves: If the institutional apparatus of terror and its operations were put in place and are supported by the United States, is it not likely that the abusive results are expected and acceptable, if not intended? Is it not therefore also likely that these expressions of concern are only nominal and designed to placate public opinion? Wouldn't a serious attack on the "abuses" go to the heart of the supported enterprise? The press does not ask such questions, however, and allows the official claims of deep concern over abuses to prevail.[36]

There is, in fact, substantial evidence that the primary role of U.S. officials in dealing with "difficult" cases of state terror—i.e., those that establishment institutions are unable entirely to overlook and that must therefore be explained and reconciled with our benevolent purposes—such as the holocaust in Guatemala from 1978 to 1984, the rape-murder of four U.S. religious women in El Salvador in 1980, and the army's murder of six Jesuit priests and their two employees in

November 1989, has been "damage containment," designed to protect the institutions of terror. Cover-ups and false denials have been systematic and U.S. officials and client-state terrorists have been in consistently friendly alliances of mutual support and protection.

During the early 1980s era of mass killings in Guatemala, Reagan administration officials not only engaged in continuous apologetics and serial lying on Guatemalan government actions and responsibility,[37] they carried out a systematic campaign of derogation and intimidation against AI, Americas Watch, and other human-rights groups in an attempt to discredit and silence them.[38] In the case of the rape-murders of the four U.S. religious women by members of the Salvadoran National Guard in December 1980, it took three-and-a-half years and a congressional threat to cut off U.S. funds to get a few low level Guardsmen tried and convicted of the murders. With the help of U.S. officials, the involvement of higher-level Salvadoran political and military leaders was kept out of the press and trial in an outstanding example of protection of a regime of terror.[39]

In connection with the November 1989 murder of the six Jesuits and their two employees, the record of protectionism of the terrorists was so blatant that even the *New York Times* used the word in reference to the case.[40] For over a month the U.S. Embassy suggested that the murders were carried out by the rebels. When a Salvadoran soldier came forward with evidence of Salvadoran army responsibility, U.S. officials released his name to the Salvadoran military, thereby jeopardizing his life and warning others to remain silent.[41] A woman who witnessed the murders was taken to the United States, threatened, and treated as a hostile witness.[42] A CBS "60 Minutes" program on the murders reported that the U.S. Ambassador had coached the Salvadoran army chief on probable questions and appropriate answers for the program. Shortly thereafter, the *New York Times* reported that four army witnesses in the case had "disappeared." It soon turned out that the reporter had neglected to note that the soldiers had "disappeared" to Fort Benning, Georgia, which apparently put them out of the jurisdiction of Salvadoran law![43] On August 11, 1990, it was reported that U.S. officials were refusing to release documents pertaining to the murders on "national security" grounds.[44]

Attempting to explain the tacit U.S. support of torture in Greece in the late 1960s, AI pointed out that as the Greek military regime met the U.S. criteria of strategic compliance and suitable political stability, and with other matters being of little account, U.S. policy on Greek torture "has been to deny it where possible and minimize it, where denial was not possible. This policy flowed naturally from general support for the military regime."[45] This analysis has wide applicability.

In the Reagan years, Congress imposed a requirement that the administration certify each year that human rights were improving in El Salvador, as a condition for further aid to the Salvadoran government. It is well known that during this period over 50,000 Salvadoran civilians were killed by the armed forces and death squads, without any officer ever being brought to trial for murder. Nevertheless, the administration never failed to find improvement and Congress never failed to accept these findings. The fact that mass killings at the rate of some 1,000 civilians per month occurred in the base years of 1980-1981 helped support the claims of improvement, but it is a notable fact that the immense height of the initial level of state terror never caused Congress to refuse support. This process, which did not interfere with U.S. aid to the Salvadoran government, allowed the establishment institutions to show U.S. devotion to human rights by reporting these concerns and debates, while ignoring their largely nominal character and deflecting attention from the main human-rights decision—to support the regime of terror in the first place.

The Role of National Security and Anti-communism

It is often argued that U.S. support for human-rights violators is based on "national security" considerations, rather than any mundane motives. This rationale for intervention, however, even if valid, which it is not (see below), does not eliminate U.S. responsibility for the regimes of terror and human-rights violations which it supports; it merely tries to explain them in more acceptable terms.

The great virtue of the national security argument from the standpoint of U.S. economic and military elite interests is its combination of apparent virtue, compelling importance to politicians and press, and virtually unlimited elasticity. Politicians and mainstream editors and journalists cannot withstand the accusation that they are damaging U.S. national security, especially as "communists" are usually alleged to be standing in the wings waiting to take over and commence their march on Washington. Anti-communism and national security in tandem have thus been a primary control mechanism that allows the political and military machinery of the state to serve the larger interests that benefit from the global expansion of the U.S. economy.[46]

It must be acknowledged, however, that these ideologies and fears are internalized and take on a life of their own, and that the "threat" of Grenada, Nicaragua, and a virtually disarmed Guatemala in the early 1950s may seem real to national security managers and mainstream editors. The NSC Policy Statement on "U.S. Policy in the Event of Guatemalan Aggression in Latin America," dated May 28, 1954, conveys an aura of panic, as if Guatemala, "increasingly [an] instrument of Soviet aggression in this hemisphere," was truly about to launch an attack.[47] In the real world, Guatemala had not moved one inch outside her own borders,[48] and was to be easily toppled by a U.S.-organized invasion within one month of the date of the NSC statement. Did the NSC members believe their own claptrap, or was it tongue-in-cheek? Whatever the answer, the service of such claims to the U.S. policing and removal of deviants from its backyard is real and hardly coincidental.

National security has the merit of vagueness and thus easy extensibility to anything that stands in the way. Especially with Moscow to "link" to the local radicals, governments that show signs of excessive independence, allow local communists and radicals to proselytize, tolerate, and even encourage union and peasant organization, and worst of all, take positive steps to serve the majority (as did the Sandinistas), quickly become national security threats. I have long contended that one of the main purposes of the boycotts of countries like Guatemala, 1948-1954, and Nicaragua in the early 1980s, was to force a greater dependence on the Communist powers, thus proving a desired linkage and justifying actions allegedly based on such connections.

One form of evidence that national security is convenient pathology is the extent to which neighbors of the states allegedly threatening U.S. security, who are closer to and less able to defend themselves from the menace than the United States, are much less concerned than the pitiful giant, and have had to be bribed and browbeaten to join the U.S.-sponsored opposition. Arm-twisting was notorious in the case of the U.S. attack on Guatemala in the early 1950s.[49] With the Nicaraguan "revolution without borders" in the early 1980s, the supposedly threatened local governments formed a Contadora group whose main function was to try to contain the United States by confronting it with an unwanted negotiating option. For the neighboring states, U.S. intervention was a far greater threat than Nicaragua.

The history of Contadora provides further evidence that the national security threat was nominal only, and a cover for a great power's determination to brook no opposition in its backyard. The moment of truth came in 1984, when Nicaragua suddenly agreed to sign without reservation a proposed Contadora agreement that would have precluded all foreign advisers and bases and cross-border aid to rebels, and would have provided for continuous and virtually unrestricted on-site monitoring by third parties. This caused the Reagan administration to panic, and it quickly got its most amenable dependencies, Honduras and El Salvador, to find serious objections to the Contadora provisions.[50] An agreement that resolved the alleged national security concerns of the United States was an annoyance, for reasons that are all too clear.

Elections and Democracy

While U.S. sponsorship of regimes of terror, and the human-rights implications of this support, are not discussed very much in the mainstream media, and are typically explained away in terms of our alleged national security interests, a great deal of attention is given to U.S. support of free elections and thus democracy in vindication of the genuineness of U.S. concern for human rights. This proof suffers from several serious limitations, however. One is its narrow conception of democracy. A second is the selectivity of application even within its own limited frame of reference. A third limit is that it ignores the ability of a great power to use free elections in ways that pervert them to its own ends and cause them to have an inverse relation to the substance of democracy.

On the concept of democracy, the focus on elections addresses only political rights and powers, not the economic and social aspects of democracy. This conforms to the Western emphasis on rights that do not directly address inequality of wealth and income and the structural basis of inequality,[51] which in turn affect the substance of personal and political rights. Where structural change is needed for the attainment of basic needs for the majority, it is a precondition for political justice and rights as well, and the focus on elections may not only be a diversion, it may be a means of *combatting* the struggle for human rights.[52]

In the case of Nicaragua in the 1980s, the Sandinista government put great weight on economic and social rights, pursuing what the Latin American Studies Association team called the "logic of the majority,"[53] mobilizing a long repressed majority to participate in organizations, and carrying out educational, medical, and economic programs oriented to majority interests. These programs were highly regarded by Oxfam and the Inter-American Development Bank (IADB). The former noted that: "...from Oxfam's experience of working in 76 developing countries, Nicaragua was to prove exceptional in the strength of that government's commitment 'to improving the condition of the people and encouraging their active participation in the development process' [quoting a World Bank report]."[54] The IADB stated in 1983 that "Nicaragua has made noteworthy progress in the social sector, which is laying a solid foundation for long-term socio-economic development."[55]

The "logic of the majority" was not appealing to the Reagan administration and U.S. establishment, which quickly built up the exiled Somoza National Guard to attack the new order in Nicaragua. A variety of nominal reasons were given for this assault, reasons which shifted over time and were often based on fabricated evidence.[56] However, it is important to recognize that Sandinista failings on political and personal rights, while vociferously alleged and strenuously protested by the Reagan government, merely provided public relations ploys whose use involved the Reaganites in remarkable hypocrisy. This same administration was entirely oblivious to the absence of political rights in Saudi Arabia and Pakistan, and to what AI described as "A Government Program of Political Murder" in Guatemala,[57] among many other cases.

It should also be reiterated that the absence of political rights under the Somozas never elicited U.S. hostility. The Somozas, however, pursued the "logic of the *minority*." There may have been other variables affecting their relations with the United States, such as the Somozas' artful acknowledgment of inferiority and willingness to serve Godfather,[58] but it is striking that their systematic violations of human rights of all types caused no substantial negative U.S. reaction.[59]

When the Sandinista government held an election in November 1984, the Reagan administration went to great pains to discredit it, to prevent it from legitimizing the Nicaraguan government and thereby interfering with the ongoing program of destabilization and low intensity warfare. This effort at discrediting, based on an intense focus on official censorship and harassment of the newspaper *La Prensa* and the voluntary withdrawal from the election of a potential candidate, Arturo Cruz, was largely successful.[60] The Reagan administration was thus able to continue its boycott, harassment, and military attacks on Nicaragua via a proxy army.

By 1990, with the Nicaraguan economy virtually destroyed and per capita real income reduced by more than 50 percent, in a further free election the candidate sponsored and aided by the United States finally ousted the Sandinista government. This was almost universally regarded in the United States as proof that the patient pursuit of the electoral option works![61] The complementarity of the incessant, decade-long and large-scale intervention damaging to the governing (and elected) party to the benign electoral result was hardly noticed.[62]

Elections were also held in El Salvador in 1982 and 1984 and in Guatemala in 1984 and 1985. These elections were sponsored and supported by the United States to legitimize governments that were engaged in very severe human-rights violations, but which pursued the "logic of the *minority*." They were held under conditions of army rule and ongoing state terror, and only after any Left oppositional organizations and parties had been decimated, eliminated, or pushed underground.[63] These were "demonstration elections," demonstrating that democracy prevailed, as evidenced by free elections, and thus vindicating the terrorist regimes. In these cases, in contrast with the Nicaraguan election, the Reagan team focused not on press constraints and the inability or unwillingness of an alleged "main opposition" to run, but on the long voting lines, the guerrilla opposition to the elections, and the extent to which the elections met formal procedural criteria. The Western media followed this agenda, and El Salvador and Guatemala, unlike Nicaragua in 1984, were found to be democracies run by elected governments.[64]

These were not free elections in substance but the power of superstate propaganda, with media support, allowed them to be portrayed as such. The Salvadoran and Guatemalan elections therefore served to *damage* human rights by improperly accrediting regimes of terror, thereby facilitating (for El Salvador) continued financing and underwriting further oppression. Through the same process of superpower propaganda and media cooperation, the relatively free Nicaraguan election of 1984 [65] was not permitted to legitimate the government and therefore failed to bring an end to a program of external intervention and state-sponsored terror designed to terminate the pursuit of the logic of the majority. The Nicaraguan election of 1990, successfully portrayed in the United States as fair, was not fair at all—it was an electoral ratification of the defeat of the Sandinista program by foreign aggression. Not only had the position of the ruling party been undermined by incessant foreign economic and military attack, the elections were held under conditions of de facto extortion, as the hostage voting population was openly threatened with continued boycott, harassment, and renewed violence for casting their ballots the wrong way.[66]

Concluding Note

The image of the United States as a protagonist of human rights is a result, in part, of patriotic sentiments and the self-serving claims of officials and their establishment supporters. It is also widely believed that a democracy must support democracy abroad; facts to the contrary are handled by muted coverage or rationalizations in terms of national security and the threat of communism. The possible dominance of the "investment climate" as the operational criterion of policy in the Third World, its implications for human rights, and the "insurance policy" strategy, are simply not discussed. The possibility that the assertion of national security concerns may be a cover for the support of clients whose rule violates all of our nominal values is also avoided.

The United States is, in fact, a strong supporter of political and trade union rights—in enemy states. In the early 1980s, the public would have had reason to be impressed with the passionate official concern with trade union rights in Poland. They would not be aware of the same officials' almost simultaneous support of the Turkish military government and its violent crackdown on Turkish trade unions.[67] Turkey was an ally and client.

Bringing about change in U.S. policy toward human rights is a formidable task as it is rooted in a structure of interests and power. As these interests dominate the state and are able to shape media agendas, they have also been able to engage in effective role reversals, making themselves appear to be fighters for democracy and human rights, and hostile to terrorism and the use of force. In the light of the facts, this is an achievement that a totalitarian state could strive to equal but could hardly surpass.

—*Harvard Human Rights Journal, Spring 1990*

Chapter Nineteen

Western State Terrorism and Its Apologetics

Despite the great media interest in terrorism in recent years, William Perdue's *Terrorism and the State* has not been reviewed in any mainstream journal or national newspaper. It was issued by a publisher that charges library-oriented high prices (here, $42.95) and provides modest follow-up support (including copy editing as well as advertising). But that is not the main reason this book has fallen still-born from the press. The problem with Perdue's book is that it frames the terrorism issue outside the mainstream paradigm, and will necessarily repel, and may even be incomprehensible to, mainstream editors and reviewers.

In the mainstream paradigm, the West is the *victim* of terrorism, because of its openness and the envy and hatred of the subversive forces of the world (Saddam Hussein and Iraq, Muammar Qadaffi and Libya, and, in the Evil Empire years and the vision of Ronald Reagan, Claire Sterling, and A. M. Rosenthal, the Soviet Union). The focus of Western officials, experts, and media is therefore on insurgent and Left terrorism, with selective admission of state terrorism by politically convenient villains.[1]

Perdue not only fails to use this supremely biased Western model of terrorism, he analyses and rejects it as a blatant ideological apparatus designed to rationalize Western state terror. For Perdue, the main form of terrorism is "regime terrorism," a "higher terrorism" managed by the leading Western states, to help them mobilize the world's resources and people to serve their own interests. They employ their superior power to advance and protect the transnational corporate system which they dominate and "to keep the world safe from change" (pp. 16, 18). These states use a wide array of means to dominate through fear. Thus Perdue includes under the rubric terrorism not only the state's employment of force to keep its own populace in line, but also the warfare state and its operations, racial terrorism, settler terrorism, surrogate terrorisms, and a vast array of other forms of state intervention (listed on pp. 42-43).

Concept and Ideology

As Perdue notes, terrorism is "a label of defamation, a means of excluding those so branded from human standing" (p. 4), and it is a powerful one. He situates it not only in an ongoing structure of power relations, but in a history of domination and supremacist thought. In an earlier age of imperialism, slavery was legitimized by various racist ideologies, and terrorism is in the same tradition of ideologies in the service of domination. Essentially, terrorists are those who stand in the way of the West: it is "a form of international deviance," a resort to uncivilized forms of violence. These outsiders and deviants "are often portrayed as irrational or crazed, exercising a twisted thirst for blood....History is reduced to the behavior of notorious persons (whether good or evil) locked in an international morality play....Combined with appeals to nationalism, faith, and other traditional symbols, the war on terror unites the social audience against the forces of barbarism and heresy" (pp. 8-9).

Perdue observes that each anti-colonial movement has been delegitimized as terrorist, and that each enemy resisting the United States, such as the National Liberation Front in Vietnam, is quickly given the terrorist label. He also points out that the "paranoid style of anti-communism projected on a world scale" has conveniently linked together domestic opposition to U.S. intervention and foreign communist terrorists. He stresses also the flexibility of usage of terrorism in a regime of modern propaganda servicing the state, illustrated by the emergence of "narco-terrorism," tying Reds and enemies of the state to drug suppliers, and merging together all the enemies into a compote of negative symbolism (pp. 10-11). Meanwhile, of course, in Southeast Asia in the 1960s, and in the case of the Nicaraguan contras in the 1980s, the establishment media ignored or downplayed the very real links between the CIA and other government agencies, the immediate Western tools of state terrorism, and the drug trade.

Perdue has a good account of the "academic" construct of terrorism, showing how nicely aligned it is with the demand of the Western establishment for an exclusive focus on threats and violence from below, simultaneously ignoring regime terrorism. He calls this the "order paradigm of terrorism" which "is clearly committed to a control perspective" (p. 14). Occasionally discussions of state terrorism by mainstream analysts mention notorious regimes (Hitler and Stalin, but never Pinochet or Botha) or take illustrations from African tribal communities. "Absent from this entire type of inquiry is an analysis of Western state violence, much less the global relations that give it form" (p. 15).

Regime Terrorism

Perdue provides a broad account of regime terrorism, describing its multi-leveled characteristics, but its invariable reliance on control through fear. He includes internal wars through death squads as well as pacifying armies, but he also embraces all of the external manifestations of the warfare state, which reflect "a real developmental stage in the productive forces" (p. 23). The resultant imperial terror, aided by a bellicose patriotism, is far and away the most important form of terrorism. It rests on and is at the same time a part of the ideology of a dominant global system, designed to open and serve transnational investment. It is a partner of a growth (as opposed to distributional) model of development. "Thus what is 'modernized' is a system of global inequality, and what is 'developed' are the dependency relations of peripheral underdevelopment. This, simply put, is real terrorism" (p. 42).

Most of Perdue's later chapters are case studies of various forms of regime terrorism. He is unusual in treating the testing of and threat to use nuclear weapons as a form of state terrorism. For the Western establishment, the threat of nuclear terrorism is confined to the possible acquisition and use of such weapons by Qadaffi, Saddam Hussein, and other enemies of the West. Perdue argues, however, that "the real nuclear terrorism is already here," manifested by actual possession and threatened use of nuclear weapons by Western governments pursuing their alleged national security interests. For the West, only its members have legitimate security interests, and the imperial demands of the elites of the dominant states are readily made into "security" questions. But this is the self-serving perspective of the powerful; in fact, the nuclear powers have transformed "the whole of humanity into nuclear hostages," always in the name of keeping the peace, but as part of a system of domination by fear (p. 83).

Racial terrorism is analyzed in a chapter focusing on the apartheid system of South Africa. Perdue puts that system into a historic and global context: a racialist tradition; the long record of South African oppression and aggression; the tie-in of South Africa's needs and the Red menace; and the various modalities of U.S. and other Western support for racial terrorism. Perdue's other chapters on forms of state terrorism cover the British in Ireland (Chapter 2), the Israeli-Palestinian conflict ("settler terrorism," Chapter 7), Iranian state terror under the Shah and pre- and post-Shah developments (Chapter 8), and the U.S. attack on Nicaragua as a case study in surrogate terrorism (Chapter 9).

These chapters are rich in historic and global context, unusual in the terrorism literature.

His most original work in this series is that on Libya and terrorism, in Chapter 6, entitled " 'Terrornoia' and Zonal Revolution." Terrornoia is of course Western frenzy over terrorism, which reached its zenith in the Reagan-orchestrated anti-Qadaffi campaign of 1981-87. Perdue reframes the issue, making Libya the victim of western terrorism, for two main reasons: its (and particularly Qadaffi's) serviceability as a target of opportunity and, most important, Libya's own independent development and support for programs, movements and regimes not fitting the global requirements and development model being enforced worldwide by the United States and its allies.

The Selling of International Terrorism

Perdue also has a very good account of "the selling of terrorism" (Chapter 3). He describes how the media readily adopt the official identification of terrorists, confine the discussion to ways of meeting a self-evident terrorist threat, and ignore Western terror or make it into "counter-terror." He shows how really gullible the Western media are, swallowing lies, small and large, sometimes belatedly and unapologetically corrected in the back pages.

He stresses that terror stories concerning the proper terrorists are highly salable and "commodified" in the Western media, not only meeting the standard of high marketability in a commercial media setting, but serving well the ideological interests of the transnational corporate economy. Commodified terror stories build audiences and sell commercial messages, and also serve to mobilize people and justify attacks against threats to global corporate interests.

As Perdue points out, the commodification of terrorism—confined to cases fitting systemic needs—also comes very easily to the mass media by virtue of their ownership, frequent conglomerate linkage, and literal membership in a mutually supportive global corporate system.

Perdue effectively ties the Western media's selling of terrorism into the long debate over a New World Information Order (NWIO). He notes how the extremely self-serving Western media perspective on terrorism is transmitted through powerful Western-dominated agencies to the entire world as *the* view on terrorism. This is a compelling proof that a NWIO that would not frame important issues solely in accord with the demands of dominant Western power is desperately needed. A section on the stereotyping of Arabs in the media reinforces this point.

Perdue also provides an extended case study of the Reagan era demonization of and attacks on Qadaffi and Libya, showing in detail the media's extreme bias and service as a propaganda agency of the state. He examines the 1981 "hit squad" episode, as well as various others designed to make Libya the model of a modern terrorist state, in an interesting and persuasive account of real terrorism portrayed in the U.S. media as a response to terrorism.

Conclusion

William Perdue provides a critique that deserves close reading and wide distribution and debate. It reverses the dominant Western frame of discussion, locating the most intimidating and destructive forms of terrorism in the Western states and their clients and in the needs of the global political economy dominated by the West. Perdue shows convincingly how the West and its intellectual and media agents have transformed the victims of terrorism into the terrorists, in a great feat of system-supportive word management and intellectual legerdemain. His work has the additional merits of providing historic and institutional context, describing the semantic and ideological background of Western practice, and tying the whole picture together as part of a global system of control.

This is an important and useful work that raises questions that would be openly debated in a truly free society. The book has a contribution to make to an understanding of the Bush policies of selective opposition to "naked aggression" and the differential labeling of the insurgencies in Angola, Israel, Lebanon, Central America, the Gulf, and elsewhere. In fact, it provides an excellent background for understanding the Persian Gulf War, which fits the notion of a higher terrorism employed once again by the West to smash a threatening independent locus of power in the Third World.

—Monthly Review, April 1991[2]

Chapter Twenty

Reparations

Reparations as Exactions of the Powerful

Reparations imply payments that compensate for damages unjustly inflicted on the recipient individual, group or country. At the height of the Black upheaval in the United States in the late 1960s, Black activists sometimes invaded White churches and demanded acknowledgement of and reparations for past crimes. These occupations and demands got some publicity, and perhaps had some marginal educational value, but they had no material consequences. Historically, reparations have only been exacted by victors from the vanquished, and have been unrelated to matters of justice. Reparations reflect strength and power, and are hard to distinguish from looting and the exaction of tribute.

Weak countries and exploited peoples cannot obtain reparations because they rarely if ever vanquish their oppressors, and also because there is no world system that enforces reparations for law violations, except where consistent with the interests of the dominant powers. It has often been said that Vietnam "won" the Vietnam War, but the fact that Vietnam could not obtain a penny of reparations and could not even escape a U.S.-organized 18-year-long ostracization and boycott is one piece of evidence that they did not "win." They were not conquered, and their tenacious resistance imposed such costs that the aggressor eventually gave up the effort. But the *aggressor* was clearly not defeated, and the Vietnamese people and countryside suffered a devastation and disorganization from which they have not yet recovered. The United States attained a partial victory by disrupting and shattering another threatening socialist experiment, and by providing an object lesson in the costs of refusing to accept Western domination ("freedom").

If a minimal system of justice and enforceable rules of international law existed, a powerful aggressor would not be able to get away with destroying and making an object lesson of a small country like Vietnam—but the UN never interfered with U.S. aggression, and Vietnam had no legal recourse for obtaining reparations, which would have run to many hundreds of billions. Instead, Western nations cooperated with the United States in further impoverishing the victim of aggression.

The double standard was dramatically illustrated when the United States succeeded in imposing reparations on Iraq for its damage to Kuwait, while ignoring the bill for damages to Nicaragua called for by a World Court decision of 1986, which had found the U.S. guilty of the "unlawful use of force" and owing reparations. The Bush administration eventually bullied the Chamorro government into withdrawing the $17 billion Nicaraguan claim, which the United States had refused to pay and would have continued to ignore if Chamorro had continued to press it. It is clear that "reparations" can only be exacted from parties that fall afoul of the United States, and perhaps its principal allies. No reparations will be required of South Africa for its depredations against its Black population, Namibia, and the frontline states, although a system of just compensation would call for sums in excess of $100 billion. The best that victims of the West can hope for is a termination of the violence perpetrated against them.

Salgado and the Workers

I was inspired to write on reparations after seeing the wonderful photo exhibit "Workers," by Sebastiao Salgado at the Philadelphia Art Museum. (The exhibit traveled subsequently to Louisville, Sioux City, Dallas, and New York.) A former economist, Salgado overcame this structural obstacle to a humanistic perspective and in 1973 became a photojournalist with a specialty in photographing people at work. His coverage is global and his message is humane and radical: that workers are remarkable in their diversity, beauty and ugliness, ability to cooperate, and willingness to struggle, suffer and overcome obstacles; and that they are grossly abused and exploited in the service of the world's affluent minority. It was a bit startling to see Salgado's printed message greeting entrants to the exhibit:

> The images offer a visual archeology of a time that history knows as the industrial revolution, a time when men and women at work with their hands provided the central axis of the world.

> Concepts of production and efficiency are changing and, with them, the nature of work. The highly industrialized world is racing ahead and stumbling over the future. In reality, this telescoping of time is the result of the work of people throughout the world, although in practice it may benefit few.

The developed world produces only for those who can consume—approximately one-fifth of all people. The remaining four-fifths, who could theoretically benefit from surplus production, have no way of becoming consumers. They have transferred so many of their resources and wealth to the prosperous world that they have no way of achieving equality.

So the planet remains divided, the first world in a crisis of excess, the third world in a crisis of need, and, at the end of the century, the second world—that built on socialism—in ruins.

The destiny of men and women is to create a new world, to reveal a new life, to remember that there exists a frontier for everything except dreams. In this way, they adapt, resist, believe, and survive.

Salgado shows sugarcane workers in Brazil and Cuba, tea workers in Rwanda, shipyard workers in Poland and France, textile workers in Bangladesh and Kazakhstan, stockyard workers in South Dakota, gold mine workers in Brazil, fishermen in Spain and Italy, sulfur workers in Indonesia, and canal builders in India, among many others. He provides textual backgrounds to each set of pictures, and in some cases the question of reparations owed strikes one forcibly. In the accompaniment to the superb photos on Coal India, he tells us that

For nearly two centuries, small British companies in the Dhanbad region were interested in short-term investment and immediate results. Miners drilled a hole in the center of the coal vein and removed only the quantity found in that tunnel, leaving whatever surrounded it. This practice, called "gallery mining," circumvented the investment needed for extensive tunnels. When the British finally left, nearly 90 percent of Indian coal reserves remained untouched.

Though this extraction method had some immediate advantages, the long-term consequences of gallery mining were disastrous. Many of the tunnels had been badly drilled: oxygen circulation caused underground fires that broke out around 1940, not only causing enormous damage to the Dhanbad coal reserves but allowing parts of towns built on ground above the mines to collapse. The fires continue to burn today. The loss is estimated at five billion U.S. dollars, not counting the waste of surface area and the destruction of roads and buildings. In addition, gases emitted from the underground combustion cause heavy pollution.

Most of the workers shown by Salgado are simply working hard under technologically backward conditions at low, often impossibly low, wages. His incredible pictures of the gold miners in Serra Pelada, Brazil, with 50,000 mud-soaked men digging for gold on a hillside, calls up an image of slaves building pyramids in ancient Egypt. Teams of three men dig and six men haul the ore from 65-square-foot concessions leased by the state to private contractors. Each sack weighs between 65 and 130 pounds, and the workers are paid 20 cents per sack, which must be carried up a myriad of ladders to the top of the mines. The

Indonesian sulfur miners have a four-hour climb up to the top of a volcano, then a 2,000-foot descent to the edge of a sulfuric lake. Clouds of poisonous sulfuric fumes bubble up from the crater; these are captured through tubes, cooled, solidified, broken up, and put in wicker baskets placed on the ends of carrying poles. The wicker baskets, with 155-pound loads, are carried up the 2,000 feet to the top by men "who often weigh no more than 130 pounds themselves, [which] is an exercise in suffering." For each such load, the workers receive the equivalent of $3.50, down from the level of $6.70 a decade previously.

Forms of Abuse Calling for Reparations

There is a continuum in the spectrum of human exploitation and abuses from the simple and local to the complex and large scale, national and global. Workers are exploited by overwork under terrible conditions, underpayment and fraud, and their exploiters use the proceeds to accumulate property. Powerful people also obtain property by the use of inside information, market manipulation, taking advantage of favorable market conditions to buy cheaply, exploitation of monopoly power and the capitalization of market power in stock values, and of course by the privileged acquisition of publicly owned property. In the history of the Third World, many hundreds of millions of people have been killed, enslaved, and exploited as part of the "social history of the machine gun" in the service of imperialism. P. J. Proudhon's famous dictum, "property is theft," is a fundamental truth that is made obvious in any serious history of the past 500 years (see, for example, L. S. Stavrianos' excellent survey *Global Rift: The Third World Comes of Age* [1981], and Chomsky's *Year 501* [1993]; both have extensive references to supportive writings).

That truth is obscured by a static and individualistic view which takes existing arrangements as a given. In the neo-classical economic perspective, the Brazilian gold miners, Indian coal miners, and Indonesian sulfur workers get low wages because of their large numbers and low productivity. Vietnam also suffers from low productivity and a lack of market discipline. But Brazil, India, Indonesia, and Vietnam had a long colonial and neo-colonial heritage that helped build Western fortunes and the Western industrial base, shaped the ownership and direction of use of indigenous resources, and caused them to remain within the control orbit of the global financial and market system up to the present (with the partial exception of Vietnam). Vietnam fought off full integration by decades of devastating warfare that left the country prostrate. The low productivity, income distributions, and economic structures of these countries (again, partly excepting Vietnam) have been decisively shaped by Western "primitive accumulation" in the past and the continuing influence of neo-colonialism.

In a just world, Vietnam would collect reparations for its colonial experience with France and the massive and devastating aggression by the United States from 1954 through 1975. Further reparations are due from the West for economic aggression thereafter and its support of Pol Pot and Chinese attacks on Vietnam as part of a further bleeding operation. Comparable obligations are owed to the rest of the Third World. Enormous sums are due the American Indian survivors in Guatemala, Mexico, and the United States. Black citizens of the United States, descendants of the victims of the slave system, still suffer severe damaging effects of a continuing racism, physical, and cultural isolation, limited opportunity, and poverty, while the dominant White population considers them to have benefited excessively from "reverse discrimination"! Proper reparations would be enormous. And in general, the list is long and the bill would be huge. I would guess that a valid system of reparations payments to victims and their descendants would reduce Western real incomes by two-thirds or more. It might be worth putting up such a balance sheet, which would be difficult but interesting and valuable even on a very tentative basis.

The Ideological Defenses

As past exploitations and abuses have yielded a status quo very comfortable to the dominant classes, they bury and rewrite the history of property accumulation. Like the military goons of El Salvador (etc.) they favor "mutual" forgiveness for past sins, without retribution or reparations. The clean slate starts now. In the dominant ideological perspective, too, Blacks and Indians in the United States are now free and live in a land of opportunity, so let *them* accumulate. God knows we don't want to repeat the abuses of the past by reverse discrimination in their favor, which would also erode their character and create a White backlash!

Furthermore, here, and in Indonesia and Brazil, the "market" reigns or is taking hold, so that proper values are now being placed on the services of sulfur workers and gold miners. We certainly wouldn't want to reduce efficiency by subsidizing these workers, and the history leading to their present unpleasant position is just history, best forgotten.

Concluding Note

These obfuscating rationales should never fool people of the Left or remain unanswered. Just reparations are hard to compute and even harder to obtain for those who have moral entitlement, but this is because of lack of both power and a system of justice, national and international. The "market" does not rectify historical injustices, and more often than not reinforces them by consolidating structures and imbalances in power dominated by the unjustly rich and their heirs. The world's poor continue to increase rapidly in numbers and misery as the rich get richer in a vicious circle that the dominant order does everything to maintain.

The task of the Left is to replace unjust structures and inequalities built in the past with new ones that will focus on the well-being of ordinary people, and enhance human solidarity and concern for long-run planetary survival. For the Left, it is as important to keep the real history of economic development and exploitation front and center as it is to maintain a critique of the market as the exclusive organizing principle of human life. One of the great legacies of the 1960s and new activist movements has been a revisionist history of Columbus, the settlement of the West, slavery and the slave trade, the history of racism, women's' history, and the history of the 500-year colonization process. This is important for understanding, organizing, and contesting establishment ideology and apologetics. The acute discomfort of the establishment with these "politically correct" critiques is excellent testimony to their value and importance. A rule for the Left should be: never let the establishment use the word "reparations" without insisting that it be put into a proper historical context.

—Z, June 1993

Part Four

THE MEDIA

Chapter Twenty-One

Market System Constraints on Freedom of Expression

The Hyde Park Soapbox Model

The U.S. tradition of freedom of expression has focused heavily on the need for protection from governmental encroachments and restrictions. It rests on what we may call the "Hyde Park Soapbox" (HPS) model of freedom of expression according to which the condition of freedom of expression is met if people are permitted to speak and pass out handbills to passersby in the streets and other public places without interference.[1] The U.S. tradition (and application of the HPS model) has never considered positive government acts and policies necessary to make free expression a reality, except possibly for public education needed to foster a literate and minimally knowledgeable populace.

It is also assumed in the HPS model that no threat to freedom of expression can arise from private-sector developments and policies. This assumption reflects both a preoccupation with the threat of government and the classic liberal faith in free competition and the market. The lack of concern over private restraints on freedom of expression may also manifest the class bias of constitution makers and legislators, who often owned (and own) property and represented (and represent) property interests. In James Madison's Federalist Paper Number 10, the class bias was clear: the "permanent interests" of society (i.e., property) were threatened by majority rule, but fortunately the pursuit of majority interests was encumbered by fragmentation and geographic dispersion.[2] That Madison viewed effective majority rule as a threat, and welcomed structural impediments, suggests that inequality of access to and control over the means of communication would not have bothered him, and would in fact have been seen as another valuable protection against the leveling tendencies of the general population.[3]

Acceptance of the HPS model and its assumptions, along with the evolution of the structure of the communications industries, has yielded a system in which private rights of free expression are protected, but rights to public access, insofar as these entail outreach through privately owned communications facilities, are not. Decisions on access are left to the "marketplace" and those who control it. This means that individuals with facts, ideas, and proposals important to the public interest may be effectively ignored (or relegated to marginal forums) if the controllers of the marketplace disapprove of and refuse to disseminate their messages. But in the frame of free-market thought and ideology, competition among media already operating, and freedom of entry, assure that all views that are important to substantial numbers—and to the truth—will be expressed. As stated in A. J. Liebling's famous irony: We are all free to start our own newspaper if we don't like those available to us.[4]

The Free-Market Model

A free market model can readily be constructed, however, that shows how market processes naturally constrain free expression and marginalize dissent. And there is evidence that such constraints and processes are operative and have large effects. It is well known that the market "rations" goods by price, and that people without "effective demand" will be excluded from, that is, priced out of, the market. The point is not often applied to the media and free expression, possibly because those who might make the point have already been priced out of the market and denied access!

Access is restricted, first, by the requirement that one have capital to enter the media industries.[5] From the earliest times, capital requirements ensured that the media "gatekeepers" are members of the economic elite, with associated class biases; other interest groups, some with enormous constituencies but without substantial capital, like trade unions, racial and ethnic minorities, environmentalists, and consumer organizations, have to depend on the elite gatekeepers for access to the general public.[6]

This control mechanism has been strengthened over the years as the scale of production and capital requirements have steadily grown, the wealth of mass media owners has greatly increased,[7] newspaper chains and television and cable networks have grown in importance, the media have become parts of conglomerates, and the media industries have spread beyond single country borders. The media have been further integrated into the market by increasing competition and an active takeover market. The result of all this has been both delocalization and steadily greater pressure to focus on profitability.

The bias of the media toward the status quo and the interests of the corporate system is assured by this set of considerations alone.[8] But beyond this, profit-oriented media are extremely sensitive to advertiser, governmental, and other powerful interest group wants, needs, and pressures, and tend to avoid controversy and oppositional views even more comprehensively than government-funded media enterprises.[9]

While the owners of the media are wealthy individuals and companies, their operations are funded mainly by advertisers; that is, by business firms trying to sell goods and corporate messages. These have a powerful impact on the media, especially on television but also on the print media.[10] Their influence is exercised under a competitive system mainly by advertisers' demands for a suitable "program environment" for their commercial messages, and their power to choose among stations and programs according to these preferences.[11] The biases of corporate advertisers, whose ideological assumptions and fondness for the status quo is similar to that of the media's owners, should reinforce establishment positions and tend to marginalize dissent.

A third factor that causes market forces to limit free expression arises from the media's quest for cheap, regular, and credible sources of information. Dissident sources are expensive to locate and their claims must be checked out carefully. Claims of the Secretary of State and other high officials, or police officers in charge of investigating an act of violence, are readily available, are newsworthy in themselves, are supplied by credible sources, and do not require careful checking (although a media concerned seriously with truth and *substantive* objectivity would treat all sources with the same degree of scrutiny). A symbiotic relationship develops between dominant sources and the media, which makes the latter more reluctant to transmit dissident claims, as these would embarrass and annoy the media's primary sources.

The dominant sources within the government and corporate system also finance and otherwise support quasi-private institutes and think-tanks, where experts who will preempt further space in the mass media for proponents of establishment views are funded and accredited.[12] Dissidents have no comparable endowed funding and accrediting agencies[13] and are therefore further limited in access to the mass media.

A fourth route through which the market limits free expression is by the generation and use of "flak." Flak is negative feedback that threatens, imposes costs upon, and therefore constrains the media. The importance of flak to the media is a function of money and power, which allow monitoring and serious media challenges, including advertising boycotts, threats of libel suits, congressional hearings, and FCC and anti-trust actions. Just as the American Enterprise Institute, Hoover Institution, and Georgetown Center for Strategic and International Studies serve the establishment by providing accredited experts, so Accuracy in Media, the American Legal Foundation, and Capital Foundation are funded to discipline the media by systematic challenges for "liberal bias," unfairness, and libel.

A final factor in media control by market forces is the ideological premises of the system, which reflect a culture centered in private property. The merits of free enterprise, the threat of state ownership and intervention, the benevolent role of the government in international affairs, and anti-communism are central. Anti-communism has been especially strategic as a disciplinary device, keeping the media and Democratic Party in line by their fear of being tagged unfaithful to the national religion, when they might otherwise be inclined to respond to mass demands by raising questions about tax equity, the size of the military budget, and the propriety of destabilizing and attacking countries not governed in accord with U.S. establishment interests and demands.[14]

These free-market mechanisms, working in concert, and on foreign policy matters usually geared closely to a government agenda, provide a powerful means of filtering out dissident and inconvenient information and opinion. One of the great merits of this system of control is that it operates so naturally, without collusion or explicit censorship, merely by the decentralized pursuit of a set of micro-interests. It "just works out that way." If Poland, a Communist power aligned with a then-hostile Soviet Union, cracks down on the Solidarity union, this is extremely newsworthy, whereas if at the very same time Turkey (a U.S. client state) is cracking down on its trade unions, the filters work to keep this out of the news. If it is serviceable to the Reagan administration to inflate the Libyan menace, the market causes Qadaffi to become a featured "terrorist," while at the same time if state policy toward South Africa and Guatemala is accommodation and "constructive engagement," their far more severe terrorism is found not newsworthy, is largely suppressed, and the word terrorism is not applied to these states and their leaders.[15] If it serves state propaganda needs to focus on the abuses of the Khmer Rouge in Cambodia, the market does this energetically and with great indignation; and if at the same time client state Indonesia invades East Timor and decimates its population with at least equal ferocity, the market-based media avert their eyes.[16] The ease and naturalness with which this is done by uncoordinated self-censorship makes for extremely effective propaganda and allows the creation of a virtually Orwellian world of doublespeak via free- market processes.

A second great merit of the evolving market system of control is that it is not total and responds with some flexibility to the differences that frequently crop up among elite groups. This allows controversy to rage within the mass media, but confined almost entirely to tactical matters, and not challenging fundamental premises. Thus, during the Vietnam War, it was fiercely debated whether we could win, how this could be done, and whether the costs (to us) were too great. The premises: that we had a right to be there, were not invaders and aggressors, and were seeking self-determination and "protecting South Vietnam," were rarely questioned in the mainstream media.[17]

Similarly, in the case of the subversion and proxy warfare against Nicaragua in the 1980s, the view that this was plain aggression and international terrorism, and that the U.S. design was to oppose independence, self-determination, and the pursuit of the "logic of the majority," was simply not addressed in the mainstream media. The access to the mass media of individuals and groups anxious to make such points, in both news columns and opinion pages, was so low as to approach total exclusion.[18]

With the mainstream "Left" lauding our benevolent ends and the eventual achievement of a "democratic election" through "patience" (i.e., not invading Nicaragua with large U.S. forces)[19] following the destruction of the Nicaraguan economy, and with the election held under the ongoing threat of more of the same in the absence of a U.S.-approved outcome,[20] the market system of control performed a propaganda feat that a system of state censorship could hardly improve upon.

A third merit of the market-based system is that a dissident media is allowed to function, but without the capacity to reach large numbers. This is interpreted in the mainstream as evidence that the public does not want the excluded products. But their producers can rarely raise the capital or attract advertising support sufficient to allow a valid product test. For those products that do come into existence, advertiser disinterest, and the benefits of advertiser support for rival publications in price charged, promotion, technical quality, etc., make the survival of dissident media difficult. In Great Britain, the *Daily Herald*, with a large working class audience, failed in the 1960s despite a circulation larger than *The Times*, *Financial*

Times and *Guardian* combined; but its 8.1 percent of national circulation yielded it only 3.5 percent of advertising revenue.[21]

Furthermore, the excluded dissident "product" is a complex of products that often includes elements of the news and perspectives that are highly relevant to issues discussed by mainstream media, but which simply fail to meet their criteria of newsworthiness. This means that literal lies may be institutionalized in the mainstream media, with corrections in the *samizdat* press. [22] More important is the fact that unpalatable matters may be ignored or downplayed, while system-supportive facts, developments, and claims (including fabrications) may be pushed front and center to mobilize the citizenry.[23] But, meanwhile, the establishment points triumphantly to the *samizdat* press, free to operate, but not reaching a mass audience allegedly for reasons of "insufficient demand."

Concluding Note

In sum, a market system of control limits free expression largely by market processes that are highly effective. Dissident ideas are not legally banned, they are simply unable to reach mass audiences, which are monopolized by profit-seeking large organizations offering advertising-supported programs, from which dissent is quietly and unobtrusively filtered out. Excluded individuals are free to say what they want, and may have access to a marginalized media, but do not have the power to contest the market-dominated mass media's system-supportive selectivity and propaganda with the larger public.

This system is extremely difficult to attack and dislodge because the gatekeepers naturally do not allow challenges to their own direct interests to reach the public consciousness. Nonetheless, structural change is imperative for increasing freedom of expression in the United States. This will only happen with greater public understanding of the stakes and important grassroots support for a democratic media.

—Journal of Communication Inquiry, Winter 1991

Chapter Twenty-Two

Commercial Broadcasting on the March

The Deepening Market in the West (5)

The balance between commercial and public broadcasting in the West has shifted steadily, and perhaps decisively, in favor of the former in the 1970s and 1980s. Public broadcasting has been under siege from commercial interests and conservative governments throughout this period, with the tempo of attack stepped up in the 1980s. Public broadcasting monopolies have been broken in Belgium, France, Italy, Norway, Portugal, Spain, Switzerland, and elsewhere, and commercial broadcasters have been rapidly widening their domains, encroaching on public system advertising, putting public broadcasters' funding by the state under further pressure by reducing their audience shares, and forcing them to alter their programs to compete for audiences.

In the United States, public broadcasting was marginalized in the early 1930s; the defeat of an amendment to the Communications Act of 1934 that would have reserved 25 percent of broadcasting space for educational and nonprofit operations confirmed the triumph of commercial broadcasting, and its power was steadily increased thereafter. A small place was carved out for educational and other nonprofit broadcasting in the 1950s and after, but federal sponsorship and funding of public broadcasting did not come about until 1967, and one of the functions of public broadcasting was to relieve commercial broadcasters of a public service obligation that they did not want and were sloughing off. Even in the small niche reserved for it, public broadcasting has been a target of steady conservative attack for its excessive preoccupation with public affairs, and was subjected to a further financial crunch and politicization in the Reagan era.

Although many democratic and progressive critics of the media have been harsh on public broadcasting, most of them have looked upon its decline as a distinctly adverse and threatening development. The most common view is that while public broadcasting has never realized its potential, it has nevertheless contributed modestly to a public sphere of debate and critical discourse and has provided information and viewpoints essential to the citizenship role. By contrast, commercial broadcasting is viewed as an entertainment vehicle that tends to marginalize the public sphere in direct proportion to its increasing dominance and profitability.[1]

Commercial Broadcasting and "Market Failure"

Commercial broadcasting, in fact, offers a model case of "market failure" in both theory and practice, although you will rarely see this point discussed in the mainstream media. But broadcasting has important "public goods" properties, with a potentially important yield of positive externalities; and negative externalities, such as the effects of the exploitation of sex and violence to build audiences, are a likely (and observable) consequence of commercialization.

Externalities are, by definition, things that the market does not take into account, like pollution, worker injuries (when the employer can escape liability), and, on the positive side, aesthetic beauty in well planned and maintained private gardens and buildings, and greater productivity from technological advances that serve industry in general (see Chapter Two, note 1). Broadcasting can be a powerful educational tool and contributor to democratic participation and citizenship. From the time of the Communications Act of 1934, and even earlier, its "public service" possibilities were widely recognized in the United States, and it was accepted even by the broadcasters that their grant of rights to use public air channels was in exchange for their serving "the public convenience, interest, and necessity." In the 1934 hearings, the National Association of Broadcasters acknowledged that it is the "manifest duty" of the Federal Communications Commission (FCC) to assure an "adequate public service," which "necessarily includes broadcasting of a considerable proportion of programs devoted to education, religion, labor, agricultural and similar activities concerned with human betterment."

The 1946 FCC report, *Public Service Responsibilities of Broadcast Licensees*, contended that "sustaining programs" (i.e, those put on at the station's expense, unsupported by advertising) are the "balance wheel" whereby "the imbalance of a station's or network's program structure, which might otherwise result from commercial decisions concerning program structure, can be redressed." It even quotes CBS's Frank Stanton to the same effect. The report referred to the sustaining programs as an "irreplaceable" part of broadcasting, and public service performance in the interest of "all substantial groups among the hearing public" as a fundamental standard and test in approving and renewing licenses.

Commercialization and the Decline of Public Service

But a funny thing happened as the commercial system matured. It became possible to sell time to advertisers for all hours of the day, and the price at which time could be sold depended on "ratings," which measure the audience size (and from 1970, its "demographics"). As time became salable and its price rose, the pressure for high ratings increased; and as Erik Barnouw noted in *The Sponsor*, "The preemption of the schedule for commercial ends has put lethal pressure on other values and interests."[2] One effect was the steady trend away from "controversial" and modestly rated public service programs and toward entertainment. Richard Bunce found that by 1970, public affairs coverage had fallen to 2 percent of programming time, and the entire spectrum of public interest programming was far below that provided by public broadcasting systems in Canada, Great Britain, and elsewhere in the West.[3]

The decline in public service performance of the U.S. commercial broadcasters paralleled a steady increase in broadcasting station and network profitability. By 1970 the profits of major station owners were in the range of 30-50 percent of revenues, and much more on invested capital. Bunce estimated that for the period 1960-72, the ratio of pretax income to depreciated tangible investments for the broadcast networks never fell below 50 percent a year.[4] These staggering profits did not alleviate broadcaster pressure for additional profits, as the workings of the market cause profits to be capitalized into higher stock values, which become the basis of calculation of rates of return for both old and new owners.

The force of competition and stress on the rate of return on capital, which comes to prevail in a free market, compels firms to focus with increasing intensity on enlarging audience size and improving its "quality," as these will determine advertising rates. A recent audience decline for NBC's morning "Today Show," moving it a full rating point behind ABC's "Good Morning America," was reportedly the basis of a $280,000-a-day advertising income differential between the shows. Managements that fail to respond to market opportunities of this magnitude will be under pressure from owners and may be ousted by internal processes or takeovers. There will be no room for soft-headed "socially responsible" managers in a mature system, and in the United States, the three top networks have in fact been taken over by strictly market-driven corporate owners.[5]

The maturing of commercial broadcasting not only steadily reduces the public service component, the U.S. experience also suggests that maturation brings with it a decline in variety of viewpoints and increased protection of establishment interests. A telling illustration was in the coverage of the Vietnam War, where, as Erik Barnouw notes, "The Vietnam escalation of 1965-67 found commercial network television hewing fairly steadily to the administration line. Newscasts often seemed to be pipelines for government rationales and declarations...Though a groundswell of opposition to the war was building at home and throughout much of the world, network television seemed at pains to insulate viewers from its impact...Much sponsored entertainment was jingoistic." The U.S. networks not only made none of the seriously critical documentaries on the War, during the early War years they barred access to outside documentaries. As Barnouw points out "this policy constituted de facto national censorship, though privately operated."

But while the mass protest against the War rarely found any outlets in commercial TV, it "began to find occasional expression in NET [National Educational Television, precursor to the Corporation for Public Broadcasting] programming in such series as *Black Journal*, NET *Journal*, *The Creative Person*, and—explosively—in the film *Inside North Vietnam*, a British documentarist's report on his 1967 visit to 'the enemy.'"[6] This pattern helps explain why Presidents Johnson and Nixon fought to rein in public broadcasting, with Nixon quite openly seeking to force it to de-emphasize public affairs. The commercial systems did this naturally.

In depth news presentations on commercial TV reached their pinnacle with Edward R. Murrow's "See It Now" programs in the mid-1950s. There was a resurgence of news documentaries in the early 1960s, in the wake of the quiz-show scandals of 1959, but subsequently the decline continued, despite occasional notable productions. Sponsors don't like controversy and depth—in either entertainment or non-fiction. In the years when environmental issues first became of national concern, NBC dropped the environmental series "In Which We Live" for want of sponsorship, although the major companies were all busily putting up commercials and other materials on the environment. Their materials, however, reassured, and did not explore the issue in depth and with any balance, as had the NBC series. More recently, a program with Barbara Walters on the abortion issue was unable to obtain sponsors, who openly rejected participation for fear of controversy.

Fear of "Fairness Doctrine" requirements of balance also made serious programs that took a stand on an issue a threat to broadcasters; and watering them down to obviate challenges for lack of balance made them lifeless. Documentaries that appealed to sponsors were about travel, dining, dogs, flower shows, life styles of the rich, and personalities past and present. In short, under the system of commercial sponsorship, the documentary was reduced to "a small and largely neutralized fragment of network television, one that can scarcely rival the formative influence of 'entertainment' and 'commercials.' " The form survived mainly in an aborted quasi-entertainment form called "pop doc," specializing in brief vignettes, with a focus on individual villains pursued by superstar entertainers, and settling "for relatively superficial triumphs." "Infotainment" has also come to the fore, with entertainers titillating audiences with "information" about other entertainers.

Other public affairs programs, like discussion panels, with lower ratings were placed in weekend ghetto slots, and consisted mainly of unthreatening panels asking unchallenging questions of officials. In the years before the death of the Fairness Doctrine, the "public service" obligation was met largely by public service announcements cleared through the Advertising Council, which provided a further means for the broadcasters to establish a record of public service without addressing any serious issue.

Public broadcasting, by contrast with commercial, is likely to provide programs that give substantial weight to positive externalities. This is because the broadcasting media were recognized from the beginning as potentially valuable tools of education and citizen training, capable of universal outreach and service to both mass audiences and minorities, and public broadcasting took an early responsibility for realizing this potential. Most important, public broadcasting has not been driven by the profit motive or funded primarily by advertising, so that its functional role has not been as incompatible with its funding source or institutional linkage as the market-tied and profit-oriented commercial systems have been. It should be noted, however, that insofar as public broadcasting is forced to compete with growing commercial systems for a mass audience, with limited funding, there should be an erosion of original purpose and quality.

The evidence from Western Europe on the treatment of public service and positive externalities by commercial and public broadcasters is similar to that from the United States. Public broadcasting systems offer wider ranges of choice and significantly more national news, discussion programs, documentaries, cultural, and minority programs than commercial systems in the United States or in any other country.[7] The spread of commercial systems within Europe has not increased diversity and in fact threatens it through its damaging effects on the capabilities of public broadcasters. The first commercial broadcast channel in Italy offered literally zero news and public affairs programming, and Murdoch's Sky Channel provided 95.6 percent entertainment and under 1 percent information.[8] French commercial TV has been notable for "the lack of variety...the tendency of the stations to align their programming on each other; the excessive screening of films and the neglect of the documentary; and...the haziness of the frontier between the commercial and the programme..."[9]

Children's Programming

Broadcasting offers a potentially major and efficient vehicle for educating and entertaining children. Children, however, are not very important buyers of goods, especially small children, and are therefore of little interest to advertisers. The positive social benefits of quality radio and TV to children are externalities, and U.S. experience demonstrates that they will be ignored or marginalized by commercial broadcasters.

As in the case of public affairs programming, the U.S. commercial system eventually ghettoized children's programming with Saturday and Sunday morning fare that was largely cartoon entertainment with very heavy doses of commercials. Between 1955 and 1970, weekday programming for children on network affiliated TV stations in New York City fell from 33 to five hours. Only on Saturday did the children continue to get substantial time, but not with any new or non-entertainment programs.[10] A major FCC study of children's television published in 1979 concluded that children are "drastically underserved."

The failure of commercial TV in children's programming was so severe that a number of citizens groups were formed during the 1960s to fight the commercial system. One, Action for Children's Television (ACT), formed in 1968, lodged a protest with the FCC in 1970 demanding reform. The FCC response in 1974 admitted the industry's failures and responsibilities, but left the resolution to the voluntary actions of the broadcasters. In 1983, the Reagan-era FCC, in a further response to the ACT petition, declared that the broadcasters had *no* responsibility to children. The situation deteriorated thereafter. Programming of substance for children was left to public broadcasting, but there was no national policy or regular funding of children's programs. The poor performance of U.S. school children is often noted in the mass media, and is sometimes attributed in part to the underfunding of schools, but the foregone potential of TV broadcasting is rarely mentioned.

Negative Externalities

While the failure of commercial broadcasting to produce public affairs, cultural, and children's programs that promise important positive externalities has been subject to only modest study and even less publicity, its exploitation of the audience-enlarging vehicles of sex and violence has aroused important elements of the mainstream and has received greater attention. The aggressive use of themes of sex and violence, often in combination, can produce externalities in the form of distorted human and sexual attitudes, insecurity and reduced ability to function in a social order, and aggressive and violent behavior.

Television violence builds audiences. It therefore tends to dominate the TV screen under the pressure of commercial imperatives. Since 1967, Professor George Gerbner and his associates have compiled an annual television program Violence Profile and Violence Index. They have found that on average seven of ten prime-time programs use violence, and the rate of violent acts runs between five and six per hour. Some half of prime-time dramatic characters engage in violence and about 10 percent in killing, as they have since 1967. Children's weekend programming "remains saturated with violence," clocking more than 25 acts of violence per hour, as it has for many years.[11]

Violent programming has grown in Western Europe, along with the new surge in commercialization and in direct relation to the shift to action-adventure and movies. With the proliferation of commercial channels and the high cost of original programming, there has been a heavy demand for mainly foreign movies and series to fill the program gap.[12] Sepstrup points out that the great increase in use of U.S. movies and serials is not based on a special preference for U.S. products, it is grounded in commercialization and the proliferation of commercial channels with slots to fill and sell.[13] With market-based imperatives in place, violence as an important ingredient of programming follows. In reference to their transnational study of TV violence, Huesmann and Efron point out that "of the violent programs evaluated in the first wave of the study in Finland, Poland, and Israel, about 60 percent have been imported from the United States."[14]

While there has been little dispute that commercial broadcasting has been associated with a large diet of violence, there are ongoing debates over the effects of violent programs. There are problems of causality: does alienation and aggression come from watching violence on television, or do alienated and violence-prone people tend to watch programs that express their world view? Is TV violence an incitement and stimulus to violence or a catharsis? Despite continuing debate, the overwhelming consensus of experts and studies over several decades, covering a number of countries and supported by a variety of models of behavior and controlled experiments, is that TV violence makes a significant contribution to real world violence by desensitizing viewers, making people insecure and fearful, and habituating, modeling, and sometimes inciting people to violence.[15]

Commercial Broadcasting and Anti-democratic Power

The threat of a centralized, monolithic, state-controlled broadcasting system is well understood and feared in the West. What is little recognized or understood is the centralizing, ideologically monolithic, and self-protecting properties of an increasingly powerful commercial broadcasting system. U.S. experience suggests that once a commercial system is firmly in place it becomes difficult to challenge, and as its economic power increases so does its ability to keep threats at bay and gradually to remove all obstacles to commercial exploitation of the public airwaves and without any charge for their use. Commercial broadcasters do compete with one another, but this competition is for large audiences through offering entertainment fare under the constraint of advertisers, and it ignores externalities as a matter of structural necessity and the force of competition.

As one illustration of the power of the industry to fend off virtually any threat, in the liberal environment of 1963 the FCC leadership decided to try to impose a formal restraint on commercial advertising, but only to the extent of designating as the regulatory standard the limits suggested by the broadcasters' own trade association. This enraged the industry, which went quickly to work on Congress, and the FCC quickly backed down.[16]

Another important illustration of the commercial broadcasting industry's self-protective power is found in the area of children's television. The country claims to revere children, and child abuse is given frequent and indignant attention. But although the erosion of children's programming, and the commercial exploitation of the residual ghettoized programs, occurred as the commercial networks were making record-breaking profits, and although substantial numbers of adults have been angered by this programming, it has taken place with only a muted outcry. The FCC has been pressed hard to do something about the situation by organized groups like ACT, but the mass media have not allowed this matter to become a serious issue. When, after a 13-year delay in dealing with an ACT petition to constrain abuses in children's television, the FCC decided in December 1983 that commercial broadcasters had no obligation to serve children, this decision was not even mentioned in the *New York Times*. In fact, between 1979 and 1989, although many important petitions were submitted by ACT and decisions were made by the FCC that bore significantly on the commercial broadcasters neglect and abuse of children, the *New York Times*, *Washington Post*, and *Los Angeles Times* had neither a front-page article nor an editorial on the bject. The dominant members of the press, most of them with substantial broadcasting interests of their own, simply refused to make the huge failure of commercial broadcasters in children's programming a serious issue.

It is also enlightening to see how the principles of broadcasters' public service responsibility were gradually amended to accommodate broadcaster interests, without discussion or debate. As advertised programs displaced sustaining programs, and the "balance wheel" disappeared, what gave way was any public interest standard. The industry defense was in terms of "free speech" and the Alice-in-Wonderland principle that if the audience watches, the public interest is served. But the industry hardly needed a defense: raw power allowed the public interest standard to erode quietly, the issues undiscussed in any open debate, even as regards the enormous abuses and neglect in children's programming.

—Communication (Quebec), Spring 1995

Chapter Twenty-Three

The Government Shouldn't Have Lied

A fundamental fogging process carried out again and again by the mainstream media is to report uncritically government propaganda claims—even when contrary evidence is available—then retrospectively acknowledge that they had been duped, but complaining that the government shouldn't have lied. Rarely if ever do the media admit, apologize for, or reflect on their own major role in helping make the government lies effective propaganda.

This system has manifold advantages. It allows the government to carry out its propaganda operations without the inconvenience of an "adversary" press, or even one that does a minimal job of checking and verification. It permits both the government deceptions and media failures to be explained away as a result of liars in the prior administration, now out of office and safe targets. The decent folk currently in power are offended by the earlier deceptions, and may even appoint a commission to establish the truth and see that we don't do such things in the future. Thus, the country is also shown to be good, its benevolent course only briefly diverted by bad people momentarily in power.

To a fog watcher, however, it appears that we are witnessing an effective propaganda system in operation, with the media conniving in the dirty work, then later cleaning up their image and readying us for the next round of propaganda service.

The KAL 007 Case

A classic illustration of this process took place after the USSR shot down Korean airliner 007 in September 1983. The Reagan administration took advantage of the incident to vilify the Evil Empire. A key element was the official lie that the Soviets knew that 007 was a civilian airliner. The media accepted the lie without question and gave the event enormous and morally indignant publicity. Years later, in an editorial entitled "The Lie That Was Not Shot Down" (Jan. 18, 1988), the *New York Times* admitted it (and its colleagues) had been gulled. The exposure of the lie came long after the propaganda campaign had done its useful work, and was so muted that most of the public, insofar as they recalled the case at all, would retain the impression of Soviet villainy. Furthermore, the media didn't even uncover this lie themselves; they were reporting a disclosure by Congressman Lee Hamilton, who had the enterprise to use the Freedom of Information Act which the adversary press had never mustered up. The media never apologized or took blame for having helped turn a lie into an effective propaganda weapon. They were just innocent dupes, for the umpteenth time, although their business is supposed to be the professional gathering and dissemination of information.

The Truth About El Salvador

The media are now going through this routine on El Salvador, reporting on a UN Truth Commission's findings of massive state terror and Salvadoran and U.S. government lying and cover-ups in the 1980s, and ignoring or downplaying their own collaborative role. A *New York Times* editorial of March 26, 1993 goes so far as to admit that "coverage was intermittent and at times timid," a serious misrepresentation of the facts, as discussed below. The necessary work of pacification having been concluded, the media are now more forthcoming; the new administration, appointing a commission to examine the lying, shows itself to be dedicated to a return to truth after the accidental decade; and the media, no longer being deceived, can once again be their usual truth-loving selves.

Timidity or Tacit Collusion?

The mainstream media, and especially the major institutions like the *New York Times*, *Washington Post*, major news weeklies, and television networks, were not "timid" about reporting the El Salvador struggle—they were active collaborators in protecting state terrorism. There were occasional exceptions, but the generalization holds for the institutional thrust and principal reporters employed in the mainstream media. In fact, it could even be said that the major institutions were enthusiastic salespersons for the U.S. policy and therefore de facto supporters of what novelist Juan Corradi called "a deranged killing machine" (the Salvadoran army).

1. Accommodation to propaganda themes. This was dramatically evident in the media's regular acceptance of official propaganda lines. A very important one from late 1979 onward was that the ruling Salvadoran junta was "centrist," "moderate," and struggling to find a middle way between the extremists of right and left who were killing people. This was a huge misrepresentation: an October 1979 coup was carried out by young military officer-reformers, but the junta it appointed found itself stymied by old guard military officers (with active support of the Carter administration), and the last of the reformers had resigned by March 1980, leaving the army in full charge and the junta a mere military front.[1] The military had already embarked on a rampage which lasted for several years and in which thousands of unarmed civilians were murdered. Although the army and their 'security forces' and specialized 'death squads' did virtually all the killing of civilians, the official line was that an uncontrolled right and left were more or less equally at fault. The mainstream media's acceptance of the propaganda line of "a weak centrist government...beset by implacable extremes"[2] that were doing the killing helped rationalize support for the "deranged killing machine."

Another tremendous propaganda achievement of the government-media team was in portraying the elections of 1982 and 1984, held under conditions of extreme terror, obligatory voting, and with the Left off the ballot by necessity and plan, as triumphs of democracy. The purpose of these U.S.-sponsored "demonstration elections" was to persuade the U.S. public to accept official support for a regime of terror by showing its democratic character in holding and winning an election. The mainstream media cooperated fully in portraying these elections, in which *none* of the conditions essential to a free election were met, as genuine and legitimizing.[3]

The media also helped put over a multitude of smaller propaganda ploys, sometimes making themselves ludicrously gullible conduits of official propaganda. One of my favorites was the work of James LeMoyne and the *New York Times*, collaborating with the Salvadoran government in pretending that the murder of human rights activist Herbert Anaya in October 1987 was the work of the rebels. Anaya had been imprisoned by the government, and was their bitter critic. At the time of his murder he was under constant government surveillance and threat. After his murder, which created an international furor, the government got a 19-year-old student to "confess" that he did the killing for the rebels, in order to make the government look bad! This was a rerun of an earlier 1983 murder in which the government obtained a confession under torture, which was later retracted, as the student accused of Anaya's murder subsequently retracted his. But LeMoyne and the *New York Times* took the Salvadoran propaganda seriously and featured it in two substantial articles. The retraction was noted in a tiny AP dispatch. This was knowing gullibility in the service of propaganda.[4]

2. Refusal to publish readily available materials. The mainstream media protected the Salvadoran army and death squads, and Carter-Reagan-Bush policy, by their muted coverage of "negatives" and by their failure to report vast numbers of unpleasant facts. The deranged killing machine made a practice of exposing mutilated bodies in the outskirts of San Salvador and other towns in the early 1980s as a form of "public education." The media protected the terrorists by avoiding discussion of this practice or showing pictures of these horrors. A few days before the March 1982 election, the Salvadoran army took the press corps to the San Salvador morgue to see the bodies of four Dutch journalists, whose mutilated genitals were in full view. Again, the media failed to report the event. The destruction of the two independent Salvadoran newspapers (and associated murders) and multiple attacks on the church's radio station in 1980-81 were barely mentioned in the *New York Times*, which referred to the trials and tribulations of *La Prensa* in Nicaragua 263 times in a four-year span.

The massacre of some 600 Salvadoran civilians by the Salvadoran army at the Rio Sumpul river in May 1980 was not covered at all by the mainstream media, although it was reported abroad. This was a microcosm of the enormous media coverup—mass murder was in progress in El Salvador in 1980-82, but because the mainstream media kept this in the distant background, the March 1982 election could be portrayed as a plausible electoral experience, disturbed only by rebel threats. The huge massacre at El Mozote was reported, but it led to a government and right-wing assault on the reporters involved. The subsequent demotion of Raymond Bonner at the *New York Times* was an object lesson to other reporters and testimonial to the quality and priorities of the dominant media (see below).

In March 1981, the army produced a death list of 138 Salvadoran liberals and Leftists, which included virtually all politicians and organizational leaders of the Left. This list dramatized the danger to Left politicians if they ran for office, and made it clear that the election was a farce. The list was never mentioned by the *New York Times* in 1981 or 1982. In 1989, however, the *New York Times* finally referred to the 1981 death list, noting that "In 1981...the armed forces put a bounty on the heads of 138 leftists by publishing a list of their names and describing them as wanted traitors."[5] In 1989 the Left was making a tentative electoral bid, and the earlier death list could be used to contrast the "bad" old days with the new openness, and was therefore brought out of the black hole to which it had been consigned in 1982.

3. Treatment of D'Aubuisson and Vides Casanova. The Truth Commission reported that Roberto D'Aubuisson was a key organizer of the murder of Archbishop Oscar Romero in 1980, and that the U.S. government had information pointing that way which it sat on. With minor exceptions, such as an outstanding 1983 *Los Angeles Times* series by Craig Pyles and Laurie Beckland on the the extreme right in El Salvador, the mainstream organs were not interested in D'Aubuisson or in any search for who murdered the Archbishop. After the murder of Polish Priest Jerzy Popieluszko in 1984, the *New York Times* and other media focused incessantly on how far up the ladder responsibility went. In the case of Romero, the media had more important matters to concern themselves with. The *New York Times* never examined D'Aubuisson's ties to the U.S.-organized intelligence apparatus of El Salvador, or to the World Anti-Communist League; nor did it ever report his statement to European journalists in 1982, published in Mexico's *El Día*, that: "You Germans are very intelligent; you realized that the Jews were responsible for the spread of communism and you began to kill them." When the election of 1982 approached, and the Reagan administration was preparing the ground for a possible D'Aubuisson presidency, the *New York Times* obliged with an article that softened his image in perfect accord with the new political line. The piece, by Warren Hoge, entitled "Rightist Flag Bearer" (April 1, 1982), was accompanied by a flattering picture of D'Aubuisson, and criticized him gently for "impulsiveness" and "uneven" behavior.

In the case of the murder of the four U.S. religious women by members of the Salvadoran National Guard in December 1980, again the U.S. mass media were remarkably unenterprising in searching for top-level responsibility. Journalist John Dinges uncovered evidence that the "threat" posed by the four women had been discussed at the highest government levels just weeks before the murders, but his report was never picked up by the *New York Times* and his lead was never pursued by the mainstream media.[6] When Vides Casanova, the head of the National Guard at the time of the women's murders, was elevated to Minister of Defense in April 1983, Lydia Chavez noted in a flattering *New York Times* portrait that he "is considered a political moderate" and was named to head the National Guard back in 1979 "in an effort to end its reported excesses."[7] Can you imagine the *Times* doing this for the head of the Polish security service that had murdered Popieluszko? This is not "timidity," this is active collusion.

4. Treatment of sources. The mainstream media used official sources very heavily in reporting on the Salvadoran struggle even though it was obvious from the start that these sources were completely unscrupulous. It is true that government officials in the Reagan years used strong-arm methods to keep the media in line; and it is also true that honest reporters in El Salvador faced real threats of bodily harm. But instead of fighting back and refusing to be bullied, the mainstream media caved in. Belatedly, the *New York Times* castigated Elliott Abrams as a liar.[8] At the time when it counted, however, this liar was given generous space and no attempts were made to evaluate and correct his false claims.[9] Church sources on the mass killings in El

Salvador were virtually ignored, as were peasants, rebels, and U.S. and foreign observers whose views differed from the government's line. This was very clear during the elections of 1982 and 1984, when officials and official observers were given publicity and credence, but dissidents and foreign observers were ignored, allowing an election "theatrical" to be effectively staged.

The *New York Times* editorial of March 26, 1993 mentioned that the "courageous Ambassador Robert White found deaf ears in Washington in 1980 and 1981 when he cabled unwelcome news about the murder of Archbishop Romero and of four American church-women." But did the *New York Times* follow up on White's earlier courageous efforts by using him as a source, pressing to find out the exact content of his cables, and making other efforts to get to the truth about these murders? Clearly they did not. Not only did the paper fail to pursue the Romero case, as White was anathema to the Reaganites, it didn't take long for Juan d'Onis of the *New York Times* to write that "even Robert White" acknowledged an administration claim,[10] as if Robert White was a far-out extremist.

5. Treatment of reporters. The *New York Times* editorialized on March 16, 1993 that Raymond Bonner's reporting on the El Mozote massacre had been vindicated by the Truth Commission. This was remarkably hypocritical, given that following the attacks on Bonner by the government and Right-wing (*Wall Street Journal*'s editors, Reed Irvine of Accuracy in Media, etc.), the *New York Times* soon relieved Bonner of his duties in Central America and put him on the financial-page beat. Bonner resigned shortly thereafter. While Bonner was demoted, Warren Hoge, whose reporting on the Salvadoran election of 1982 never deviated from official propaganda claims, was in due course promoted to head the paper's foreign desk. Richard Meislin and Lydia Chavez, like Hoge reporters who deferred to state propaganda, remained in Central America. Eventually the *New York Times* hired Shirley Christian, an aggressive proponent of the Reaganite line, and James LeMoyne, who served the state propaganda apparatus with sleazy efficiency,[11] to cover Central America.

This pattern of promotion, demotion, and overt selection of reporters points to a deliberate policy of support for government propaganda, not timidity, as the guiding thread in news decision-making. So does the entire record of studied ignorance, selective indignation, and frequent enthusiastic participation in propaganda campaigns. Insofar as timidity and fear were factors, they add the sin of cowardice to that of deliberate propaganda service to a system of sponsorship of state terrorism.

−Z, May 1993

Chapter Twenty-Four

David Broder and the Limits
of Mainstream Liberalism

Several years ago, a Central America activist in Philadelphia asked the editor of the *Philadelphia Inquirer (PI)* where on his opinion page there was a Leftist to offset his regular offerings of George Will and Charles Krauthammer? The editor named David Broder. Broder himself would quite properly deny this designation, but it is significant that he would be so categorized, and it is a fact that in the spectrum of opinion of leading syndicated columnists he *is* on the Left. Eric Alterman points out that "Broder is the only non-right-wing pundit who begins to challenge the circulation numbers of the likes of Will, Kilpatrick, and Buchanan," and that in the print media "the 'responsible' political dialogue on the Great Issues of the Day is thus often perceived to fall between Will on the one hand and Broder on the other."[1] We may recall, also, the neo-conservative opinion that the elite media has been captured by the Left. It may be of interest, therefore, to examine Broder's positions on major issues,[2] to see just how far Left opinion reaches in the mainstream press today.

Since 1966 Broder has been a reporter and (from 1975) syndicated columnist based at the *Washington Post (WP)*. He won the Pulitzer prize in 1972 and has received many other awards within the journalist fraternity. Although alleged by some to be a card-carrying liberal, he is rarely attacked by right-wing media enforcers and politicians, as Anthony Lewis sometimes is and as Drew Pearson used to be. It will be shown below that this is understandable given that Broder takes conservative positions on many issues, and in those instances where he is inclined toward liberal and dissident views, his voice is faint and he leans over backwards to cause no conservative distress.

No Agenda and No Pugnacity

Broder has no discernible agenda as a columnist, with the possible exceptions of the threat of budgetary deficits, and the need to fend off attacks that suggest fatal flaws in the two-party system or basic U.S. institutions. Furthermore, in contrast with right-wingers like Krauthammer, Safire, and Will, he does not press issues. He shifts from topic to topic like a butterfly, touching lightly on a point of current interest and moving quickly on. But he avoids many of the tough issues that the conservatives repeatedly address. For example, on Nicaragua, during the 1980s Broder several times noted in passing that he opposed the contra war, but his only full column on the subject lauded Reagan for finally "turning to diplomacy" and working on "a sounder premise than the maintenance of a mercenary army of 'contras'" (WP, Aug. 19, 1987). In fact, Reagan was trying to undercut the efforts of several Central American governments to stop the war, so that in this one and only column Broder misrepresented the facts and issues and served as an instrument of official propaganda.[3]

On numerous other important but controversial issues, Broder has been silent or evasive. He has written only passing phrases on the Israeli-Palestinian conflict. Racism, environmental issues, gender and sexual preference questions, and developments in and policies toward problematic states like Pinochet's Chile and Guatemala he rarely if ever discusses. His two articles on feminism over the past dozen years dealt with infighting among feminists: one was on the possibility of working within the Republican Party (WP, Aug. 26, 1987), the other on who deserves feminist political support (WP, July 18, 1993). He avoided taking a position in his several columns on abortion by writing in a "horse race" mode—merely reporting on the balance of factional power in the political arena (WP, May 29, 1991) and on who is winning and losing in the court battles (PI, May 30, 1991). A column on Clinton's early compromise on the issue of gays in the military did stress the historic significance of Clinton's rally with gay activists in May 1992 and the "important step [of the compromise itself] toward eliminating one of society's last prejudices," but framed it all in terms of Clinton's weakness and inability to carry through on commitments (WP, July 25, 1993). In another article touching gay-lesbian issues, Broder described his attendance at Tony Kushner's *Angels in America-Perestroika* (PI, June 29, 1994); but again, while the column was sympathetic in tone, it failed to address real issues. Broder has been entirely silent on Guatemala, Chile, El Mozote, Oscar Romero, the Contadora agreement, the U.S. withdrawal from UNESCO, Otto Reich and the Office of Public Diplomacy, the Boland amendment, Cuba and the Torricelli bill.

Kindness Toward Conservatives

Broder not only doesn't fight on the tough issues, he is exceedingly kind to conservatives. Thus, Lee Atwater, the organizer of the Willie Horton campaign of 1988, is "tough and effective" (*PI*, Nov. 26, 1990); campaign manager James Baker was merely "manipulating paranoia" in using Willie Horton (*WP*, Apr. 9, 1989); and George Bush, ultimately responsible for the Horton ploy, did this despite a "life-long history of tolerance and decency in racial matters" (*PI*, June, 10, 1991). Broder was apparently unaware of Bush's opposition to the crucial Civil Rights Act of 1964 (on the ground that it "violates the constitutional rights of all people"). He wrote this phrase while commenting on Bush's new "quota bill" campaign against civil rights. Bush was also described as a "man of moderate temperament and pragmatic instinct" (*WP*, Dec. 21, 1988) and his foreign policy was one of "practical idealism" (*WP*, Sept. 11, 1991). Dick Cheney had "an emotional balance and a mental discipline remarkable" in government (*PI*, Feb. 28, 1991). Reagan himself was repeatedly lauded for his "presidential" qualities and "national leadership of a high order" in handling Grenada and in pushing through his economic program (*WP*, Nov. 14, 1984), and any shortcomings as chief-of-state were "overshadowed by the grace with which he functions as chief-of-state in moments of national tragedy and triumph" (*WP*, Dec. 22, 1985).

Broder's generosity to the Reaganites went far beyond any he extended to Democrats, except New Democrats. Those who attacked the Bork appointment, Broder spoke of as "quick-lip liberals" who "pop off in opposition" (*WP*, Aug. 14, 1987). Those signing a petition opposing the invasion of Panama he dismissed as "left-wing politicians and activists" (they included former Senator J. W. Fulbright, WP, 1-14-90). Jerry Brown, campaigning in 1992, Broder paired with Buchanan, and dismissed harshly as a "loud-voiced protester" offering "left-wing populism" and "phony salvation" (*PI*, Feb. 26, 1992).

Lazy Insider

One of Broder's favorite themes is the danger of reporters getting too close to their sources, and he congratulates the press for "its determination to keep its distance from government, not only to avoid censorship, but to avoid co-optation" (*WP*, Dec. 4, 1988). He clearly puts himself in the class of outsiders who are "inquisitive, impudent, incorrigibly independent," who "hold their [government officials] feet to the fire and devil them with questions and make them, if they can, explain and justify what they do."

But Broder is describing somebody like the late I.F. Stone, or Robert Parry, formerly with Associated Press (AP) and *Newsweek*, surely not himself. Broder's columns never display a serious investigative effort. His citations to scholarly articles and books are infrequent; he rarely if ever refers to government hearings and out-of-the-way government documents. In his numerous articles on economics, he never cites Ralph Nader, Jeff Faux or the Economic Policy Institute, Robert McIntyre or Citizens for Tax Justice, or representatives of the Center for Budget Priorities or the Center for Defense Information. Rather, he quotes spokespersons of the right-wing Cato Institute, the New Democrat's Progressive Policy Institute, the Georgetown Center for International and Strategic Studies, the Hoover Institution, and other conservative thinktanks. The farthest left Broder goes in tapping policy institute sources is the Brookings Institution, now run by former Republican officials and safely back in the conservative fold.

And Broder's reliance on government officials is heavy. He reports on interviews with Bush, Cheney, Moynihan, William Gray, Lee Hamilton, Les Aspin, Colin Powell, and William Bennett, and he cites many other officials. He handles them lightly, rarely comparing their claims with evidence from independent sources. He never questions their motives, and with rare exception takes what they say at face value. On Reagan's bombing of Libya in 1986, Broder assured his readers that "Reagan has been insistent that every possible step be taken to spare the innocent" (*WP*, Apr. 20, 1986), an unverifiable claim of no value except as official propaganda. As noted, Broder praised Reagan for having taken the diplomatic track in Nicaragua in 1987, lazily accepting official claims at face value and failing to consider other possible reasons for the new line, as would a pundit who holds officials "feet to the fire and devils them with questions" (in the theoretical Broder model of the non-insider press).

In a speech before the National Press Club in which he spoke on the threat of co-optation, Broder flattered the press and public, saying that the U.S. system of journalism "somehow works." The voters "sniff out the phoney from the real, the poseur from the politician who merits trust" (*WP*, Dec. 4, 1988). This was asserted in December 1988, after the Iran-Contra affair disclosures and toward the end of actor-president Reagan's second term in office.

Elitism and Anti-Democracy

Broder's touching faith in the voters finding their way to essential truths is hyperbole in the service of the status quo. If the voters don't agree with an elite agenda, his respect for their grasp of the truth vanishes. This was dramatically evident in the struggle over NAFTA. The general public didn't like NAFTA, according to a steady stream of polls (55 percent were "against" compared to 27 percent "for" in July 1992 [CBS/NYT]; 63 percent to 31 percent in March 1993 [Gallup/CNN]; 65 percent to 28 percent in July 1993 [Gallup/CNN]), despite overwhelming press bias in NAFTA's favor. And the elected Democrats didn't like it either. But the Business Roundtable and corporate elite were enthusiastic—so Broder sneers at those Democrats in opposition who were once again siding with "the losers" instead of "the winners." He made it clear that the winners are the affluent upwardly mobile suburbanites whom the Democrats have foolishly neglected, whereas the losers were "the older, poorer and black Democrats" (*WP*, Nov. 19, 1993).

Broder ignored the polls, which suggested that the "losers" were a majority of the population and constituted the great majority of those who had voted for Clinton. He did not mention the backroom construction of NAFTA, its capacity to override domestic law, and the fact that Clinton had to engage in egregious bribery to win enough pro-NAFTA votes. Apparently, democracy for Broder means that elected representatives should pay no heed to their voting constituencies when the "winners" have spoken.

Similarly, in discussing the health-care debates of 1993 and 1994, polls have indicated that the public strongly prefers a single-payer system and universal coverage. Broder's articles on the subject never mention the polls or discuss the Canadian system, and only once addressed the single-payer plan—one of three Broder interviewees favored single-payer, but Broder did not ask this individual to state the reasons for his preference (*WP*, Apr. 28, 1993). As the elite had declared single-payer impracticable, Broder doesn't allow voter and democratic preference to influence *his* assessment of health care politics.

Politics Lite

Broder attacked Jerry Brown in 1992 on the ground that "politics is more than protest. For people's anger to be salved, policies must be put in place that address their needs and right the wrongs of which they properly complain. The problem with populism...is that it is long on indignation but notably short on solutions" (*PI*, Feb. 26, 1992). But what solutions do Broder or his favored New Democrats have for the big problems? In a 1992 apologia for New Democrat Paul Tsongas, Broder stressed Tsongas's alleged integrity, religious faith, and fighting qualities; he mentioned only in passing his "belief in capital-gains [tax] cuts and industrial policy" and Broder didn't discuss how Tsongas's policies would address the needs and wrongs of ordinary people (*PI*, Feb. 12, 1992). Apparently only "populists" have to produce viable policies; New Democrats are acceptable on the basis of faith and personal qualities.

Broder sometimes writes about the unaffordability of political office and the rise of rich people to Senate preeminence (*PI*, Aug. 4, 1993), but he never discusses who owns newspapers and TV stations, who funds elections, who can move capital in and out of the country according to investment climate, and how these together might constrain policies serving ordinary citizens and affect publicity and votes on an issue like NAFTA. He offers only "politics lite"—horse racing, personal qualities of establishment politicians, programmatic failings of populists, inexplicable public anger and frustration at policy failure in a system that is a triumph and with a media that is "working well" to serve the public interest.

Court Appointments

Broder was extremely kind to the Reagan-Bush court appointees of the past decade, and raised no objection to the resultant ideologically based restructuring of the courts. In discussing Scalia's nomination, Broder's article was entitled "Finally the Reagan Stamp" (*WP*, June 22, 1986); that is, Broder treated the topic "objectively," using as a peg the fact that Reagan was merely conforming to expectations, which allowed him to avoid addressing substantive issues. He even compliments Scalia and Rehnquist as "of commanding intellect and considerable personal charm," and offers no critique of these strongly ideological jurists; presumably intellect and "charm" are enough. Souter was "a superb choice—both substantively and politically" for Broder (*WP*, July 27, 1990)—despite "grumbles from the political extremes." Broder failed to provide one fact or argument in support of the alleged "substantive" merits of Souter; most of his article was on the political adeptness of the appointment.

On Clarence Thomas, Broder was once again "objective," devoting most of his attention to the politics of the selection, very little to qualifications and none to the ideological stacking of the court (*WP*, July 7, 1991). And Broder took no position on the merits of the appointment. He did mention Thomas's somewhat esoteric notion of "natural rights," and civil rights leaders' objections to Thomas's having worked for the Office of Economic Opportunity under Reagan (where he helped gut poor people's claims). But Broder never mentioned Thomas's close association with two Black lobbyists for the South African apartheid government (Jay Parker and William Keyes), or the terrible irony and racist insult that this anti-affirmative action ideologue should be named to replace Thurgood Marshall (who was himself outraged). The Anita Hill sequel was never taken up by Broder.

Guinier and Civil Rights

Broder's virtual enthusiasm for Scalia and Souter, and acceptance of Thomas and the final Republican construction of an extremist court, contrasted sharply with his critique of Lani Guinier and approval of Clinton's decision to drop her nomination (*PI*, June 16, 1993). No mention was made of Guinier's "intellect and personal charm"; in this case an analysis of the alleged theoretical position of the appointee on voting rights in scholarly law reviews (which Broder gave no evidence of having read) was the basis for a conclusion on fitness for office. The right-wing court nominations that Broder approved were lifetime appointments, unlike Guinier's, yet Broder felt no obligation to examine those closely and try to see where they might take the country in the future.

His response to Guinier (and Thomas et al.) did not speak well for Broder's commitment to civil rights or civil liberties. He never mentioned the political and symbolic importance of Guinier—that she represented a likely reinvigorated enforcement of civil rights law that had been gutted in the Reagan-Bush years. It is significant that that gutting had never energized Broder—he had no column on civil rights or William Bradford Reynolds in the Reagan years. *After* Reagan's departure, he had one good article based on a Brookings study on *The Urban Underclass*, in which Broder summarized the grim empirical evidence of serious employer racist discrimination (*WP*, Apr. 21, 1991); and in another article he quoted Eddie Williams of the Joint Center for Political Studies, asking whether Reagan "did not allow the genie of racism to escape the bottle" (*WP*, Apr. 4, 1990). But these were late; and it was only the proposed appointment of Guinier that aroused and upset him, as it did the Republicans and New Democrats.

South Africa and Savimbi

Broder ignored South Africa during the Reagan-Bush years. He never discussed the apartheid system, the South African assault on the frontline states, "constructive engagement," or Savimbi. He had one sentence on the subject: "An American negotiated agreement promises to bring peace to Namibia, a land fought over by South Africa and Angola, with the involvement of thousands of Cuban troops" (*WP*, Dec. 21, 1988). In fact, Namibia had been illegally occupied by South Africa for decades, and used as a jumping-off place to invade Angola; Cuban troops were never in Namibia and entered the conflict in response to South African aggression against Angola. Describing Namibia as having been "fought over" by Angola and South Africa is a gross distortion of the record, and Broder's focus on Cuban aid and failure to note U.S. support of South Africa (and Savimbi) under "constructive engagement" is seriously biased reporting.

Broder made a more general statement that would seem to laud the Reagan achievement in Angola: "But from Afghanistan to El Salvador, the United States under the leadership of these Republicans effectively supported people whose values and aspirations came closest to our own—and helped them prevail" (*WP*, Jan. 17, 1993). This incredible sentence is on a par with Reagan's identifying the contras with our founding fathers—Afghan Islamic fundamentalist terrorist leader and drug dealer Gulbuddin Hekmatyar, Roberto D'Aubuisson's ARENA party, and presumably the Argentinean and Guatemalan generals as well as Savimbi "share our values." I suspect Broder was carried away with sentimental yearnings for the Reagan-Bush era in which he thrived as a columnist "on the Left," and would possibly not agree with his own statement if confronted with the details—Broder is not a very careful writer.

It is obvious that in this important area (South Africa), in which the conservative pundits pushed a reactionary agenda that cost Black South Africans dearly, David Broder offered not the slightest opposition.

Imperialist Apologetics

Except for the low intensity Nicaraguan and Salvadoran conflicts, Broder got onto the war bandwagons of the Reagan-Bush era with enthusiasm. The Grenada invasion he found entirely justifiable based on our natural imperial rights: "We are old-fashioned enough to think that, even in a nuclear age, there are such things as spheres of influence and geographical areas of vital national interest. The Caribbean is such an area for us. The use of American power against a regime of thugs backed by forces that want to weaken American influence in the area does not strike us as unconscionable" (*WP*, Nov. 2, 1983). In connection with the Panama invasion of 1989, for which Broder was equally keen, he did note that in an open letter to the president "69 left-wing politicians and activists" called attention to his violations of the UN Charter and OAS agreement. Broder's reply was: "What nonsense. This static on the left should not obscure the fact that Panama represents the best evidence yet that 15 years after the Vietnam War ended, Americans really have come together in recognition of the circumstances in which military intervention makes sense" (*WP*, Jan. 14, 1990). The evasion of the question of international law is laughable, and the "analysis" is sheer demagoguery. The public always rallies around the flag after an enemy has been demonized and "our boys" are in action. Making this into a careful calculus by the public which justifies intervention is worthy of Charles Krauthammer.

In commenting on the Iran-Contra affair, Broder wrote that the Reagan administration's "defiance of law by its own staff members [caused it to be] terribly weakened when confronting a dictator who chooses to ignore...laws that inconvenience him" (*WP*, May 14, 1989). The hypocrisy of this position, in light of Broder's comprehensive apologia for Bush's ignoring laws that inconvenienced him in invading Panama, is striking.

On Panama, Broder quoted Bush on our need "to send a clear signal when democracy is imperiled," as otherwise "the enemies of constitutional government will become more dangerous" (*WP*, Sept. 10, 1989). Broder did mention in passing that the Reagan administration had earlier supported the "tin-pot dictator" and drug trader Manuel Noriega, but he never mentioned George Shultz's presence and sanctioning of the fraudulent Panamanian election of 1984, which left Noriega in charge. He did not discuss Oliver North's negotiations with Noriega to secure help in destabilizing Nicaragua, and did not explain why the tin-pot dictator suddenly became objectionable in 1986. And in his usual superficial way, Broder failed to enumerate the vast array of tin-pot dictators supported by U.S. power, nor did he mention George Bush's 1985 toast to the tin-pot dictator Ferdinand Marcos: "We love you, sir...we love your adherence to democratic rights and processes."

During and after the Gulf War Broder exceeded himself in patriotic ardor, several times even castigating the Democrats for "dithering" in failing to give Bush immediate powers to fight ("the best hope of salvaging the peace"), and then hypocritically citing the congressional debates on the War as evidence of democracy at work (*WP*, Dec. 16, 1991; *PI*, Jan. 12, 1991; *PI*, Aug. 3, 1994). There was no patriotic lie and obfuscation that Broder did not swallow and regurgitate. In an early article, Broder quoted a Republican politician's prescient observation: "My concern is that before election day, the question will be not how well Bush reacted but whether we did all we could have done to prevent the crisis from arising" (*WP*, Aug. 19, 1990). But Broder made no effort to examine the background of appeasement, which virtually invited an invasion of Kuwait; he simply parroted the official propaganda line that it was all Saddam's fault ("the miscalculations were all on Saddam's side" [*Washington Post*, Apr. 10, 1991]). He also accepted without question that we were helping the people of Kuwait "keep their freedom"! (*WP*, Jan. 18, 1991). And he failed to question the central propaganda lie that the Bush administration made a serious effort at a diplomatic solution; he stated that Saddam was applying the "diplomatic stiff-arm," when in fact Bush and Baker fended off every diplomatic move (for a good review, see Chomsky's chapter in Mowlana, Gerbner, and Schiller, *Triumph of the Image*). Broder reported Baker's failed conference with Iraqi Foreign Minister Aziz in January 1991 as simply one more sad instance of Iraqi intransigence (*WP*, Jan. 11, 1991). This was pundit service to the war party that once again Charles Krauthammer could not surpass.

Libya and Terrorism

When Reagan bombed Libya in 1986, purportedly in response to a Libyan terrorist attack at a German discotheque, Broder, far from distancing himself from government, once again took the official version as true and asked no questions. The strike was "a necessary and proper step," and Americans "can take justifiable pride" in the President's response to "deliberate provocation" (*WP*, Apr. 20, 1986). Could Reagan be lying about Libyan involvement? Could there be a hidden agenda in this stoking up of anti-Libyan fervor? Wasn't the attack an attempt to kill Qadaffi, and therefore contrary to U.S. law which prohibits foreign assassinations? No such questions are asked by the gullible Broder. He lists as the other major "terror states" Syria and Iran—not South Africa, or Guatemala, or the U.S. in Nicaragua—in accord with the official line.

Haiti and El Salvador

Broder's only redeeming columns on foreign policy were one criticizing Clinton for following Bush's policy of repatriating fleeing Haitians, contrary to his campaign promises (*WP*, Mar. 7, 1993) and a 1983 column reporting on the slaughter of doctors in El Salvador (*WP*, June 26, 1983). The trouble is that these are, or were, major issues and demanded sustained attention; a journalist with an aim to enlighten on issues of great public importance would have held Reagan's and Clinton's "feet to the fire" on these matters and made them "explain and justify what they do" (Broder).

Reaganomics and the Deficit

Broder's finest moments were his attacks on Reagan's economic program between 1981 and 1984, in which he assailed Reagan (and the supportive Democrats) for a damaging policy mix that promised dire consequences. He stressed the implausibility of supply-side reasoning, the deficits that would ensue, the favoritism to the rich in the tax cuts that were supposed to (but wouldn't) serve the general interest (*WP*, Feb. 10, 1982; May 23, 1982; Oct. 6, 1982). Reaganomics was grounded in "greater inequality and greater poverty for millions of our fellow citizens" (*WP*, Nov. 4, 1984).

Over succeeding years, however, Broder's focus was increasingly on the deficit and its threat alone. And in urging policy changes between 1987 and 1994, he did not call for rectifying the regressive income distribution changes of the early Reagan (and late Carter) years—he stressed the menace of "runaway entitlement spending" (*PI*, Jan. 2, 1994) and the threat to the "integrity of the social security trust fund" (*PI*, Oct. 4, 1992). In other columns, however, Broder cited Moynihan's critique of deficit accounting, which stressed that the accounts for the "runaway entitlements" were in surplus and masked the real deficit (*WP*, Mar. 29, 1990). This contradiction was based on muddled thinking, but the focus on entitlements was in accord with elite priorities. Broder has also been keen on scaling down the size of government and privatization, both also in accord with corporate, Republican, and New Democrat ideology. Broder discusses these issues with great superficiality, using as his sources a Cato Institute study urging massive cuts in non-military outlays (*WP*, Aug. 22, 1982), the example of privatization by Mayor Daley of Chicago (*PI*, July 10, 1991), and recommendations of David Osborne and the New Democrats Progressive Policy Institute (*WP*, Jan. 13, 1993).

Military Budget

Broder was somewhat ambivalent about Reagan's military buildup and occasionally suggested that its rate was perhaps excessive; but in the end he accepted the level of military outlays and never regarded it—like entitlements—as a source of potentially large budget savings. He never spoke of a "runaway" military budget. In 1987 he wrote an admiring column on a Hollings budget proposal that incorporated a further 2 percent annual real growth in military spending (*WP*, May 11, 1987). He has had no column over the last 15 years devoted to the military budget and its possible excesses (although he had one full column critical of Star Wars; *WP*, Sept. 22, 1985).

Broder even lauded Reagan in retrospect for his military buildup, which made us ready for the Gulf War, and he expressed worry lest we short-change our military establishment. The Gulf crisis proved to Broder that we can't "safely solve every budget problem by 'whacking the Pentagon'" (*WP*, Aug. 29, 1990). Broder never ever hinted at the possibility that the Gulf War (or any other) could be even partially *explained* by the power of the security establishment and its need to justify its command over resources.

The Republicans, said Broder, in a final accolade, "did not let America's armed might wither away" (*WP*, Jan. 17, 1993). He did not mention that they let other things wither away instead, like human and social capital. There was no hint by this chronic worrier about entitlement excesses that the Republicans might have spent too much on America's armed might.

NAFTA and Free Trade

As noted earlier, Broder strongly favored NAFTA, on the grounds that it represented the "winners," and would enlarge U.S. markets. Furthermore, voting down the treaty would have stopped the "liberalizing trend" of Salinas and the PRI; Broder never mentioned the impact of these changes on ordinary Mexicans—he just assumed that their interests were being served by something called "reform." He did speak with Harley Shaiken, an "anti-NAFTA guru," but Broder only reported Shaiken's admission that the defeat of the treaty would shock Mexico–not a word on Shaiken's analysis of the substantive issues (*WP*, Nov. 14, 1993). Instead, he relied heavily on journalist William Orme's book *Continental Shift*, published by The Washington Post Company, which says what Broder wanted to hear on the wonders of NAFTA (*WP*, Nov. 3, 1993).

Broder argued in a number of columns for the unqualified benefits of free trade, and repeatedly claimed that the Great Depression of the 1930s resulted from the imposition of the Smoot-Hawley tariff (a position that would not be supported by most economic historians; the index to economic historian Peter Temin's well-regarded book on the causes of the Great Depression has no listing for "tariff" or the "Smoot-Hawley Act"). He congratulated Reagan for his support of free trade, apparently unaware of the great Reagan-era expansion of Voluntary Export Agreements and what has been described as a policy of "aggressive unilateralism" (the title of a book by Patrick and Bhagwati). The possible damaging effects of NAFTA on the environment and income distribution he ignored or treated as transitory; and as with his discussion of the health-care issue, Broder never mentioned the Canadian experience–in this case, under a 1988 free-trade agreement. The essence of Broder's approach is a simple-minded and demagogic support of a policy favored by the national business elite, and a failure to discuss alternative views and analyses.

Iran-Contra

Broder's dozen articles on Iran-Contra and its follow-up were an unmitigated journalistic disaster. He came to the subject late, never deviated from the lines put forward by the Reagan team and leading Democrats, and failed to follow up on the Banco Lavoro case or Walsh report. He never cited independent investigators like reporters Robert Parry or Brian Barger, or analyst Peter Kornbluh–his main source was Democratic Congressman Lee Hamilton, who was one of the engineers of the Democratic political collapse over Iran-Contra (protecting a dubious "national interest" in unity that the Republicans never honor in connection with a Democratic president). His leading secondary sources were George Bush and "an influential Republican." He never criticized the extremely limited scope of the congressional investigation, its granting of immunity to Oliver North, and the incompetence and cowardice of the Democrats, who let North take over the proceedings. Most important, Broder saw the whole affair as mainly executive mismanagement–the very serious law violations he underplayed or ignored (*WP*, June 17, 1987, Aug. 9, 1987, Nov. 10, 1987). The main problem was the failure of Reagan to control his subordinates and inform the congressional intelligence committees what they were up to (*WP*, July 9, 1987). He therefore agreed with Hamilton that no legislative change was necessary (*WP*, June 7, 1987), and expressed satisfaction that Reagan had taken steps to put his house in management order (*WP*, Aug. 14, 1987).[4]

Broder's downgrading of the legal and constitutional issues in Iran-Contra was shown further in a column in which he equated the Democrats' attempts to legislate limits on contra aid with the Iran-Contra actions of the Reaganites (*WP*, Apr. 9, 1989). The former, which were entirely within the bounds of law, he characterized as "legislative usurpation"; the Iran-Contra actions, which involved hidden, direct violations of law and an overriding of constitutional provisions on the separation of powers, was "executive usurpation" for Broder.

Broder had columns arguing against both the trial and then the imprisonment of Oliver North. He argued that North did violate the law, but had already suffered by being fired from the White House and retired from the Marines; and a trial and imprisonment would be "a copout for our failure to ban—or shun—a prominent ne'er do well" (*WP*, Apr. 5, 1989). The "critical question" is "whether we as a society are prepared to treat him as someone who has betrayed his trust," etc. That "is up to us," not a jury.

The notion that the law should be enforced as a matter of principle, and that the *jury* is "our" representative in treating matters of trust that are also law violations, escapes Broder; as does the fact that his own opinions feed into how the public views North and his legal position (and help exonerate him). Broder's evasions can be explained as follows: large numbers felt North should not be tried or imprisoned (believing him justified, or a secondary character and fall guy), and Broder doesn't want to offend this substantial constituency, so he works both sides of the issue—he castigates North, but constructs a pathetic argument that rationalizes the non-application of the law in this particular case.

Crime

On crime and crime legislation Broder deserves commendation for several pieces in which he argues that imprisonment as a main solution to the crime problem is both enormously expensive and ineffective as well. He doesn't delve very deeply into what would be effective, but he mentions policies addressing jobs, education, gun control, and identifying and treating drug and alcohol abuse (*WP*, Mar. 23, 1994; Apr. 17, 1994).

Welfare and Family Values

On welfare and family values, however, Broder joins the Republican-New Democratic throng as they focus on family stability and values while downgrading economic conditions and racism. Broder cites as main sources William Bennett, the "estimable" David Gergen, Clinton's in-house Moynihan clone, William Galston, and of course Deborah Dafoe Whitehead's *Atlantic Monthly* article, "Dan Quayle Was Right." Broder quotes Gergen at an Aspen Seminar on the participants' agreement that "the best anti-poverty program for children is a stable, intact family" (*WP*, Mar. 24, 1993), a remarkable statement that makes family instability the *cause* of poverty and doesn't even admit the possibility that family instability might be a *result* of poverty. Broder says that "liberals now acknowledge the centrality of values like family stability, personal responsibility and work." This is a misleading partial truth; many liberals contend that family values, while important, are fundamentally derivative, not central in a causal sense. Broder features Whitehead's claim that Dan Quayle was right that two-parent families are best for children, implying that family instability is primarily a matter of personal morality, not economic and social conditions. That Whitehead's views are contestable, and that "Dan Quayle's attack on Murphy Brown was an attempt to play the Willie Horton card in whiteface" (Judith Stacey, "The New Family Values Crusaders," *The Nation*, July 25/Aug. 1. 1994) is beyond Broder's vision, as he follows the elite in making welfare a moral issue, with conservative (and money-saving) policy conclusions that follow.

Education

Broder had two columns on the Reagan educational aid cutbacks of the early 1980s. Although superficial, they did offer a serious critique on grounds of damage to the less affluent and to the educational system (and national interest) in general (*WP*, Feb. 24, 1985, Apr. 3, 1985). In an article on school choice, however, Broder framed the story around the failure of organized conservatism to support a school-voucher plan referendum in California (*WP*, Oct. 27, 1993). He makes it a story of betrayal, and in the process failed to discuss the merits and demerits of school-choice and -voucher plans.

Environment

Although environment is an exceedingly important issue, over a 15-year period Broder provided no coverage of the problem in general, Reagan policies in specific, national forest policy, or Bush and the Rio Summit. Surprisingly, in the one article during the Reagan era in which he devoted a few paragraphs to environmental policy, he sided with the Reaganites and castigated Carter as an environmental extremist.

Speaking of Beaver Island, Michigan, his vacation site, he wrote: "Deregulation—and particularly the change in the Environmental Protection Agency since Anne Gorsuch took over—has helped the island. For a time, under what Interior Secretary James Watt would rightly call the environmental extremism of the Carter administration, the Beaver Island dump was threatened with closure. There were rumbles we would have to take our tax money and build an incinerator. Let me tell you, an incinerator would be as out of place on Beaver Island as an All-Star on the Chicago Cubs. But, thanks to Reagan, the dump is still in business" (*WP*, July 25, 1982) This is all Broder had to say about Gorsuch, Reagan's gutting of EPA (which went too far even for the chemical industry), and environmental issues, in the 1980s.

In 1990, in connection with Earth Week celebrations, Broder addressed environmental issues once again (*WP*, Apr. 22, 1990). One main point was that everybody now agrees that the environment is important and "the 'conservation ethic' has become one of the fixed guiding stars of American politics." This vacuous statement confuses the nominal and real; the *words* must now be used, but that tells us nothing about real beliefs, and obscures the likelihood that powerful interests may find public concern over the environment an obstacle to overcome. His second prominent theme is the threat of environmentalist alarmism and too frequent pushing of the panic button, which may discredit environmentalism. There is no suggestion that the strength of the business interests opposing genuine environmental protection might be a major problem. The experience of the EPA under Reagan is not mentioned.

Broder on the Press

Broder is a Pollyanna on the press, which "has always been tough on itself" and is notable for successful maintenance of a "distance" and "apartness" from government, despite the attraction of closeness to insiders and the existence of a revolving door between media and government, which Broder acknowledges (*WP*, Dec. 4, 1988). Broder never gets beyond these superficial assertions. He does not discuss the economics of the media that make for dependency on powerful sources, nor does he examine the economic interests, power, and policy of media owners and advertisers. That Katherine Graham and Ben Bradlee were part of the dominant power structure and close friends of many government leaders he doesn't consider salient.

Although the 1980s witnessed a major merger movement in the media, Broder never dealt with the issue. The Reagan administration's attacks on the media and its major propaganda and disinformation effort, paid for by the taxpayer and based in the Office of Public Diplomacy, were never discussed by Broder, although he did have a celebratory (but fact-free) column on our wonderful Bill of Rights (*PI*, Nov. 16, 1991).

Broder did criticize the Reagan censorship of the media during the Grenada invasion and Gulf War, but in neither instance did he discuss government disinformation (which he failed to recognize as such) or the media's de facto collaboration in propaganda. With the Gulf War, he didn't even object to the pool system of censorship—only to the delays in release of information and the government's lack of trust in the press (*PI*, Mar. 21, 1991).

On "the deterioration in the tone and quality of public discourse in this country," Broder is encouraged by the recent "sensible dialogue between press and government" which is "a start on improving public understanding and reducing cynicism" (*PI*, July 6, 1994). He has no further recommendations on the subject.

Forecasts

David Broder doesn't often offer prognostications of the future, but when he does the results are not impressive. Although his forte is politics, in 1987 he predicted that poor George Bush was not likely to be a candidate given his vulnerable record and political innocence. If Bush did venture into today's "shark tank" political environment, we were likely to witness "the slaughter of the innocent" (*WP*, Aug. 9, 1987). (It turned out, of course, that the sharks were on Bush's payroll, or pundits who feed only on Democrats.) Broder's forecast that the candidate would be somebody with the "spontaneity for common truth," an outsider not loaded down "with political-government connections" (*WP*, July 14, 1987), was a bit off the mark.

On international affairs, his Panglossian tendency was dramatically evident in his view that in the New World Order ethnic conflict would surely be on the downgrade; he spoke of "the waning force of the clashing nationalisms" (*WP*, Dec. 21, 1988), unfortunately timed to usher in its global resurgence.

Concluding Note

David Broder has prospered as a syndicated columnist because he never threatens the *larger* special interests—the "winners" who he advises the Democrats to heed in contests like NAFTA. When his better instincts would lead to opposition, as in the case of the contra war against Nicaragua, the Israeli-Palestinian conflict, or gay-lesbian issues, he remains exceedingly quiet and his tiny forays have no weight. On most foreign and economic policy issues, Broder lines up with the conservatives—NAFTA; the Grenada, Panama, and Iraq Wars; attacks on Libya; fear of runaway entitlements; the need for a lavish military budget; welfare as a personal morality question; the tendency toward environmentalist excesses. He relies heavily on official and conservative institutional sources, engages in minimal independent research, and rarely asks hard questions. He even helps keep debates within proper bounds by castigating those who challenge establishment premises as extremists (Jerry Brown, J. W. Fulbright), or by simply ignoring them (Ralph Nader, Jeff Faux, Robert Eisner, Harley Shaiken, Robert Parry, Peter Kornbluh, Noam Chomsky). In sum, David Broder is an ideal "Leftist" for a media and political establishment that can't even abide a serious liberal challenge.

—*Extra!, November/December 1994*[5]

Chapter Twenty-Five

The Persian Gulf TV War

The invasions of Grenada and Panama during the 1980s and the Persian Gulf War in 1991 were military successes, but disastrous media failures. In part, the failures were a result of military restrictions on access, but the media did not react to these official constraints by more aggressive investigative and reporting efforts in areas open to them, nor did they struggle very energetically to get the restraints removed. In the cases of Grenada and Panama, once the great military triumphs over two of the tiniest countries in the world were completed, and officials turned their attention elsewhere, the mainstream media dutifully did the same.

The Persian Gulf War was a larger-scale effort, with international dimensions, and its preparation and the war itself were of longer duration, even though the imbalance of forces between the West and Iraq was overwhelming. This meant that there was more room for debate and public discussion before the outbreak of hostilities. The main attention in what follows will be on this early period in which the media could have fostered a democratic debate on issues of war and peace.

Phase 1—August 2, 1990 through January 15, 1991

Following the occupation of Kuwait by Iraq on August 2, 1990, the Bush administration very quickly decided to use this invasion for Bush's and the security state's political advantage by compelling Saddam Hussein to leave Kuwait in total defeat and humiliation ("with his tail between his legs," in Defense Secretary Dick Cheney's memorable phrase). This required fending off all attempts at a negotiated settlement that would have allowed Saddam a dignified exit, and readying the public for war.

The media's role was crucial. The Reagan-Bush administration had actively supported Iraq's aggression against Iran, 1980-88, and subsequently the Bush administration continued to aid and appease Saddam Hussein through July 31, 1990. On July 25, 1990, a week before the invasion, U.S. Ambassador to Iraq April Glaspie had assured Saddam that the United States had "no opinion" on his conflict with Kuwait which was "Arab" business. And on July 31, John Kelly, the highest ranking Bush official directly concerned with Middle Eastern affairs, told a congressional committee that this country had no obligation to defend Kuwait.[1] Numerous CIA alerts that Iraq was massing troops on Kuwait's border and that an invasion was imminent did not cause the Bush administration to issue a word of warning. This was either entrapment or colossal incompetence and blundering. It was important for Bush's freedom of action that his virtual go-ahead to the invasion, and the prior appeasement policy, be buried. The media obliged.[2]

As Bush was allegedly taking a high moral stance against "naked aggression," it was also important that the background of Reagan-Bush support of Iraq's aggression against Iran be ignored. Furthermore, less than a year before Iraq's invasion, the Bush administration had invaded Panama, in violation of the UN and OAS Charters and in the face of a UN oppositional majority, vetoed by the United States. South Africa had been ordered to leave Namibia by UN and World Court orders from 1968, and it regularly invaded Angola from Namibia from 1975 into the 1980s. But Reagan-Bush policy in that case was "quiet diplomacy" and "constructive engagement," with the United States supporting a "linkage" between South Africa's gradual withdrawal from Namibia and the departure of Cuban troops from Angola. Israel, also, was in long-standing violation of Security Council orders to leave the occupied territories, which led to no cutbacks in massive U.S. aid, let alone sanctions or bombing. Attention to these double standards would have called into question the purity of Bush's insistence that aggression could never be allowed to stand or to pay. The media obliged by rarely, if ever, allowing these matters to surface.[3]

Similarly, the United States had long failed to meet its legal obligations to UN financing, had withdrawn from UNESCO, and was far and away the dominant user of the veto against UN attempts to oppose violations of international law. It simply ignored a 1986 World Court decision that its attacks on Nicaragua constituted an "unlawful use of force." In the case of Iraq's invasion of Kuwait, however, with the Soviet veto and military capability no longer an obstruction, the United States was able to mobilize the UN to attack this particular law violator. The double standard here, and the turnabout in treatment of UN authority, were dramatic, but were essentially ignored in the mainstream media, which reproduced the U.S. official view that the UN was finally resuming its proper role in maintaining the peace, etc.[4]

In addition to the decontextualization of issues just described, the Bush administration depended heavily on mass-media cooperation in its various strategies for mobilizing consent, all of which involved the use of traditional propaganda techniques. One technique was the demonization of Saddam Hussein, who, like Qadaffi and Manuel Noriega in earlier years, was made into the embodiment of evil and "another Hitler." Effective propaganda here required that the mass media repeat the propaganda claims and disclose the evidence of the new villain's evil acts, but avoid mention not only of any positive features of his rule, but the fact that the villain was for a long time nurtured by the U.S. government as a valuable ally, and treated with parallel apologetics by the mainstream media (a "pragmatist," with the evils now featured then glossed over).[5] Demonization was accompanied by new atrocity stories, often inflated and sometimes wholly fabricated. A classic was the alleged Iraqi removal from incubators of several hundred babies in Kuwaiti hospitals following the occupation. This story, created by a Kuwait-financed propaganda operation, was accepted and transmitted without verification by the mainstream media, and was still repeated by CNN and others long after it had been shown to be a complete fabrication.[6]

An important part of the Bush war program was to place a large U.S. contingent in Saudi Arabia and elsewhere in the Middle East, to get the media focused on military maneuvers and to bond them and the public with our fighting men facing a ruthless enemy. This was accomplished, first, by claiming that Iraq was planning to invade Saudi Arabia. This claim was a propaganda lie, as Iraq not only denied any such intention, it had insufficient troops and supplies for such an operation, and such action would have been a suicidal declaration of war against the United States. The U.S. mainstream media nevertheless accepted the official version without question and quickly urged vigorous military action against Iraq.[7]

Having gotten a large U.S. force in place, the Bush team enlarged it substantially immediately after the November elections. With "our boys" over there, the media cooperatively spent a large fraction of their organizational resources in exploring military deployments, possible scenarios of war, and the conditions and opinions of our boys. This not only diverted attention from real issues, it readied the public for war.

The most important official lie and greatest media service to the war policy was on the question of diplomacy. It was crucial to the Bush strategy that a diplomatic solution be averted—as noted by Thomas Friedman in the *New York Times* of August 22, 1990, the diplomatic track must be blocked lest negotiations "defuse the crisis" while allowing Iraq "a few token gains." The administration therefore carefully subverted an early Arab effort at resolution of the crisis.[8] Iraq itself, taken aback by the Bush administration's furious reaction, made at least five diplomatic approaches and proposals, all summarily rejected by the United States.[9] The French and Russians also tried to open diplomatic lines, to no avail.[10] In this process, the mainstream media not only served administration policy by giving these diplomatic efforts and their immediate summary rejection by the United States minimal attention, in the end, when the Bush administration kept repeating that the United States had tried and exhausted the diplomatic option, the media accepted this lie as true.[11]

The significance of this Big Lie and its media support is highlighted by a national public opinion poll reported in the *Washington Post* on January 11, 1991, which indicated that two-thirds of the public favored a conference on the Arab-Israeli conflict if that would lead to an Iraqi withdrawal from Kuwait.[12] The poll was biased against a positive response, as it indicated that the Bush administration was opposed to the proposal. As it happens, about one week earlier a diplomatic proposal had been floated by the Iraq government, supported by the Iraqi democratic opposition,[13] which embodied the elements of the resolution supported by at least two-thirds of the U.S. public. The Iraqi proposal was flatly rejected by the Bush administration, and went virtually unreported by the U.S. mass media. That is to say, the media suppressed and failed to allow or encourage a debate on a political solution favored by the public; instead it allowed the administration to pull the country into war, based on a media-sustained lie that all the diplomatic routes had been exhausted.

The War—January 16 through February 27, 1991

During the War proper, access to military personnel was closely controlled by a pool and censorship system, causing exceptional reliance on government handouts. The aim was to get the media to focus on the new weaponry, to convey the image of a clean war, to minimize images of human suffering, and to give the impression of warmakers in excellent control of the situation.

The result was one of the great successes in the history of war propaganda. The media were incorporated into a system of serious censorship with only mild protests,[14] focused throughout on precisely what the censors wanted them to, and helped produce a genuine war hysteria. The control of information by government "couldn't have been better," stated Michael Deaver, the number two image-making official in the Reagan administration.[15] Douglas Kellner, in his extensive examination of media coverage, concludes that the mainstream media

[P]resented incredible PR for the military, inundating the country with images of war and the new high-tech military for months, while the brutality of war was normalized and even glamorized in the uncritical media coverage. Throughout the Persian Gulf TV War, the culture of militarism became *the* mainstream culture after a period when war and the military were in disfavor.[16]

During the War, the media passed on innumerable rumors and official and unofficial fabrications concerning Iraqi atrocities, the size of Iraq's forces in Kuwait and chemical and other arms capabilities, alleged exclusive Iraqi responsibility for oil spills, the number of Iraqi hostages taken from Kuwait in the final Iraqi exodus, and the legitimacy of U.S. targeting and "turkey shooting."[17] Although it was clear from official statements during the War that the United States was deliberately destroying the infrastructure of Iraq beyond military necessity, the media never picked this up or discussed its compatibility with the UN mandate or international law and morality. When U.S. officials adamantly claimed that an infant-formula milk factory destroyed in Baghdad actually made biological weapons, the U.S. media accepted this as true, despite the fact that Peter Arnett's and Iraqi officials' denials were confirmed by numerous independent sources.[18]

When the U.S. military engaged in its final orgy of massacre on the Highway of Death, destroying many thousands of fleeing Iraqi soldiers and, almost surely, thousands of Kuwaiti hostages and other refugees, the U.S. media provided an apologetic cover: averting their eyes to a maximum degree; failing to discuss the use of napalm, fragmentation bombs, and fuel air bombs; stressing that the fleeing Iraqis were "looters" and ignoring the large numbers of hostages and refugees slaughtered along with the Iraqis (although they had given close attention to the earlier claims of Iraqi hostages taken from Kuwait); repeating the official explanation that it was important to destroy Iraq's military capability, while failing to note the limited UN mandate and international law condemning the slaughter of completely helpless and fleeing soldiers and burying large numbers of them in unmarked graves.[19] After discussing what he calls "probably the most appalling episode" in the War, and quoting an Air Force officer that "it was close to Armageddon," Kellner says: "And that's it. Armageddon for the Iraqis but no details, no follow ups, and certainly no outrage."[20]

The Aftermath—February 28, 1991 to the Present

The euphoria following the pulverizing of a completely overmatched Third World country continued for some months, but eventually faded as neglected internal problems came to the fore *and* as the results of the War came under closer scrutiny. Belated attention was given to the earlier appeasement policy and the Bush administration's role in building up Saddam Hussein's military establishment, although almost nothing was said of the administration's virtual enticement of

Iraq to invade Kuwait and its subsequent complete refusal to allow a diplomatic resolution of the conflict. The fact that the "allied" military effort stopped short of removing "another Hitler," but left him with just enough arms to crush dissident and oppressed Kurds, Shiites, and any democratic opposition, was noted, but its full implications were not discussed. There was some slight publicity given to the fact that Bush and the CIA had encouraged the Kurds to fight, but virtually none was given to the administration's refusal to provide arms to those fighting Saddam Hussein.

The fact that the United States was again selling arms to the Middle East on a massive scale was barely noted in the media, and was certainly not contrasted with earlier pious claims about bringing a new era of peace to that area. The media touched lightly on the fact that the fight for principle did not include bringing democracy to Kuwait or Saudi Arabia, and little attention was paid to the retaliatory killings in Kuwait, which may have exceeded the inflated and indignantly publicized executions in Kuwait by Iraq.[21]

Most notable in the aftermath coverage was the continued attention to Iraq's obstructions and refusals to allow inspections, overflights, and destruction of its military resources. This was the basis for the continued limitations on Iraqi trade and oil sales, and made more difficult its recovery from the "near apocalyptic conditions" reported by a UN team in June 1991.[22] In perfect accord with the U.S. foreign policy agenda, the media paid almost no attention to Iraqi civilian hunger, sickness and death, but focused unrelentingly on Iraq's alleged foot-dragging on weapons control.

In sum, in the three phases of the Persian Gulf War, U.S. mass-media coverage was to an extraordinary degree a servant of official policy. In the crucial months before the War, the mainstream media allowed themselves to be managed in the service of war mobilization, and failed to provide the factual and opinion basis for public evaluation. Then and later the mass media served ongoing government policy, not the democratic polity.

—Journal of International Affairs, Summer 1993[23]

Chapter Twenty-Six

Toward a Democratic Media

A democratic media is a primary condition of popular rule, hence of a genuine political democracy. Where the media are controlled by a powerful and privileged elite, whether of government leaders and bureaucrats or those from the private sector, democratic political forms and some kind of limited political democracy may exist, but not genuine democracy. The public will not be participants in the media, and therefore in public life, they will be consumers of facts and opinions distributed to them from above. The media will, of structural necessity, select news and organize debate supportive of agendas and programs of the privileged. They will not provide the unbiased information and opinion that would permit the public to make choices in accord with its own best interests. Their job will be to show that what's good for the elites is good for everybody, and that other options are either bad or do not exist.

Media Sovereignty and Freedom of Choice

Economists have long distinguished between "consumer sovereignty" and "freedom of consumer choice." The former requires that consumers participate in deciding what is to be offered in the first place; the latter is satisfied if consumers are free to select among the options chosen for them by producers. Freedom of choice is better than no freedom of choice, and the market may provide a substantial array of options. But it may not. Before the foreign-car invasion in the 1960s, U.S. car manufacturers chose not to offer small cars because the profit margin on small cars is small. It was better to have choices among four or five manufacturers than one, but the options were constrained by producer interest. Only the entry of foreign competition made small cars available to U.S. buyers. Freedom of choice prevailed in both cases, but consumer sovereignty did not. The cost of *producer* sovereignty was also manifest in the policy of General Motors Corporation, in cahoots with rubber and oil interests, of buying up public transit lines and converting them to GM buses or liquidating them.[1] The consumers of transportation services, if fully informed, might well have chosen to preserve and subsidize the electric transit option, but this sovereign decision was not open to them.

This distinction between sovereignty and free choice has important applications in both national politics and the mass media. In each case, the general population has some kind of free choice, but lacks sovereignty. The public goes to the polls every few years to pull a lever for slates of candidates chosen for them by political parties heavily dependent on funding by powerful elite interests. The public has "freedom of choice" only among a very restricted set of what we might call "effective" candidates, effectiveness being defined by their ability to attract the funding necessary to make a credible showing.

At the level of mass communication as well, the dominant media with large audiences are owned by an overlapping set of powerful elite interests. There is a fringe media with very limited outreach that might support "ineffective" candidates, but because of their marginal status they and the candidates they support can be easily ignored. As with the candidates, the populace has "freedom of choice" among the dominant set of mainstream media, but it lacks sovereignty[2] except in a legalistic and formal sense (we are each legally free to start our own newspaper or buy our own paper or TV network).[3] The elite-dominated mass media, not surprisingly, find the political system admirable, and while sometimes expressing regret at the quality of candidates, never seriously question the absence of citizen sovereignty regarding decisions about the effective options.

Naturally, also, the mass media hardly mention the undemocratic underpinnings of the political process in the media itself. In fact, one of the most disquieting features of the propaganda systems of advanced capitalism's constrained democracies is that the consolidation of mass media power has closed down discussion of the need for radical restructuring of the media. It has also pushed such changes off the political agenda. As the "gatekeepers," the mass media have been in the enviable position of being able to protect themselves from debate or political acts that threaten their interests, which illustrates the deeply undemocratic character of *their* role.

Occasionally, issues like TV violence have aroused public opinion and caused Congress to hold hearings and assail the TV networks, but the whole business has always been settled by appeals to corporate responsibility and self-regulation, and the assurance by the media barons of their deepest concern and commitment to rectifying the situation. In 1977, however, an unusually aggressive and naïve House subcommittee actually drafted a report calling for investigation of the structure of the television industry as a necessary step to attacking the violence problem at its source. As George Gerbner described the sequel:[4]

> When the draft mentioning industry structure was leaked to the networks, all hell broke loose. Members of the subcommittee told me that they had never before been subject to such relentless lobbying and pressure. Campaign contributors were contacted. The report was delayed for months. The subcommittee staffer who wrote the draft was summarily fired. The day before the final vote was to be taken, a new version drafted by a broadcast lobbyist was substituted. It ignored the evidence of the hearings and gutted the report, shifting the source of the problem from network structure to the parents of America. When the network-dictated draft came to a vote, members of the full committee (including those who had never attended hearings) were mobilized, and the watered down version won by one vote.

In short, the power of the "actual existing" highly undemocratic mass media is enormous.

What Would A Democratic Media Look Like?

A democratic media can be identified by its structure and functions. In terms of structure, it would be organized and controlled by ordinary citizens or their grassroots organizations. This could involve individuals or bodies serving local or larger political, minority, or other groups in the social and political arena. Media fitting these structural conditions would be bound to articulate demands of the general population because they are either part of it or instruments created to serve its needs.

In the mainstream system, the mass media are large organizations owned by other large organizations or shareholders and controlled by members of a privileged business elite. The ownership structure puts them at a distance from ordinary people. They are funded by advertising, and advertisers have to be convinced that the programs meet their needs. Thus in terms of fundamental structure the mainstream media are not agents serving the general public: the first responsibility of their managers is by law to stockholders seeking profits; and as advertisers are the principal source of revenue, their needs come second. There is no legal responsibility to audiences at all; these must be persuaded to watch or buy, but by any means the gatekeeper chooses, within the limits of law and conventional standards of morality.

As regards function, a democratic media will aim first and foremost at serving the informational, cultural, and other communications needs of the members of the public which the media institutions comprise or represent. The users would determine their own needs and fix the menu of choices either directly or through their closely controlled agents, and debate would not be limited to select voices chosen by corporate or governmental gatekeepers. The sovereign listeners would not only participate in choosing programs and issues to be addressed, they would *be* the voices heard, and they would be involved in continuous interchanges with other listeners. There would be a horizontal flow of communication, in both directions, instead of a vertical and downward flow from officials and experts to the passive population of consumers. A democratic media would encourage people to know and understand their neighbors and to participate in social and political life. This is likely to occur where media structures are democratic, as such media will be open to neighbors who want to communicate views on problems and their possible communal resolution.

At the same time, a democratic media would recognize and encourage diversity. It would allow and encourage minorities to express their views and build their own communities' solidarity within the larger community. This would follow from the democratic idea of recognizing and encouraging individual differences and letting all such flowers bloom irrespective of financial capability and institutional power. This is also consistent with the ideal of pluralism, part of mainstream orthodox doctrine but poorly realized in mainstream practice. The commercial media serve minority constituencies badly, tending toward the repetition of homogenizing mainstream cultural-market themes and ignoring the group entirely when it is really poor. In Hungary, for example, the new commercial media, "have a radio programme for tourists from German-speaking countries, but none for hundreds of thousands of gypsies living in Hungary (7 percent of the population)."[5] The same criticism often applies to state-controlled media.[6]

Talk Shows: Phoney Populism, Phoney Democracy

The talk show radio and TV "revolution" in the United States offers the facade of something democratic, but not the substance. The interaction of talk-show hosts with the public is usually carefully controlled by screening out undesired questions, and there are very limited exchanges between hosts and a "statistically insignificant" proportion of the listening audience.[7] Rush Limbaugh, for example, has a sizable audience of proudly self-styled "ditto heads," but they are entertained in pseudo-post modern monologues with a minimum of genuine interaction. There is a kind of quasi-community built among the followers, who listen, meet together, buy and discuss the master's (and other recommended) books, but the community has a cultish quality, and the master's discourse is no more democratic than was Father Charles Coughlin's radio talk show back in the 1930s. The community is led by a leader who possesses, and guides the followers to, the truth.

As is well known, many of the talk-show hosts are right-wing populists, who claim concern over the distress of ordinary citizens, but never succeed in finding the sources of that distress in the workings of corporate capital and its impact on politics, unemployment, wage levels, and economic insecurity. They focus on symptoms and scapegoats, like crime, Black welfare mothers, environmental extremists, and "family values" issues. Their service is comparable to that of the Nazi movement during the Weimar Republic years in Germany in the 1920s, diverting attention from real causes of distress and weakening any threat of meaningful organization and protest from below by obfuscating issues and stirring up the forces of irrationality.

Routes to Democratizing the Media

There are two main routes to democratizing the media. One is to try to influence the mainstream media to give more room to now excluded ideas and groups. This could be done by persuasion, pressure, or by legislation compelling greater access. The second route is to create and support an alternative structure of media closer to ordinary people and grassroots organizations that would replace, or at least offer an important alternative to, the mainstream media. This could be done, in principle, by private and popular initiative, by legislative action, or by a combination of the two.

The first route is of limited value as a long-run solution to the problem, precisely because it fails to attack the structural roots of the media's lack of democracy. If function follows from structure, the gains from pursuit of the first route are likely to be modest and transitory. These small gains may also lead both activists and ordinary citizens to conclude that the mainstream media are really open to dissent, when in fact dissent is securely kept in a non-threatening position. And it may divert energy from building an alternative media. On the other hand, the limited access obtained by pursuit of the first route may have disproportionate and catalyzing effects on elite opinion. This route may also be the only one that appeals to many media activists, and there is no assurance that the long-run strategy of pursuing structural change will work.

The second route to democratization of the media is the only one that can yield a truly democratic media, and it is this route that I will discuss in greater detail. Without a democratic structure, the media will serve a democratic function inadequately at best, and very possibly even perversely, working as agents of the *real* (dominant corporate) "special interests" to confuse and divert the public. The struggle for a democratic media structure is also of increasing urgency, because the media have become less democratic in recent decades with the decline in relative importance of the public and nonprofit broadcasting spheres, increased commercialization and integration of the mass media into the market, conglomeration, and internationalization. In important respects the main ongoing struggle has been to prevent further attrition of democratic elements in the media.

This has been very evident in Western Europe where powerful systems of public broadcasting, as well as nonprofit local radio stations, have been under relentless attack by commercial and conservative political interests increasingly influential in state policy. These changes have threatened diversity, quality, and relatively democratic organizational arrangements. In the former Soviet bloc, where state-controlled media institutions are being rapidly dismantled, there is a dire threat that an undemocratic system of government control will be replaced by an equally undemocratic system of commercial domination. The same is true of the Third World which, while presenting a mixed picture of government, private/commercial, and a sometimes important civic sector, has been increasingly brought within the orbit of a globalizing commercial media.

It is obvious that a thoroughgoing democratization of the media can only occur in connection with a drastic alteration in the structure of power and political revolution. Democratizing a national media would be very difficult in a large and complex society like the United States even with unlimited structural options, just as organizing a democratic polity here would be a bit more tricky than in a tiny Greek city-state or autonomous New England town. An important step toward a democratic media would be a move back to the Articles of Confederation, and beyond—to really small units where people can interact on a personal level. For larger political units personal interaction is more difficult; efficiency and market considerations make for a centralization of national and international news gathering, processing, and distribution, and of cultural-entertainment productions as well. Funding would have to be insulated from business and government, but it could not be completely insulated from democratic decision processes. Maintaining involvement and control by ordinary citizens, while allowing a necessary degree of specialization and centralization, and permitting artistic autonomy as well, would present a serious challenge to democratic organization. As this is not on the immediate agenda, however, I am not going to try to spell out here the machinery and arrangements whereby these conflicting ends can be accomplished.

Some partial guidelines for the pursuit of democratic structural change in the media here can be derived from the current debates and struggles in Europe, where the democratic forces are trying to hold the line (in Western Europe) and prevent wholesale commercialization (in the East). The democrats have stressed the deadly effects of privatization and commercialization on a democratic polity and culture, and have urged the importance of preserving and enlarging the *public* and *civic* spheres of the media. The public sphere is the government-sponsored sector, which is far more important in Western Europe than in this country. It is funded by direct governmental grants, license fees, and to an increasing but controlled extent, advertising. This sphere is designed and responsible for serving the public interest in news, public affairs, educational, children's, and much cultural programming. It is assumed in Europe that the commercial sphere will pursue large audiences with entertainment (movies, sitcoms, cowboy-crime stories) and that its long-term trend toward abandonment of non-entertainment values will continue.[8]

The civic sector comprises all the media that are noncommercial but not government sponsored, and which arise by individual or grassroots initiatives. This would include some mainly local newspapers and journals, independent movie and TV producers, and radio broadcasters. The civic sector has virtually no TV presence in Europe, but radio broadcasting by nonprofit organizations is still fairly important, sufficiently so to have produced a European Federation of Community Radios (FERL) to exchange ideas and coordinate educational and lobbying efforts to advance their ideals and protect their interests.

FERL has been lobbying throughout Europe for explicit recognition of the important role of the noncommercial—and especially the civic—sector in governmental and inter-governmental policy decisions. It has urged the preservation and enlargement of this sector by policy choice. In France, the civic sector actually gets some funding from the state via a tax on commercial advertising revenues. This is a model that could be emulated elsewhere. It should be noted, however, that in the conservative political environment of the past half dozen years, the policies of the French regulatory authority, the Higher Broadcasting Council, has reduced the number of nonprofit radio stations from 1,000 to under 300, and discriminated heavily in favor of religious and right-wing broadcasters as well.

Democratizing the U.S. Media

Democratizing the U.S. media is an even more formidable task than that faced by Europeans. In Western Europe, public broadcasting is important, even if under siege, and community radio is a more important force than in the United States. In Eastern Europe the old government-dominated systems are crumbling, so that there are options and an ongoing struggle for control. In the United States, commercial systems are more powerfully entrenched, the public sector is weak and has been subject to steady right-wing attack for years, and the civic sphere, while alive and bustling, is small, mainly local, and undernourished. The question is, what is to be done?

Funding. An extremely important problem for democratization is that the commercial sector is self-financing, with large resources from advertising, whereas the public and civic sectors are chronically starved. This gives the commercial media an overwhelming advantage in technical quality and polish, price, publicity, and distribution. An important part of a democratic media strategy must consist of figuring out how to obtain sizable and more stable resources for the public and civic sectors. The two promising sources are taxes on commercial media revenues and direct government grants. Commercial radio and television are getting the free use of the spectrum and satellite paths—which are a public resource—to turn a private profit, and there is an important record of commercial broadcasting and FCC commitments to public service made in 1934 and 1946 that have been quietly sloughed off.[9] These considerations make a franchise or spectrum use tax, with the revenues turned over to the public and civic sectors that have taken on those abandoned responsibilities, completely justifiable. We could also properly extend a tax on spectrum-use to cellular and other telephone transmission, which also use public airwaves, possibly placing the tax revenue into a fund to help extend telephone service as well as other communications infrastructure to Third World areas at home and abroad.

The funding of the public and civic sectors from general tax revenues and/or license fees on receiving sets is also easily defended, given the great importance of these sectors in educational, children's, minority group and public affairs programming. These services are important for democratic citizenship, among other aims.

In sum, local, regional, and national groups interested in democratizing the media should give high priority to organization, education, and lobbying designed to sharply increase and stabilize the funding of the financially strapped public and civic sectors. Success in these endeavors is going to depend in large measure on the general political climate.[10]

The Commercial Sector

The commercial sector of the media does provide some small degree of diversity, insofar as individual proprietors may allow it and advertisers can be mobilized in niche markets of liberal and progressive bent (*The New Yorker*, *Village Voice*, urban alternative press). But this diversity is within narrow bounds, and rarely if ever extends to support for policies involving fundamental change. Furthermore, the main drift of commercial markets is absolutely antithetical to democratic media service (see Chapter Twenty-Two), and while we may welcome the offbeat and progressive commercial media institutions, we should recognize the inherent tendencies of the commercial media.

It will still be desirable to oppose further consolidation, conglomeration, cross-ownership of the mainstream media, and discriminatory exclusions of outsiders,[11] not only because they make the media less democratic, but also because they help further centralize power and make progressive change in the media and elsewhere more difficult. I also favor "fairness doctrine" and quantitative requirements for local, public affairs, and children's programs for commercial radio and TV broadcasters. Part of the reason for this is straightforward: it is an outrage that they have abandoned public service in their quest for profit. A more devious reason is this: pressing the commercial broadcasters, and describing in detail how they have abandoned children and public service for "light fare," will help make the case for taxing them and funding the public and civic sectors.

In Europe, commercial broadcasters are sometimes obligated by law, or by contract arrangements made when spectrum rights were given, to provide a certain amount of time to quality children's programs at prime hours, or to give blocks of broadcasting time to various groups like labor organizations, church groups, and political parties, in proportion to their membership size (not their money). In Europe, and elsewhere as well, broadcasters are obligated to give significant blocks of free time to political parties and candidates in election periods. These are all desirable, and should be on the agenda here. They are not being considered because the media would suffer economic costs, so that the public isn't even allowed to know about and debate these options.[12]

Various groups have been formed in this country to lobby and threaten the media, the most important and effective regrettably being those of the Right.[13] Notable among those representing a broader public interest was Action For Children's Television (ACT), organized in 1968 to fight the commercial media's degradation of children's programming.[14] Also worthy of special mention is Fairness and Accuracy in Reporting (FAIR), a media monitoring group that has published numerous special studies of media bias as well as an ongoing monitoring review, *EXTRA!* FAIR also produces a weekly half-hour radio program, "Counterspin," heard on over 80 (mostly public, community, and college) stations, which provides media criticism and alternative news analysis.

The Public Sector

The Corporation for Public Broadcasting was brought into existence in 1967, with the acquiescence of the commercial broadcasters, who were pleased to transfer public-interest responsibilities elsewhere as long as these were funded by the taxpayer. Over the years, public radio and television have been more open to dissent and minority voices than the commercial broadcasting media, partly as a result of original design, but also because, despite their ties to government, they have proven to be somewhat more independent of government and tolerant of controversy than the commercial broadcasters[15] (which shows how awful the latter have been).

The independence and quality of the public sector depends heavily on the political environment. As long as it is kept on a short financial leash, underfunded, and worried mainly about attacks from the Right, it will feature a William Buckley and McLaughlin, with McNeil-Lehrer on "the Left," and offer mainly bland and cautious news and commentary plus uncontroversial and cultural events.[16] Not surprisingly, it went into serious decline in the Reagan-Bush years. It needs a lot more money, longer funding periods, more autonomy, and less threatening pressure from the right wing to perform well. There is an important role for the public sector in a system of democratic media, and its rehabilitation should definitely be on the democratic media agenda.

The Civic Sector

For real progress in democratizing the media, a much larger place must be carved out for the civic sector. This is the nonprofit sector organized by individuals or grassroots organizations to serve the communications interests and needs of the general population (as opposed to the corporate community and government). The building of a media civic sector is important as part of community building and the democratic process itself. Democratic media analysts stress that ordinary citizens must *participate* in the media, which is part of the public sphere in which public opinion is formed, to be genuine members of a political community.[17]

Alternative press. There is an alternative local press in many cities in the United States, usually distributed without charge and funded by advertising, but catering to a somewhat offbeat audience and providing an opening for dissent and debate, within limits. This alternative press has a national Association of Alternative News Weeklies with 95 members and claims a readership of some 5.5 million. Its performance is spotty and often unimpressive, but it is a small force for diversity.

It *is* possible to depend on advertising and to maintain alternative press substance. The costs of serious dissent may be heavy, however, and compromises are endemic. The *Village Voice* has provided significant dissent in the huge market of New York City. Even more interesting is the *Anderson Valley Advertiser* of Boonville, California, a local paper which has survived in a small town despite the radical perspectives of its editor. It has been subjected to advertising boycotts and is avoided regularly by some advertisers on political grounds, but its advertising penalties are partially offset by a wider readership generated by its exciting quality and vigor. *AVA* covers local news well and its exceptional openness to letters and petitions, and the continuous and sometimes furious debates among readers and between readers and editors constitute a kind of town meeting in print. The paper addresses a host of local issues, and the columns and letters debate national and global issues, though no attempt is made to provide national or international news coverage. A thousand papers like *AVA* would make this a more democratic country.

With the demise of the New York *Guardian* in 1992, the only national alternative newspaper is the bi-weekly *In These Times*, with a circulation of only 25,000, despite its high quality and avoidance of the doctrinaire. Even this one publication struggles each year for greater circulation and other funding to keep afloat. It deserves support; helping it continue to exist and grow, and supplementing its coverage with other national papers, is important in a democratic media project.

Alternative journals. There are a fair number of liberal and left alternative journals in the United States, including *The Nation*, *Z Magazine*, *The Progressive*, *Mother Jones*, *Dollars & Sense*, *Monthly Review*, *Ms. Magazine*, *The Texas Observer*, *CovertAction Quarterly*, *EXTRA!*, and others. Apart from *Mother Jones*, which has sometimes crossed the quarter-million mark in circulation, based on large promotional campaigns, *The Nation* has the largest readership, with about 100,000. Most of the alternative journals have circulations between 2,000 and 30,000, and experience chronic financial problems. By contrast, *Time* has a circulation of 5.6 million (4.4 million in North America) and *Reader's Digest* 29.6 million (16.7 in North America). Some of the alternative journals could expand circulation with aggressive and large-scale publicity and higher quality copy, but this would cost a lot of money. Not many of the 78 U.S. billionaires are inclined to set up trust funds to help enlarge the circulation of alternative journals.[18] Advertisers are also not bending over backwards to throw business their way.

Alternative Radio. Radio may promise more for the growth and greater outreach of alternative media than does print media. More people are prone to listen to the radio and watch television than read journals, or even newspapers, which are also harder to get into the hands of audiences. And radio broadcasting facilities are not expensive. Community radio made a large growth spurt in the early 1970s, then tapered off, in part as a result of the shortage of additional frequencies in the larger markets. Of the roughly 1,500 noncommercial radio licenses outstanding, half are held by religious broadcasters. Many of the remaining 750 are college- and university-linked, and perhaps 250 are licensed to community organizations.

Many of the community stations have languished for want of continuity of programming and spotty quality. Discrete and sporadic programs do not command large audiences; building substantial audiences requires that many people know that particular types of programs are going to be there, day after day, at a certain time period. (This is why stations become "all news," or have talk shows all morning and rock music all afternoon.) There are also the usual problems of funding, as well as threats to licenses by more powerful commercial interests seeking to enlarge their domains. Nonetheless, these stations are precious for their pluralism in programming and diversity among staff and volunteers, and they meet the democratic standard of community involvement and serious public debate. Noam Chomsky "has observed that when he speaks in a town or city that has an alternative radio station, people tend to be more informed and aware of what is going on."[19]

Pacifica's five-station network and News Service have done yeoman work in providing alternative and high-quality radio programming and in developing a sizable and loyal listenership. Under constant right-wing attack and threat, it deserves strong support and emulation. Radio Zinzine in Forcalquier, a small town of Upper Provence in France, also provides an important model of constructive radio use. Organized by the members of the progressive cooperative Longo Mai, Radio Zinzine has given the local farmers and townspeople a more vigorous and action-oriented form of local news (as well as broader news coverage and entertainment), but also an avenue for communication among formerly isolated and consequently somewhat apathetic people. It has energized the local population, encouraged its participation, and made it more of a genuine community.

In a dramatic example of how democratic media come into existence out of the needs of ordinary people who want to speak and encourage others to communicate, M'Banna Kantako, a 31-year-old Black, blind, unemployed public-housing resident in Springfield, Illinois organized Black Liberation Radio in 1986 out of frustration with the failure of the major media to provide news and entertainment of interest to the Black community. Operating illegally on a one-watt transmitter with a range of one mile, Kantako provides a genuine alternative to the Black community. Kantako was ignored by the FCC and dominant media until he broadcast a series of interviews with Blacks who had been brutalized by the local police. Soon thereafter the FCC tried to get him off the air, and a court order was issued to close him down, but it remains unenforced. Undefended by the local media, Kantako has gotten considerable national publicity and support. Grassroots organizers and student groups from practically every state and a number of foreign countries have contacted him, and numerous other similar "micro-radio" stations have gone on the air.[20] This is genuinely democratic media: may it spread widely.

David Barsamian's Alternative Radio is another important model; it has produced and distributed a weekly one-hour public affairs program since 1986, using rented space on a satellite channel to provide U.S. stations solid alternative programming. Alternative Radio, using both taped speeches and a one-on-one interview format, has focused on "the media, U.S. foreign policy, racism, the environment, NAFTA/GATT and economic issues and other topics," with guests like Elaine Bernard (Canadian labor activist, on Creating a New Party), Juliet Schor (Overworked American), Ali Mazrui (Afrocentricity and Multiculturalism), Noam Chomsky (Manufacturing Consent), and Herbert Chao Gunther (GATT).[21] These are quality offerings of unusual depth and commentators of high merit rarely encountered in the mainstream media. Some 400 stations are able to receive Alternative Radio's offerings; foreign stations in Canada, Australia, and elsewhere can send for the show on tape.

Alternative TV. In the 1980s, the mainstreaming and commercialization of public television led to the emergence of several new public television stations designed to serve the public-interest function abandoned by the dominant PBS stations. In an embarrassing episode for PBS, an internal PBS research study found that the new entrants would not compete much with the older stations, as the latter had moved to serve an upscale audience.[22] Meanwhile, the older stations have lobbied aggressively to prevent the new ones from sharing in government funding slotted for public television stations. It goes without saying that the new stations deserve support as a democratizing force, although the older ones should not be written off—rather, they need reorganization and regeneration to allow them to throw off the Reagan-Bush era incubus and better serve a public function.

The growth of cable opened up democratic options, partly in the greater numbers of channels and potentially enlarged diversity of commercial cable, but more importantly in the frequent obligation of cable systems to provide public-access channels and facilities. First imposed as a requirement by the FCC in 1972, partly as an impediment to cable growth by an FCC still serving the commercial broadcasters' interests, the move was eventually institutionalized as part of negotiated agreements between cable companies seeking franchises and community negotiators. In many cases the contracts require cable companies to provide facilities and training to access users, and in some instances require that a percentage of cable revenues (1 to 5 percent) be set aside to fund the access operations.[23]

This important development offers a resource and opportunity that demands far more attention from media activists than it has gotten. Spokespersons for the public-access movement call attention to the fact that there are some 1,000 sites where public-access TV production takes place and over 2,000 public-access facilities, and that more than 15,000 hours of original material are transmitted over public-access channels per week to an unknown but probably fairly sizable audience. The problems here, as with community radio, lie in the spotty quality of original programming, the frequent absence of the continuity that makes for regular watching, and the lack of promotional resources. The existing levels of participation are worthy, but public-access remains marginal and has been under increasing attack from cable owners who no longer need public-access supporters as allies and have been trying hard to throw off any responsibility to their host communities. Along with community radio, this *is* democratic media, but public access is under threat; the relevant cable contracts are up for renewal over the next few years and cable access needs to be protected from attrition as well as used and enlarged.

A strenuous effort has been made by some media democrats to fill the TV programming gap with centrally assembled or produced materials, made available through network pools of videotapes and by transmission of fresh materials through satellites. Paper Tiger TV has been providing weekly programs on Manhattan Cable for years, and making these programs available to public-access stations and movement groups wanting to use them in meetings.[24] An affiliated organization, Deep Dish Network, has tried to provide something like a mainstream TV network equivalent for public-access stations, assembling and producing quality programs that are publicized in advance and transmitted via satellite to alerted individual dish owners, groups, and university and public-access stations able to downlink the programs. There are some 3 million home satellite dish owners in North America who can receive Deep Dish offerings, and it is programmed on more than 300 cable systems as well as by many individual TV stations.

In addition to a notable 10-part Gulf Project series, which provided an alternative to mainstream TV's promotional coverage of the Gulf War, Deep Dish has had a six-part program on Latino issues (immigration, work exploitation and struggles, history, etc.), a major series on the Reagan-Bush era attacks on civil liberties, and during 1992, counter-celebratory programs on Columbus' conquest of the "New World." On December 1, 1991, it transmitted an hour-long live program by Kitchen Center professional artists in conjunction with

Visual AIDS, entitled "Day Without Art," as part of a day of action and mourning in response to the AIDS crisis. Performed in New York City, there were live audiences receiving the program in eight cities, and a much wider audience call-in operation organized as part of the program. Group viewings and cable showings were encouraged in advance. More recently Deep Dish had a program on "Staking a Claim in Cyberspace," and a 12-part series on the U.S. health-care system in 1994 entitled "Sick and Tired of Being Sick and Tired."

Deep Dish has tried to use its productions as an organizing tool, working with community groups to help them tell their stories and getting them to mobilize their constituencies to become aware of access and other media issues. This is extremely valuable, but Deep Dish suffers from the sporadic nature of its offerings, which harks back to the basic problem of funding. An excellent case can be made for funding Deep Dish and similar services to the civic sector out of franchise taxes on the commercial stations or general tax revenues.

Internet. The Internet affords a new mode of communication that opens some possibilities for democratizing communications. It allows very rapid communication locally, nationally, and internationally; it is relatively cheap to send messages to a potentially wide audience; and up to this point it has not fallen under the control of advertisers, governments, or any other establishment institutions. This was important in the Chiapas revolt in Mexico and its aftermath, allowing the Zapatista rebels to get out their messages at home and abroad quickly, and interfering with government attempts to crush the rebellion quietly, in the traditional manner.[25] This caused Rand Corporation analyst David Ronfeldt to speak of "netwar" and a prospective problem of "ungovernability" in Mexico flowing in part from an uncontrollable media.[26] This recalls Samuel Huntington's and the Trilateral Commission's fears of ungovernability in the United States and other Western countries based on the loss of apathy of the unimportant people in the 1960s. In short, the new media-based "threat" of ungovernability is establishment code language for an inability of government to manipulate and repress at will, or an increase in democracy.

However, it is important to recognize the limitations of Internet as a form of democratic media, currently and in the more uncertain future. As noted in Chapter One, access to the Internet is not free; it requires a powerful computer, programs, the price of access, and some moderate degree of technical knowhow. Business interests are also making rapid advances into the Internet, so that problems of more difficult and expensive access, and domination and saturation by an advertising-linked system is a real possibility. Furthermore, the Internet is an individualized system, with connections between individuals requiring prior knowledge of common interests, direct and indirect routes to interchanges and shared information, and the buildup of information pools. It is well-geared to efficient communication among knowledgeable and sophisticated elites and elite groups, but its potential for reaching mass audiences seems unpromising. This is extremely important, as producing ungovernability is not likely to have positive consequences unless supported by a mass movement, some rational understanding of social forces, and a coherent vision of an alternative set of institutions and policies. Otherwise, those in command of access to mass audiences (and military forces) will eventually restore "law and order" in a more repressive environment, with business institutions and priorities intact.

Technological Change. More generally, the sharp reductions in price and increased availability of VCRs, camcorders, fax machines, computers, modems, E-mail, Internet, and desktop computer-publishing have made possible easier communication among individuals, lower cost production of journals and books, and new possibilities for TV production and programming. Of course, the telephone, mimeograph, offset printing and Xerox machines had the same potential earlier and were put to good use, but they never put the establishment up against the wall. Those with money and power tend to guide innovation and put technologies to use first, and frequently have moved on to something better by the time citizens gain access to these things. Camcorders do not solve the problem of producing really attractive TV programs, let alone getting them widely distributed and shown. While books may be produced more cheaply with new desktop facilities, changes in commercial distribution—blockbusters, saturation advertising, deals with the increasingly concentrated distribution networks—may easily keep dissident books as marginalized as ever. It remains to be seen whether the Internet will prove an exception to this tradition of commercial domination.

In perhaps the most dramatic illustration of the problem of catch-up, the new communications technologies in the possession of the Pentagon and mainstream media during the Persian Gulf War—video, satellite, and computer—conferred a new and enormous power to mold images, block out history and context, and make instant history. John M. Phelan entitles his analysis of the new, centrally controlled communications technology, "Image Industry Erodes Political Space."[27] And George Gerbner points out that "past, present, and future can now be packaged, witnessed, and frozen into memorable moving imagery of instant history—scripted, directed, and produced by the winners."[28]

The point is that it is important for democratic media advancement that democratic participants be alert to and take advantage of every technological innovation. The growth of common dissident carriers like EcoNet, LBBS, and PeaceNet has been important in providing tools for education,[29] research, and a means of communication among activists. But the problems of reaching large audiences, as opposed to democratic activists being able to communicate more efficiently within and between small groups, remain challenging and severe.

Concluding Note

The trend of media evolution is paradoxical: On the one hand, there is an ongoing main drift in the West toward increasing media centralization and commercialization and a corresponding weakening of the public sector. On the other hand, the civic sphere of nongovernmental and noncommercial media and computer networks linked to grassroots organizations and minority groups has displayed considerable vitality; and even though it has been pressed to defend its relative position overall, it has a greater potential than ever for coordinating actions and keeping activists at home and abroad informed.

It has been argued in this chapter that the civic sector is the locus of the truly democratic media and that genuine democratization in Western societies is going to be contingent on its great enlargement. Those actively seeking the democratization of the media should seek first to enlarge the civic sphere by every possible avenue, to strengthen the public sector by increasing its autonomy and funding, and lastly to contain or shrink the commercial sector and try to tap it for revenue for the civic sector. Funding this sector properly is going to require government intervention. Media democrats should be preparing the moral and political environment for such financial support, while doing their utmost to advance the cause of existing democratic media.

—Z Papers, January 1992

Chapter Twenty-Seven

Epilogue

The market, in its twofold sense of the dominant global firms, and the system of organizing human existence through market exchanges, has gone from triumph to triumph over the past 15 years. The collapse of the Soviet bloc and rapid moves to private-market economies by its separate elements; the Chinese steps toward integration into the world market; and the disintegration of the Non-Aligned Movement of Third World countries in the wake of the 1980s recession, debt crisis, and aggressive tactics employed by the Great Powers, were important features and landmarks of these successes. So also has been the decline in numbers and power of labor unions in the West, whose weakening has paralleled the increasing resources, mobility, confidence, and boldness of business leaders.

The triumph has extended to politics, ideology, and economic and social policy. Business's campaign for privatization at home and abroad has given the private sector added resources and reduced both the power of governments to manage economic affairs and the ability of ordinary citizens to use government for their own ends. To the citizenry and politicians there appears to be no viable option to establishing a favorable business climate as the means of providing jobs and improving well-being. The consequences have been increasing inequality, economic and social polarization, and growing unemployment and insecurity for ordinary people across the globe. Any protests have thus far been channeled toward scapegoats, including government, but not the market itself, although it is the market that is doing much of the dirty work while stymying any constructive government response. The market is on a roll.

In its further ideological expression, the triumph of the market is seen as the victory of "freedom" (and the "end of history"). In this version, freedom is, first and foremost, economic freedom, which is not conditioned on there being either equality of opportunity and resources or competition—it requires only the right of those with capital to use it freely. This suggests that labor organizations might be seen as incompatible with "freedom," and that democracy itself, with its potential for mobilization by ordinary citizens to regulate and tax business, might also threaten "freedom." This may help explain why bankers, the IMF and the Chicago School of economists welcomed Pinochet's abrogation of democracy in Chile in 1973, which crushed labor unions and terminated government interventions that "repressed" capital markets.

It is of course argued that it is the market economies that have democratic political institutions, and that even Chile has returned to the democratic fold. But if the maintenance of democratic institutions was not contingent on the adequacy of their service to capital—if it were not a means, rather than an end—why would the termination of democracy and a system of ruthless state terror be supported in the first place? And Chile was far from unique in its military establishment's obliteration of democracy with the tacit or open support of capital, private and international financial institutions, and political leaders of the democratic West.[1] Furthermore, although Chile did return to democratic forms, it did so only after an extended period of deadly attacks on oppositional sectors (labor, peasant organizations, left political groups and leaders), a restructuring of government, elite land seizures, corporate mergers, and massive borrowing abroad. The terrorizing army that had illegally seized power, killed thousands, and made radical changes in the economic, social, and political order not only suffered no punishment for its crimes, it remains above the law, with special constitutional powers and rights in the area of "security."

The new democracy is therefore crippled by the long "class cleansing" by state terror, the continued military power and threat, and other internal and external constraints on structural or policy change. As in the case of NAFTA, which "locked in" the people of Mexico to economic arrangements that they did not choose,[2] the new institutions imposed during the dictatorship locked the people of Chile into a market system stripped of many of its earlier social democratic features. They are no longer free to choose their basic institutional arrangements or policies.

The phrases "market democracies" or "market-based democracies"—now regularly invoked by President Clinton and other spokespersons for the New World Order (NWO) to describe the kinds of societies spreading throughout the world that they want to support—are more and more clearly oxymorons. The market in its modern manifestations, with agents like Pinochet, Salinas, and the IMF doing much of its dirty work, removes the substance from democratic forms, leaving a largely empty shell.

In his book, *The Stages of Economic Growth*, Walt W. Rostow contrasted the Soviet Union, which was "expansionist," with the West, which sought only "partnership" in the Third World, and to "keep open the possibility of progressive, democratic development."[3] But with whom does the West seek partnership in the Third World? In Chile, its partner was the dictator Pinochet; in the Philippines in 1972 the United States supported Ferdinand Marcos's elimination of democratic forms, with Marcos openly asking U.S. transnational corporations what he could do to serve them.[4] In Zaire, the United States entered into a partnership with Mobutu—one of the most brazen looters of the 20th century—willing to subordinate any popular interests to the demands of U.S. bankers and businesspeople.[5] There are no known cases where the Western "partnerships" in the Third World extended to non-elite (and therefore non-minority) elements of a society.

It is also increasingly clear that Rostow's assertion that the West wants to "keep open the possibility of progressive, democratic development" in the Third World is completely false, unless the words are used tautologically so that only the neoliberal agenda sponsored by the TNCs and IMF is consistent with "progressive, democratic development." Any alternative routes, like following a basic-needs strategy, putting a first priority on reducing inequality and protecting and strengthening the weak, or attempting to protect indigenous culture and national independence by maintaining distance from powerful foreign sharks, are not only unacceptable to the market, they elicit boycotts, subversion, and military threats and attacks.

All through the Cold War era, an important part of Western propaganda was that the enemy was prone to use force and compel adherence to their preferred development path, and that in the absence of communism people would be free to choose. But the dominant powers of the West are enforcing in each and every country the rule that only an open, free-enterprise system—with the rights of the local populace subordinate to the demands of the market—is tolerable. The West has *closed down* "the possibility of progressive, democratic development" in the Third World.

The coercive features underlying the triumph of the market are underrated. Under the guise of "containment" the West opposed every case of indigenous radical institutional change by using economic warfare and subversion, and very often direct or proxy military attack as well. The Russian and Chinese revolutions were fought militarily and then subjected to decades of economic warfare, including an arms race designed in part to divert resources that might otherwise be used for constructive development. Radical or even social democratic transformations in Vietnam, Cuba, Guatemala, Iran, Nicaragua, Mozambique, and Angola were opposed by devastating direct or sponsored military attacks, along with sustained boycotts and other forms of economic and political warfare. This does not exhaust the list.[6]

Trade, aid, and lending policies have been used systematically to coerce recalcitrants; and these instruments are being employed currently on a massive scale to force Second and Third World countries into the market order and to compel them to follow its rules.[7] The rules require that institutions be established and policies followed that give first priority to the needs of foreign investors and a local elite, and that place the burdens of any requisite adjustment and austerity mainly on the local non-elite majority.[8] These rules are imposed on the "market democracies" by external, market-friendly forces, without the consent of the indigenous governed.

The rule of the market is a serious threat to human welfare. Adam Smith himself regarded a government-by-merchants as the worst possible for the community interest.[9] The market threatens, first, because it presses its own short-term interests relentlessly. Even where its individual members might tend to give some weight to long-term effects, they are constrained by the need to show short-term results and by the force of competition.[10] The market has a long record of myopia, forgetting past calamities in the heat of competitive battle and immediate experience. The market may also be influenced by the ideological rationalizations thrown up by its own sponsored intellectuals, who explain why markets can do it all.[11] The problem of thinking long term is also made more difficult by globalization, which has increased competition and enlarged and diversified the numbers of firms and governments that would have to accept broader perspectives.

The market therefore tends to take aggressive advantage of its immediate opportunities and power. It can stymie governments that want to take a larger view, and eventually replace them with others more amenable. Only the parties of the market will be able to act decisively—those not adequately market friendly will be defunded, discredited by the corporate media, and penalized by responsive market actions (capital flight, higher interest rates). Unable to serve their popular constituency, insufficiently market friendly governments will lose popularity and the political spectrum will ratchet to the right. With No Other Option, ordinary citizens will look for scapegoats, and the market friendly parties, intellectuals, and media will provide them—the threat of the government itself (except for the police and military establishment), immigrants, the criminal proclivities of genetically inferior races, narcoterrorists and Islamic terrorists.

Environmental protection will be difficult in the new market-friendly order, given the short planning horizon of the TNCs, their sizable numbers and the force of competition, their power over governments and the mass media, and the pressures on the environment that result from growth and immiseration. Neoliberalism erodes the value of community, human solidarity, and the concept of limits to human acquisition and encroachments on nature. It encourages a blind faith in market processes and technological fixes to solve all problems. The environment suffers grievously as TNCs reveling in unconstrained growth and arbitrage ruthlessly strip and mine land, forests, rivers, and oceans, and poor people do the same on a lesser scale in a struggle to survive.[12]

It is hard at this juncture to imagine the global community attacking environmental issues by collective, planned action. In addition to the previously mentioned factors of ideology, private interest and power, and the force of competition, the effects of environmental damage are diffuse and some are long term and uncertain. And the forces of the market are able to co-opt experts, obfuscate issues with the help of hired "science" and propaganda, and play up job loss as a cost of environmental protection. They are also able to deflect threatening policy by sponsoring and supporting forces of irrationality: The "Wise Use" movement is well funded by the polluting community, and the market was pleased with, and in important respects responsible for, the coming into power of Newt Gingrich and his barbarian cohort in the election of 1994.[13] They are busily mistranslating general dissatisfaction with the performance of the government and economy into further attacks on labor, the welfare state, and environmental regulation.[14]

Prognosis

The naïve forecaster's rule is that tomorrow will be much like yesterday and today. This rule is a sound one, or at least a good first approximation, if the forces clearly shaping yesterday and today are in full bloom and are still consolidating their position of power, and if their opponents and victims are in disarray and without any strategic or programmatic answer to their difficulties. As this is the current reality, the prognosis here for the short and intermediate terms cannot be optimistic. The market is still extending its sway, and its economic, political, and ideological power continues to overwhelm any potential opposition and push the political spectrum to the right. Furthermore, the victories of capital, defeats of the Left, and weakness of existing oppositional groups create a sense of hopelessness that further impedes organization and action. The power of capital is still cumulating, making non-market friendly institutional changes or policy actions impractical and virtually unthinkable.

In the longer term, however, and perhaps even within the next decade or so, the neoliberal regime is going to run into serious difficulties that may well terminate its rule. By its aggressive exploitation of immediate opportunities that benefit a small elite, and its vetoing of structural changes and policies serving the bottom 80 percent, the NWO is witnessing a rapid social and economic polarization and a global "marginalization of the people." As several billion people remain mired in poverty in the Third World and hundreds of millions in the West suffer wage and benefit attrition, increased unemployment, and growing insecurity while a small elite thrives, the ground is being laid for upheavals and "crises of democracy" that will make the 1960s pale into insignificance. The gross inequalities are likely to produce slower growth from a deficiency of effective demand along with instability from social pain and outrage. The problems will be exacerbated and the challenges will escalate when ecological/environmental damage takes a further and greater toll on human health and well-being (beyond merely slowing down the rate of growth).

It is obvious that economic growth rates of 2-3 percent per year are not sustainable on this small planet for another 100 years, and that a new regime of values and economic organization and distribution will be necessary for human survival in the long run. The present system of neoliberal growth has no long-term future for this reason, but it may not last even that long because the current processes of exploitation and marginalization are rapidly creating serious "contradictions."

It is possible that the ongoing marginalization/polarization process can continue for quite a few years by a combination of propaganda, selective co-optation and bribery, the preservation of some social services, moderate repression, and the absence of any plausible alternatives—witness the Mexican people's passivity up to the time of the localized Chiapas rebellion in the face of large real-income declines, staggering inequality, and massive abuses of state power over many years. But passivity is by no means assured and is unlikely to hold for long in the West where expectations of material advance are strong and the peoples increasingly disrespectful of traditional authority. They are not likely to be bamboozled indefinitely with diversions and scapegoats; they will insist on real gains, and that is what the NWO and neoliberal project serve to prevent.

If the restless multitude gets too demanding we may see increasing resort to more serious repression. But without the Red Menace to justify massive secret police operations, repression may be more difficult than in the past and the objective of "restoring order" may not permit operations adequate to actually restore order. The Russian and Eastern European experience suggests that "moderate" law-and-order regimes confronting mass disaffection might now be threatened with uncontrollable disorder and potential state fragmentation.

It is possible that increasing distress might produce law-and-order regimes with strong leaders who would attempt to discipline capital, impose controls on global capital movements, and try to contain mass unrest by actually redistributing wealth and income and reconstructing welfare states. It is also possible that more brutal regimes might emerge to keep the rabble in line by advanced state terror à la Pinochet or Hitler.

It is at least conceivable that the reality of an interdependent global economy might, under conditions of great distress, produce a single global political entity with real powers to deal with high-priority global problems. It is difficult to imagine how this new political order could be democratic in any sense. However, it is possible that it could serve the global TNCs and dominant states in the same fashion as national states serve their dominant interests.

A final possibility is that genuine democratic forces might revive or organize under the pressures of neoliberalism and help rehabilitate national, regional, and local politics to serve a popular interest. Admittedly this possibility does not look promising at this moment, but it is the only road to a democratic, or perhaps any, future and there are some very elemental grounds for hopefulness in the longer pull. There are vast numbers of local activists at work trying to organize their communities and building networks to others. The rapid changes in communications technologies have opened up space for community and solidarity work, and there is a ferment in local communications[15] as well as in other community actions.[16]

Beyond this, democrats can build from the grassroots with two important bases of hope and confidence: one is that neoliberalism is sure to fail and will generate ever larger global forces of resistance; the second is that the temporarily victorious market order is inhuman, immiserates vast numbers, and is designed to serve a tiny elite, so that not only numbers but justice is on our side. It is for this reason that the great Brazilian Catholic Bishop Pedro Casadaliga believes "we are the defeated soldiers of an unbeatable army."[17]

Notes

Notes to the Preface

1. *Business Week* reports that the basic method used by businesses in their "successful anti-union war" has been "illegally firing thousands of workers for exercising their rights to organize." "Unlawful firings occurred in one-third of all representation elections in the late '80s, vs. 8 percent in the late '60s." Aaron Bernstein, "Why America Needs Unions, But Not the Kind It Now Has," May 23, 1994, p. 70.
2. Tony Horwitz, "9 to Nowhere: These Six Growth Jobs Are Dull, Dead-End, Sometimes Dangerous," *Wall Street Journal*, Dec. 1, 1994, p. 1.
3. Describing an international conference in Indonesia, reporter Merrill Goozner writes: "But there will be little, if anything, said about the Dickensian world only a few miles away created by some of that investment." "Asian labor: Wages of shame," *Chicago Tribune*, Nov. 6, 1994, p. 20.
4. Fred Block et al, *The Mean Season: The Attack on the Welfare State*, New York: Random House, 1987; Linda Gordon, ed., *Women, the State, and Welfare*, Madison: University of Wisconsin Press, 1990; "Women and Welfare Reform," *Social Justice*, Spring 1994 (full issue on topic).
5. Goozner, above, note 3; Goozner and Uli Schmetzer, "Growing workplace fatalities dim glow of Chinese economy," *Chicago Tribune*, Nov. 8, 1994; Noam Chomsky, *Year 501: The Conquest Continues*, Boston: South End Press, chaps. 3, 4, and 7, 1993; Kevin Danaher, ed., *50 Years Is Enough: The Case Against The World Bank and the International Monetary Fund*, Boston: South End Press, 1994.

Notes to Chapter 1

1. As in Michael Novak's vision; see Chapter 8 below.
2. Ronald Alsop, "Seven-Up's Ads on Children's TV Shows Risk Alienating Health-Conscious Parents" Dec. 9, 1988, Sec. 2, p. 1.
3. Erik Barnouw, *The Sponsor: Notes on a Modern Potentate*, New York: Oxford University Press, 1978, pp. 96-97.
4. "Credit cards pay prostitutes," *Financial Times*, Nov. 3, 1994, p. 9.
5. "Sex tourism booming in northeastern Brazil," *Latinamerica Press*, March 3, 1994, p. 2.1.
6. Marlise Simons, "In Europe's Brothels, Women From the East," *New York Times*, June 9, 1993, p. A1.
7. Huntly Collins, "HIV is spread in Asia by the sex industry and its captives," *Philadelphia Inquirer*, Aug. 15, 1994, p. A1.
8. Marlise Simons, "The Sex Market: Scourge on the World's Children," April 9, 1993, p. A3.

9. See Noam Chomsky, *World Orders Old and New*, New York: Columbia University Press, 1994, pp. 134, 137 and citations given there.

10. Several clandestine networks devoted to the buying and selling of babies operate in Bolivia, for example, according to Lisselotte Bauer de Barragan, president of the government's National Institute for Children, Women and the Family. These networks allegedly pull in $370,000 a month from the trafficking in children; they operate houses known as "fattening centers" to which the children are sent after being bought or stolen from their mothers, so that the "merchandise" will look good (Ramiro Lopez, "Bolivia: Trafficking in children," *Latinamerica Press*, Dec. 22, 1994, p. 6).

11. As was pointed out by Amnesty International, "Despite protests to the contrary by the governments concerned, they [death squads in Latin America] operate with impunity, outside the law but fully integrated into the regular security network" (*Disappearances: A workbook*, AI, 1980, p. 101.). On the U.S. support and sponsorship of the "regular security network" itself, see Edward S. Herman, *The Real Terror Network*, Boston: South End Press, 1982, pp. 121-132. One Salvadoran death squad was even named for Jeane Kirkpatrick, the Reagan administration Ambassador to the UN in the early 1980s, in recognition of her political and spiritual support of death squad activities in Central America in that era.

12. On the U.S. role in organizing and funding the contras, see Holly Sklar, *Washington's War On Nicaragua*, Boston: South End Press, 1988; Thomas Walker, ed., *Reagan Versus the Sandinistas*, Boulder: Westview, 1987.

13. The "strategy of tension" was an effort by the Italian right wing in the late 1960s to destabilize the country by a series of terrorist bombings and massacres, effectively blamed on the Left, and designed to produce a moral environment for a rightist coup (several were tried in this period). The strategy was implemented and protected by important sectors of the state apparatus (see Edward Herman and Frank Brodhead, *The Rise and Fall of the Bulgarian Connection*, New York: Sheridan Square, 1986, pp. 85-87).

14. The Atlanta Olympic Conscience Coalition estimates that the 1996 Atlanta games will displace over 9,700 low-and moderate-income residents (Metro Atlanta Task Force for the Homeless, *Homelessness in Metropolitan Atlanta*, 1994, Appendix B). And a Greek restaurant in Atlanta was forced to change its name from Olympic to Olympia to ensure exclusive name benefits to the sponsors (Karen Heller, "Selling the Olympics," *Philadelphia Inquirer Magazine*, June 23, 1995).

15. An internal audit of Brown Williamson Tobacco Company made public in 1994 showed that the company had spent a million dollars over a four-year period to get its cigarettes exhibited in movies. Sylvester Stallone was paid $500,000 to use its cigarettes in five feature films (including *Godfather III*, *Rambo*, and *Rocky IV*); Paul Newman got a $42,307 car and other amenities for helping advance cigarette images. (Philip Hilts, "Company Spent $1 Million to Put Cigarettes in Movies, Memos Show," *New York Times*, May 20, 1994, p. A26.)

16. Kyle Pope, "Product Placements Creep Into Video Games," *Wall Street Journal*, Dec. 5, 1994, p. B1.

17. Teri Agins, "Is It a TV Show? Or Is It Advertising?," *Wall Street Journal*, May 10, 1994, p. B1.

18. Barnouw, *The Sponsor*, p. 95.

19. Richard Barnet and John Cavanagh, *Global Dreams: Imperial Corporations and the New World Order*, New York: Simon and Schuster, 1994, pp. 37-38.

20. An illustration of bargaining down at the expense of schools is given in Chapter 27, note 10.

21. The number of schools involved was approximately 12,000 at the end of 1994; some eight million children were reached by Channel One.

22. "Selling To School Kids," *Consumer Reports*, May 1995, pp. 327-329.

23. Leah Brumer, "Up the Sandbox: Safe Fun in 'America's Playground,' " *Express*, Aug. 26, 1994.

24. Debora Silverman, *Selling Culture: Bloomingdale's, Diana Vreeland, and the New Aristocracy of Taste in Reagan's America*, New York: Pantheon, 1986.

25. These quotes are taken from Herbert Schiller's important book *Culture, Inc.: The Corporate Takeover of Public Expression*, New York: Oxford, 1989.

26. This concept is applied to the broadcasting field in Chapter 22, below.

27. In the spring of 1995, the advertising fraternity's leading newspaper, *Advertising Age*, was exceptionally preoccupied with the advertising and sales possibilities of the Internet, reflecting the interests of the industry. For further discussion of the Internet, and citations, see Chapter 26.

Notes to Chapter 2

1. A negative externality is a real cost that a private firm is able to pass off on the rest of society as a result of ambiguities in property rights (Who owns the air? Who has the right to use a public waterway?), traditional usage, and the power of those externalizing their costs that enables them to protect their established behavior. Externalizing costs means that the prices of the goods in question will not reflect the real social cost of production and they will tend to be produced to excess, with a resulting systematic misallocation of resources and inequitable distribution of the burden of production costs. See E. J. Mishan, *Economics For Social Decisions: Elements of Cost-Benefit Analysis*, New York: Praeger, 1978, Part III.

2. The classic article is Horace M. Gray, "The Passing of the Public Utility Concept," *Journal of Land & Public Utility Economics*, Feb. 1940, pp. 8-20.

3. See David Vogel, "Why Businessmen Distrust Their State: The Political Consciousness of American Corporate Executives," *British Journal of Political Science*, Jan. 1978; also, Edward S. Herman, *Corporate Control, Corporate Power*, Cambridge: Cambridge University Press, 1981, chap. 5 "Government and the Large Corporation."

4. Specialists in regulation have noted that the ICC, which was long famous for serving the interests of the regulated industry, was the regulatory commission most generously rewarded by Congress and the executive branch, presumably reflecting industry approval of its behavior. See Martin Glaeser, *Public Utilities in American Capitalism*, New York: Macmillan, 1957, p. 249.

5. In a nice illustration of this Republican proclivity, Lynne Cheney, formerly a Bush administration head of the National Endowment for the Humanities, joined the far-right throng in urging the complete liquidation of the Endowment which she had managed: "Kill My Old Agency, Please," *Wall Street Journal*, Jan. 24, 1995, p. 22.

6. For poll data showing the public's strong commitment to environmental protection, see Thomas Ferguson and Joel Rogers, *Right Turn: The Decline*

of the Democrats and the Future of American Politics, New York: Hill and Wang, 1986, pp.14-15.

7. Ibid., throughout. Also, Jim Sibbison, "Environmental Reporters: Prisoners of Gullibility," *Washington Monthly*, March 1984.

8. R. Jeffrey Smith, "Covering the EPA, or Wake Me Up If Anything Happens," *Columbia Journalism Review*, Sept.-Oct. 1983, pp. 29-35.

9. See R. Dan Brumbaugh, *Thrifts Under Siege*, Cambridge, MA: Ballinger, 1988; Kathleen Day, *S & L Hell*, New York: Norton, 1993; Martin Mayer, *The Greatest-Ever Bank Robbery: The Collapse of the Savings and Loan Industry*, New York: Charles Scribner's, 1990; Stephen Pizzo et al, *Inside Job: The Looting of America's Savings and Loans*, New York: McGraw-Hill, 1989.

10. Hyman Minsky, *Can "It" Happen Again? Essays on Instability and Finance*, Aronok, NY: M. E. Sharpe, 1982; Gary Dymski and Robert Pollin, eds., *New Perspectives in Monetary Macroeconomics: Explorations in the Tradition of Hyman P. Minsky*, Ann Arbor: University of Michigan Press, 1994; Jack Guttentag and Richard Herring, *Disaster Myopia in International Banking*, Princeton: Essays in International Finance, no. 164, Sept. 1986.

11. William McDonough, "The Global Derivatives Market," *Federal Reserve Bank of New York Quarterly Review*, Autumn 1993, p. 5. McDonough, president of the New York Federal Reserve, expresses serious concern over the threat of derivatives in this brief account.

Notes to Chapter 3

1. William Shepherd, ed., *Public Enterprise: Economic Analysis of Theory and Practice*, Lexington, MA: Lexington Books, 1976; Stuart Holland, *The State as Entrepreneur*, White Plains, NY: International Arts and Sciences Press, 1972.

2. David Felix, "Technological Dualism in Late Industrializers: On Theory, History, and Policy," *Journal of Economic History*, March 1974, pp. 217-228.

3. See Michael Tanzer's classic account in *The Political Economy of International Oil and the Underdeveloped Countries*, Boston: Beacon Press, 1969.

4. Richard Hellman, *Government Competition in the Electric Utility Industry*, New York: Praeger, 1972, chap. 4. According to one account, "Events seem to be establishing the T.V.A. as an effective adjunct to commission regulation in uncovering the potentialities of attracting, and rendering service economically to, wider ranges of consumption; and in forcing private industry, by threat of competition, to a fuller development of these possibilities." (Leverett Lyon and Victor Abramson, *Government and Economic Life*, Washington, DC: Brookings, 1940, vol. 2, p. 743.)

5. See "Throwing away the yardstick," chap. 7 in H. L. Nieburg, *In the Name of Science*, Chicago: Quadrangle, 1966.

6. See *Government Competition With Private Business*, Report of the Select Committee on Small Business on Discontinuance of Commercial-Type Operations by the Federal Government, Senate Rep. No. 1015, Aug. 19, 1957.

7. John Blair, *Economic Concentration*, New York: Harcourt Brace Jovanovich, 1972, pp. 380-85.

8. David Felix, "Debt Crisis Adjustment in Latin America: Have the Hardships Been Necessary?," Working Paper 170, Department of Economics, St. Louis: Washington University, Sept. 1992, p. 15.

9. Ibid., p. 16.

10. It was of course argued that the bailout was needed to avoid a financial crisis. But as the *Financial Times* noted editorially (Feb. 11-12, 1995), "Perhaps a financial crisis should be defined as one that worries Washington."

11. Ibid., p. 17.

12. Ibid., p. 19.

13. Ibid.

14. Chrystia Freeland, "Row over Russian way of making capitalists," *Financial Times*, June 15, 1995, p. 3. This article discusses in detail one case of seizure of majority control of a monopoly producer of tin by its former top manager.

15. David Mandel, "Actually Existing Privatization: An Interview With Yurii Marenich," *Monthly Review*, March 1992, p. 22.

16. Felix, above note 8, pp. 19-26.

17. Ibid., pp. 23-25. As Felix points out, the Latin American leaders never even requested help from their masters in controlling capital flight; the U.S. banks benefited enormously from the flight and had special "private banking" divisions to expedite it; and the Reagan administration backed capital flight tangibly by abolishing the withholding tax on interest income to non-resident owners of U.S. securities and by issuing "bearer bonds" to facilitate clandestine ownership (which would of course include drug money).

Notes to Chapter 4

1. See his *The New Economics One Decade Older*, Princeton: Princeton University Press, 1974, pp. 44-50.

2. From his *Political Discourses*, quoted in Edgar S. Furniss, *The Position of the Laborer in a System of Nationalism*, Boston: Houghton Mifflin, 1920, p. 173.

3. Ibid., p. 203.

Notes to Chapter 5

1. Bruce Owen and Ronald Braeutigam, *The Regulation Game*, Cambridge, MA: Ballinger, 1978, p. xv.

2. See John Saloma III, *Ominous Politics: The New Conservative Labyrinth*, New York: Hill and Wang, 1984; Lawrence C. Soley, *Leasing the Ivory Tower: The Corporate Takeover of Academia*, Boston: South End Press, 1995.

3. Alex Carey, *Taking the Risk Out of Democracy: Propaganda in the US and Australia*, Sydney, Australia: University of New South Wales Press, 1995, p. 107.

4. William Brainard and Richard Cooper, "Empirical Monetary Macroeconomics: What Have We Learned in the Last 25 Years?," *American Economic Review*, May, 1975, pp. 169-170.

5. Elton Rayack, *Not So Free to Choose*, New York: Praeger, 1987.

6. Paul Diesing, "Hypothesis Testing and Data Interpretation: The Case of Milton Friedman," *Research in the History of Economic Thought and Methodology*, vol. 3, pp. 61-69.

7. Irwin Friend and Edward S. Herman, "The S.E.C. Through a Glass Darkly," *Journal of Business*, Oct. 1964, pp. 382-405.

8. A good summary and criticism of Peltzman on drugs and auto safety is given in Mark Green and Norman Waitzman, *Business War on the Law: An*

Analysis of the Benefits of Federal Health/Safety Enforcement, Corporate Accountability Research Group, 1979.

9. Quoted in Martin Mayer, *The Greatest-Ever Bank Robbery: The Collapse of the Savings and Loan Industry,* New York: Charles Scribner's, 1990, p. 140.
10. Ibid., pp. 139-140.
11. Richard B. DuBoff and Edward S. Herman, "The Promotional-Financial Dynamic of Merger Movements: A Historical Perspective," *Journal of Economic Issues,* March 1989.
12. Ellen Magenheim and Dennis Mueller, "Are Acquiring Firm Shareholders Better Off After an Acquisition?," in John Coffee et al, eds., *Knights, Raiders, and Targets,* New York: Oxford University Press, 1988.
13. Michael Jensen and Richard Ruback, "The Market for Corporate Control: The Scientific Evidence," *Journal of Financial Economics,* 1983, p. 5.

Notes to Chapter 6

1. For a fuller account, see Richard B. Du Boff and Edward S. Herman, "The New Economics: Handmaiden of Inspired Truth," *Review of Radical Political Economics,* August 1972.
2. James Tobin, *National Economic Policy,* New Haven: Yale University Press, 1966, p. 59 (originally published in the *Yale Review,* March 1958).
3. Ibid., p. 20.
4. Walter Heller, *New Dimensions of Political Economy,* Cambridge, MA: Harvard University Press, 1967, pp. 10-12.
5. David Felix, "On the Natural Rate of Unemployment and the Impotence of Macroeconomic Policy Activism," Working Paper 48, Dept. of Economics, Washington University in St. Louis, Feb. 1983, pp. 10-21; Angus Maddison, "Western Economic Performance in the 1970s: A Perspective and Assessment," Banca Nazionale del Lavoro, *Quarterly Review,* Sept. 1980.
6. Alice Amsden, *Asia's Next Giant: South Korea and Late Industrialization,* New York: Oxford University Press, 1989; Robert Wade, *Governing the Market: Economic Theory and the Role of Government in East Asian Industrialization,* Princeton: Princeton University Press, 1990.
7. John Cavanagh, et al, *Trading Freedom,* San Francisco: Institute for Food and Development Policy, 1992, p. 56.
8. See works cited in note 6; also, Alice Amsden, Jacek Kochanowicz and Lance Taylor, *The Market Meets Its Match: Restructuring the Economies of Eastern Europe,* Cambridge, MA: Harvard University Press, 1994, pp. 8-10 and throughout; David Felix, "The Technological Factor in Socioeconomic Dualism," *Economic Development and Cultural Change,* 1977 (Supp.), pp. 183-211.
9. For a detailed account of how this happened in the large country of Brazil, see Jan Black, *United States Penetration of Brazil,* Philadelphia: University of Pennsylvania Press, 1978.
10. See Chakravarthi Raghavan, *Recolonization: GATT, the Uruguay Round & the Third World,* London: Zed, 1990.
11. A joint venture model is spelled out in Herman, *The Real Terror Network,* chap. 3.
12. Cavanagh et al, *Trading Freedom,* p. 57.
13. See Arthur MacEwan, "The 'Success' of Free Market Reforms," *Lies of Our Times,* Sept. 1991.

Notes to Chapter 7

1. The phrase is the subtitle of chap. 2 of Robert A. Brady's *The Spirit and Structure of German Fascism*, New York: Viking, 1937, which describes the accommodation of German science to the ideological and policy demands of the Nazi state.
2. Harry Magdoff, *The Age of Imperialism*, New York: Monthly Review Press, 1969.
3. "Two Myths About Mexico," *New York Times*, Aug. 22, 1993 (Op Ed).
4. Lawrence Mishel and Ruy A. Teixeira, "The Political Arithmetic of the NAFTA Vote," Briefing Paper, Economic Policy Institute, undated; Edward S. Herman, "NAFTA, Mexican Meltdown, and the Propaganda System," *Z Magazine*, September 1995.
5. "Lessons that Brazil can learn from Mexico," *Financial Times*, Oct. 16, 1991.
6. This is the title of a book by Dan La Botz, subtitled *Labor Suppression in Mexico Today*, Boston: South End Press, 1992.

Notes to Chapter 8

1. Michael Novak and Richard Shifter, *U.S. Speeches on Human Rights*, Speech of Feb. 25, 1981, p. 245. When the military government of Argentina was overthrown in 1983, the Commission appointed to study disappearances under its rule concluded that the armed forces response to terrorism was itself "a terrorism infinitely worse than that which they were combatting." As Reagan and Kirkpatrick had entered into warm relations with the military government in 1981, and were certainly not protesting its abuses, Novak engaged in the protection and support of this "infinitely worse" terrorism as he carried out his "human rights" duties.
2. An American Enterprise Institute/Simon and Schuster Publication, New York, 1982. This chapter is a review of Novak's book, published in *Monthly Review*.
3. This writer was present at a church meeting on the transnational corporation, where Novak, attending at the request of the corporate representatives, sternly addressed to the assembled churchmen two questions: Have you done as much for the poor as the businessman over the past several centuries? If not, don't you think that you should reassess your position toward Democratic Capitalism?
4. In 1981 Novak published a 55-page pamphlet entitled "Toward a Theology of the Corporation," courtesy of the American Enterprise Institute, an organization that has been extremely pleased with Novak's religious passion.
5. See the definition of externalities in Chapter 2, note 1.
6. Throughout his book Novak uses the word "community" wherever he wishes to convey a positive image. Where the corporation is about to abandon a plant, no "community" exists to be disrupted.
7. For a full account of the multileveled penetration and subversion, see Jan Black, *United States Penetration of Brazil*, Philadelphia: University of Pennsylvania Press, 1977.
8. Estimates of numbers subjected to torture in Latin America since 1964 run into the hundreds of thousands; the numbers murdered under state auspices start with over 15,000 in Argentina, over 20,000 in Chile, and over 100,000 in Guatemala. See Herman, *The Real Terror Network*, pp. 110-119.
9. In 1980-1981, 73 percent of all full professors at private four-year colleges received income from outside the institutions, the average outside income a sizable 24 percent of base salary. On the growing response of academy

economics to market demand, see above, Chapter 5, pp. 31-34. For updated information, see Lawrence Soley, *Leasing the Ivory Tower*, Boston: South End Press, 1995.

10. For example, do the mass media attack private enterprise as a system? Do they support and place in a favorable light radicals and radical change, or socialism and communism as ideals or as found in contemporary states? Some other real questions are discussed in the text below.

11. See Edward Herman, "All the Editorials Fit to Print: The Politics of 'Newsworthiness,'" in Robert Babe, ed., *Information and Communication in Economics*, Boston: Kluwer, 1994, pp. 177-181.

12. Robert Lichter and Stanley Rothman, "Media and Business Elites," *Public Opinion*, Oct.-Nov. 1981.

13. See Herbert Gans, "Are U.S. Journalists Dangerously Liberal?," *Columbia Journalism Review*, Nov.-Dec. 1985; Ferguson and Rogers, *Right Turn*, chap. 1.

14. S. Robert Lichter, Linda Lichter, and Stanley Rothman, "Video Villains: The TV Businessman, 1955-86," Washington, DC: Center for Media and Public Affairs, 1987. See also Joseph R. Dominick, "Business Coverage in Network Broadcasts," *Journalism Quarterly*, Summer 1981, pp. 179ff.

15. Todd Gitlin, "On Business and the Mass Media" (mimeo paper, 1981).

16. George Gerbner, Larry Gross, Michael Morgan and Nancy Signorielli, "Charting the Mainstream: Television's Contributions to Political Orientations," *Journal of Communication*, Spring 1982, pp 106-110.

17. "Television: The Mainstreaming of America," in *Business and the Media*, Conference Report, Yankelovich, Skelly and White, Nov. 19, 1981, p.15.

18. See David Caute, *The Great Fear, The Anti-Communist Purge Under Truman and Eisenhower*, Simon and Schuster, 1978; Charles J. V. Murphy, "McCarthy and the Businessmen," *Fortune*, April, 1954, p.180.

19. Michael Novak not only has books and articles produced and distributed lavishly with heavy subsidies, he has a degree of access to the opinion pages of *The New York Times* and *Wall Street Journal* unmatched by any radical critic in the United States. It is not just Novak's sponsors that explain this access—it is the bias of the mass media themselves, which run in the opposite direction from that asserted by neo-conservative mythology.

Notes to Chapter 9

1. As Thomas Ferguson, puts it, "Only if the electorate's degree of effective organization significantly increases...does it receive more than crumbs." *Golden Rule: Investment Theory of Party Competition and the Logic of Money-Driven Political Systems*, Chicago: University of Chicago Press, 1995, p.23.

2. See Frank Donner, *Protectors of Privilege: Red Squads and Police Repression in Urban America*. Berkeley: University of California Press, 1990.

3. Nelson Blackstock, *COINTELPRO: The FBI's Secret War on Political Freedom*, New York: Vintage, 1975; Frank Donner, *The Age of Surveillance: The Aims and Methods of America's Political Intelligence System*, New York: Vintage, 1981.

4. Ross Gelbspan, *Break-ins, Death Threats and the FBI: The Covert War Against the Central America Movement*, Boston: South End Press, 1991. On broader aspects of state repression in the 1980s, see Richard Curry, ed., *Freedom at Risk: Secrecy, Censorship, and Repression in the 1980s*,

Philadelphia: Temple University Press, 1988; Donna Demac, *Liberty Denied: The Current Rise of Censorship in America*, New Brunswick: Rutgers University Press, 1990.

5. Thomas Ferguson and Joel Rogers, *Right Turn*, New York: Hill and Wang, 1986. Ferguson's *Golden Rule* is a successor work, elaborating on and updating the investment theory.

6. Clinton won the election of 1992 on the basis of hazy and contradictory promises that gave considerable emphasis to populist aims like growth, jobs, and putting people first. However, he failed to meet those populist promises, shifting from expansionary actions to deficit reduction and putting his greatest effort into trade expansion policies. This failure was important in the Democratic election debacle of 1994. See Ferguson, *Golden Rule*, chap. 6 and postscript. See also Chapter 4, above.

7. As noted in the previous footnote, Clinton put populism on the agenda, but then couldn't or wouldn't do much in the way of implementing it. He was and remains under incessant pressure from business and its spokespersons in the press and the Democratic Leadership Council to abandon even the rhetoric and move "to the center" (i.e., cease to differ in any respect from the Republicans).

8. The same Richard Berke had an article in the *New York Times* of January 12, 1994, claiming that Democratic state chairpersons were distressed at the excessive liberalism of Clinton's new choice of party chairman, Senator Christopher Dodd ("State Democratic Chairman Criticize Dodd as Too Liberal"). Only two chairs are cited to this effect, and no alternative views are given by Berke. Berke and the *New York Times* regularly give uncritical attention to claims that push the Democratic Party further to the right. See Edward Herman, "Clinton the Leftist," *Lies of Our Times*, Sept. 1993, pp. 19-20.

9. Joel Bleifuss, "You Get What You Pay For," *In These Times*, April 17, 1995, p. 12.

10. This quote is a description of the general reaction of the business community in a Forbes-Gallup poll of 338 CEOs. Howard Banks, "A Christmas List," *Forbes*, Jan. 2, 1995, p. 121.

11. See further, Chapter 15, "The End of Democracy?" and Chapter 27, "Epilogue."

Notes to Chapter 10

1. For a review of some of these, see Noam Chomsky, *Turning the Tide*, Boston: South End Press, 1985; Mark Hertsgaard, *On Bended Knee*, New York: Farrar Straus Giroux, 1988; Robert Parry, *Fooling America*, New York: William Morrow, 1992.

2. Sir Frank Kitson, *Low Intensity Operations*, London: Faber, 1972, p. 3.

3. This statement was made in a speech by Stevenson before the National Association of Cost Accountants, as quoted by Corwin Edwards, "Can the Antitrust Laws Preserve Competition?," *American Economic Review*, March 1940, p. 167.

4. These were cases brought for the misuse of inside information by major market operators in the 1980s. See Connie Bruck, *The Predators' Ball*, New York: Simon and Schuster, 1988.

5. The U.S. prison population tripled since 1980, increasing from 501,886 to 1.5 million (with another 3.5 million on probation or parole). Fox

Butterfield, "More in U.S. Are in Prisons, Report Says," *New York Times,* August 10, 1995, p. A14. California's prison population exploded from 20,000 in 1980 to some 130,000 in 1994, and the state "is currently the third largest prison system on earth, exceeded only by China and the rest of the United States." Mike Davis, "California Uber Alles?," *Covert Action Quarterly,* Spring 1995, p. 19.

6. For many other quotes expressing support and satisfaction, see David Schmitz, " 'A Fine Young Revolution': The United States and the Fascist Revolution in Italy, 1919-1925," *Radical History Review,* no. 33, Sept. 1985. The phrase "fine young revolution" was used by the U.S. Ambassador to Rome, Richard Child.

7. Quoted from David Schmitz's *United States and Fascist Italy,* by Noam Chomsky, in *Deterring Democracy,* London: Verso, 1991, p. 41.

8. On U.S. involvement in the Brazilian military coup of 1964, see Jan Black, *United States Penetration of Brazil,* Philadelphia: University of Pennsylvania Press, 1978, pp. 27-56 and throughout. On U.S. participation in the Chilean military takeover of 1973, see James Petras and Morris Morley, *The United States and Chile,* New York: Monthly Review Press, 1975, and *Covert Action in Chile 1963-1973,* Staff Report of the Senate Select Committee on Intelligence Activities, Washington: Government Printing Office, 1975.

Notes to Chapter 11

1. Stephen J. Gould, *Ever Since Darwin,* New York: W.W. Norton, 1977, p. 247
2. Stephen J. Gould, *The Measure of Man,* New York: W.W. Norton, 1981, p. 32
3. Ibid, p. 120.
4. Stephen J. Gould, *An Urchin in the Storm,* New York: Norton, 1987, p. 126.
5. For a full discussion, see ibid., pp. 126-132.

Notes to Chapter 12

1. Joe Feagin, reviewing Chandler Davidson's *Race and Class in Texas Politics,* in the *Texas Observer,* August 23, 1991.
2. Robert Plotkin, "Injustice Department," *New York Times,* Aug. 3, 1981 (Op. Ed.).
3. "Really correct" thought is that which fits establishment premises, has establishment approval, and is therefore pushed front and center and treated uncritically by mainstream institutions. "Politically correct" is used by establishment forces to satirically designate unacceptable thought; its spokespersons are treated more harshly. See Chapter 14 below for an application of this distinction to holocausts.

Notes to Chapter 13

1. "Herman Kahn is a large man who thinks large thoughts that are largely naïve, wrong, or both," begins J. Patrick Lewis's funny and devastating review of Kahn's foray into social-economic-political issues in a 1982 book *The Coming Boom: Economic, Political and Social.* Lewis's review appeared in *Business and Society Review,* Winter 1983.
2. Drew Gilpin Faust, "Southern Stewardship: Intellectuals and the Proslavery Argument," *American Quarterly,* 1979, pp. 63-80.
3. See further, Chapter 11, "The New Racist Onslaught."
4. There was a huge exaggeration of Iraqi capabilities before and during the brief fighting (or rather slaughter) that was eventually recognized later, but

not challenged by the mainstream media at the relevant time (e.g., Eric Schmitt, "Study Lists Lower Tally of Iraqi Troops in Gulf War," *New York Times*, April 24, 1992, citing a three-fold exaggeration of Iraqi troops in place). The military casualty ratio of 150 to 150,000 (or more) is a measure of the disproportion in strength and the fact that the conflict was a massacre, not a war.

Notes to Chapter 14

1. See Edward Herman and Noam Chomsky, *Manufacturing Consent*, New York: Pantheon, 1988, chap. 4. When it was revealed during the Gates confirmation hearings in 1991 that CIA professionals had discounted the Sterling-Henze claims of a Bulgarian-KGB connection to the plot because the CIA had information based on its penetration of the Bulgarian secret services, the *New York Times*, which had used Sterling as a reporter and followed her model uncritically, failed to report this revelation. See Edward Herman and Howard Friel, " 'Stacking the Deck' on the Bulgarian Connection," *Lies of Our Times*, Nov. 1991.
2. See Christopher Simpson, *The Splendid Blond Beast: Money, Law, and Genocide in the Twentieth Century*, New York: Grove, 1993, chaps. 1-3.
3. On both the history and cover-up, see Torben Retboll, ed., *East Timor, Indonesia and the Western Democracies*, Copenhagen: IWGIA, 1980; Noam Chomsky and Edward Herman, *The Washington Connection and Third World Facism*, Boston: South End Press, 1979, chap. 3; Amnesty International, *Indonesia and East Timor: Power and Impunity: Human Rights Under the New Order*, London: AI Publications, 1994; John Pilger, "Death of a Nation: The Timor Conspiracy" (a documentary film, 1994); Peter Carey and G. Carter Bentley, eds., *East Timor at the Crossroads: The Forging of a Nation*, London: Cassell, 1995 (forthcoming).
4. Chomsky and Herman, *The Washington Connection*.
5. Hans Koning, *Columbus: His Enterprise*, New York: Monthly Review Press, 1976, p. 125.
6. See the excellent account of the history of demographic estimates by Lenore A. Stiffarm and Phil Ryan, Jr. in M. Annette Jaimes, ed., *The State of Native America: Genocide, Colonization and Resistance*, Boston: South End Press, 1992.
7. Ibid., p. 33.
8. Ibid., pp. 33-34.
9. Ibid., p. 3.
10. See especially Phyllis Johnson and David Martin, eds., *Frontline Southern Africa: Destructive Engagement*, New York: Four Walls Eight Windows, 1988.
11. L. S. Stravrianos, *Global Rift*, New York: William Morrow, 1981, p. 109.
12. Richard Cobban, *A History of Modern France*, Baltimore: Penguin, 1963, vol. 1, p. 74.
13. Ibid., p. 39.
14. "I have never talked or corresponded with a person knowledgeable in Vietnamese affairs who did not agree that had elections been held at the time of the fighting, possibly 80 percent of the population would have voted for the communist Ho Chi Minh as their leader rather than Chief of State Bao Dai." Dwight D. Eisenhower, *Mandate for Change*, Garden City, NY: Signet, 1963, p. 372.

15. Stanley Karnow, "Lessons of Running Viets' War," *Philadelphia Inquirer*, August 30, 1987.
16. H. Bruce Franklin, *M.I.A. or Myth-Making In America*, Brooklyn, NY: Lawrence Hill Books, 1992.

Notes to Chapter 15

1. Recently the name has been changed to European Union; the earlier designation, still widely used, will be retained in this chapter.
2. Tony Manwaring and Nick Sigler, eds., *Breaking the Nation: A Guide to Thatcher's Britain*, London: Pluto, 1985.
3. Joe Flexner, "Ontario Government Chooses Conservative Path," *Labor Notes*, July 1993, p. 9.
4. See Kim Moody's excellent, *An Injury to All: The Decline of American Unionism*, London: Verso, 1988.
5. Dean Baker, "Depressing Our Way to Recovery," *The American Prospect*, Winter 1994, pp. 110-114.
6. Frances Piven and Richard Cloward, *Why Amercians Don't Vote*, New York: Pantheon, 1988; Thomas Ferguson, "G.O.P. $$$ Talked; Did Voters Listen?," *The Nation*, Dec. 26, 1994.
7. The same is true of the Soviet bloc "collapsars," who are being thrust into virtual Third World status, entailing the traditional debt dependency.
8. Chomsky and Herman, *The Washington Connection*, chap. 2.
9. Edward Herman and Frank Brodhead, *Demonstration Elections: U.S.-Staged Elections in the Dominican Republic, Vietnam, and El Salvador*, Boston: South End Press, 1984, chap. 5.
10. After a huge time lag, and after the military junta had killed thousands and reneged on compromise agreements that left the army and police still intact and unpunished, in 1994 Clinton ordered the occupation of Haiti. Cedras was bought out and allowed to move comfortably to Panama; a "senior adminstration official" justified the buyout on the ground that "The social security system in Haiti doesn't work very well" (Elaine Sciolino, "Exile in Style Being Offered To Haiti Chiefs, *New York Times*, June 20, 1994). Once again, the U.S. continued to work with the military establishment and police, making it highly unlikely that Haiti will be able to escape from their clutches in the near future (see Paul Farmer, *The Uses of Haiti*, Monroe, ME: Common Courage, 1994, and introduction by Chomsky).
11. International Movement of Catholic Intellectuals and Professionals, "Voice from Northeastern·Brazil to III Conference of Bishops," Mexico, Nov. 1977, reprinted in *LADOC*, May-June 1978, p. 15.
12. Quoted in *Argentina Outreach*, March-April 1978, p. 3.
13. "La société sacrifieé au libre-échange," *Le Monde Diplomatique*, July 1993.

Notes to Chapter 16

1. Jack Heyman, "Jamaica's Manley converts to 'free marketeer'," *Guardian* (New York), Feb. 12, 1992.
2. See David Felix, "Economic Development: Takeoffs Into Unsustained Growth," *Social Research*, Summer 1969.
3. Robert Hudec, in Jagdish Bhagwati and Hugh Patrick, eds., *Aggressive Unilateralism*, Ann Arbor: University of Michigan Press, 1990, p. 114.
4. The phrase was used to describe Sandinista policies by the members of the Latin American Studies Association team of observers to the 1984

Nicaraguan election in their report "The Electoral Process in Nicaragua: Domestic and International Influences," Nov. 19, 1984.

5. Luis Echeverria, president of Mexico, 1970-76, tried a modest tilt toward equity, with the result that he "left office in a major foreign-exchange crisis and amidst rumors of a military coup, a novel and portentous phenomenon in postwar Mexico." (David Felix, in S. Hewlett and R. Weinert, eds., *Brazil and Mexico: Patterns in Late Development*, Boulder: Westview, 1982, p.295-6.) Peter Evans and Gary Gereffi point out that Echeverria's efforts led to a major capital outflow, and conclude that "Since one can hardly accuse Echeverria of being a radical, it would appear that the band of acceptable policy is exceedingly narrow and that the penalties for straying outside it are strict and swift" (ibid., p. 151)

6. This is the prime focus, and is spelled out in detail, in Herman, *The Real Terror Network*.

7. This was the phrase used in a *New York Times* editorial of July 1, 1986, which sneered at the World Court decision condemning the U.S.'s "unlawful use of force" in Nicaragua and suggested that it need not interfere with U.S. intervention.

8. In 1993, U.S. military spending was 3.8 times that of Japan and Germany combined and exceeded that of the next dozen largest military spenders combined (including Russia). The Clinton plan for 1999 envisages a level of military spending identical with that of 1980, at the height of the Cold War. Center for Defense Information, *The Defense Monitor*, vol. 23, No. 5, 1994.

Notes to Chapter 17

1. In April, 1993, at a time when the long U.S. boycott and embargo on Vietnam was showing signs of weakening, a document was discovered in Moscow files in which a Vietnamese official allegedly told Soviet officials back in 1972 that Vietnam held many more U.S. prisoners of war than they had publicly acknowledged. Despite the fact that the document was found by a man noted for a long-standing vendetta against Vietnam (Stephen Morris); that its discovery was suspiciously timed; that its authenticity was vociferously denied by the alleged Vietnamese author; and that there was internal evidence of forgery, the media gave it headline attention as presumably true (e.g., Celestine Bohlen, "Files Said to Show Hanoi Lied in '72 On Prisoner Totals," *New York Times*, April 12, 1993, p. A1). This was a rerun of previous acts of media gullibility (see H. Bruce Franklin, "Interview" in *Lies of Our Times*, Dec. 1993). It had the familiar characteristic, also, that refutations received much less attention and prominence than the original charges. For a detailed analysis of the factual errors and stylistic discrepancies in the discovered document, see Nayan Chanda, "Research and Destroy," in the *Far Eastern Economic Review*, May 6, 1993.

2. Israel Shahak shows that orthodox Judaism in Israel today retains the rampant ethnocentrism and dehumanization of outsiders that is displayed in the Old Testament, in *Jewish History, Jewish Religion: The Weight of Three Thousand Years*, London: Pluto, 1994.

3. Phillip Shabecoff, "Murder Verdict Eased in Vietnam," *New York Times*, March 31, 1990.

4. James Ferguson, *Revolution in Reverse*, New York: Monthly Review Press, 1990 (Latin America Bureau); Gordon Lewis, *Grenada: The Jewel Despoiled*, Baltimore: Johns Hopkins University Press, 1987.

5. Ron Suskind, "Made Safe By Marines, Grenada Now Haven for Offshore Banks," *Wall Street Journal*, Oct. 29, 1991.
6. Silavana Paternostro, "Casablanca without heroes," *World Policy Journal*, Winter 1993-1994, pp. 53-58; John Weeks and Phil Gunson, *Panama: Made in the USA*, New York: Monthly Review Press, 1991 (Latin America Bureau).
7. Witness for Peace, *Bitter Medicine: Structural Adjustment in Nicaragua*, Newtown, PA: Witness for Peace, 1994.
8. See Cheryl Payer, *The World Bank: A Critical Analysis*, New York: Monthly Review Press, 1982, pp. 35-38; Noam Chomsky, *World Orders Old and New*, New York: Columbia University Press, 1994, pp. 124-8.

Notes to Chapter 18

1. Given U.S. power and leadership of the Free World, its actions—which would be denounced in strong language if done by weak states—are subject only to a gentle chiding by allies and their dominant media. For example, on the Canadian media's general adherence to the double standard employed by U.S. officials and media, see Robert Hackett, *News and Dissent: The Press and the Politics of Peace in Canada*, Norwood, NJ: Ablex, 1991, chap. 9.
2. Amnesty International, *Report on Torture*, New York: Farrar, Straus and Giroux, 1975, p. 7.
3. Chomsky and Edward S. Herman, *The Washington Connection and Third World Fascism*, Boston: South End Press, 1979, Frontispiece and associated notes.
4. "United States Objectives and Courses of Action With Respect to Latin America," NSC 5432/1, Sept. 3, 1954, in *Foreign Relations of the United States, 1952-1954*, vol. IV, p. 81.
5. Ibid., pp. 82-84.
6. In 1948, George Kennan, then on the State Department planning staff, stated that: "We should cease to talk about vague and—for the Far East—unreal objectives such as human rights, the raising of the living standards, and democratization. The day is not far off when we are going to have to deal in straight power concepts. The less we are then hampered by idealistic slogans, the better." (Policy Planning Study 23, Feb. 24, 1948, quoted in Noam Chomsky, *Turning the Tide*, Boston: South End Press, 1985, p. 48.) For Vietnam, Assistant Secretary of Defense McNaughton gave value weights for our mission there as follows: 70 percent "to avoid a humiliating U.S. defeat..."; 20 percent to keeping South Vietnam out of Chinese hands; 10 percent "to permit the people of SVN to enjoy a better, freer way of life." U.S. Defense Dept., *The Pentagon Papers*, Gravel Ed., vol. 3, pp. 348-49.
7. A speech before the graduating class of the International Police Academy in 1965, quoted in Jan K. Black, *United States Penetration of Brazil*, Philadelphia: University of Pennsylvania Press, 1978, p. 143.
8. On this stress in U.S. army training, see Miles Wolpin, *Military Aid and Counterrevolution in the Third World*, Boston: Lexington, 1972.
9. See Piero Gleijeses, *The Dominican Crisis*, Baltimore: Johns Hopkins University Press, 1978, p. 285.
10. When shown a Costa Rican educational facility for the poor, the visiting Anastasio Somoza was impatiently uninterested: "I don't want educated

people. I want oxen." Quoted in Penny Lernoux, *Cry of the People*, Garden City, NY: Doubleday & Co., 1980, p. 85.

11. "United States Objectives," note 4, p. 86.
12. Addressing a New York audience in 1968, quoted in Black, *United States Penetration of Brazil*, p. 228.
13. See especially, Wolpin, *Military Aid*.
14. Quoted in Black, *United States Penetration of Brazil*, p. 194.
15. See ibid., pp. 160-61.
16. A secret 1965 Defense Department document of June 11, 1965, *Study of U.S. Policy Toward Latin American Military Forces*, which brags that the United States has already succeeded in "establishing predominant U.S. military influence," openly suggests that the Latin American military must be prepared "to remove government leaders from office whenever, in the judgment of the military, the conduct of these leaders is injurious to the welfare of the nation." Note that this is after the Latin military have been oriented to U.S. objectives, so that their judgment of the "national interest" and U.S. interest may coincide. As in the case of NSC 5432, this document has not been featured, or even mentioned, in the U.S. press.
17. Black, *United States Penetration of Brazil*, p. 161.
18. Wolpin, *Military Aid*, pp. 57, 128, 136. See also, Black, *United States Penetration of Brazil*, pp. 176-78; Edwin Liewen, in statement and testimony in *The Latin American Military*, Subcommittee on American Republics, Senate Foreign Relations Committee, Oct. 9, 1967.
19. Herman, *Real Terror Network*, p. 122.
20. Quoted in Black, *United States Penetration of Brazil*, p. 161.
21. *Foreign Assistance, 1966*, Hearings before the Senate Committee on Foreign Relations, 89th Congress, 2nd session, 1966, p. 693. On the active involvement of U.S. officials in this holocaust, see Kathy Kadane, "US aided '65 massacre of Indonesian left, ex-officials say," *Boston Globe*, May 23, 1990, p. 19; Noam Chomsky, " 'A Gleam of Light in Asia'," *Z Magazine*, Sept. 1990. On the enthusiasm for the ongoing massacre and complete lack of concern or reservations about its human consequences on the part of U.S. officials, see Kadane and Chomsky, but also Gabrial Kolko, *Confronting The Third World*, New York: Pantheon, 1988, pp. 178-85.
22. See Herman, *Real Terror Network*, pp. 115-19, 126-32.
23. Ibid., pp. 128-32; Michael Klare and Cynthia Arnson, *Supplying Repression*, IPS, 1981, p. 3; Lars Schoultz, "U.S. Foreign Policy and Human Rights Violations in Latin America: A Comparative Analysis of Foreign Aid Distributions," *Comparative Politics*, Jan. 1981, p. 162.
24. On the subservience of the Brazilian generals to the United States after the 1964 coup, see Black, *United States Penetration of Brazil*, pp. 50-52, 211.
25. Kenneth J. Grieb, *Guatemalan Caudillo, The Regime of Jorge Ubico: Guatemala, 1931-1944*, Athens, OH: Ohio University Press, 1979; Stephen Schlesinger and Stephen Kinzer, *Bitter Fruit*, Garden City: Doubleday, 1982, pp. 25-31.
26. Ibid, pp. 23-63.
27. Blanche Cook, *The Declassified Eisenhower*, Garden City: Doubleday, 1981, p. 222; see also, Richard Immerman, *The CIA In Guatemala*, Austin: University of Texas Press, 1982, pp. 82-109.

28. Piero Gliejeses, "Guatemala: Crisis and Response," in Richard Fagen and Olga Pellicer, *The Future of Central America: Policy Choices for the U.S. and Mexico*, Stanford: Stanford University Press, 1983.

29. "During the last half of Carter's term, more than $34 million worth of US military equipment wormed its way into Guatemala, mostly under contracts licensed by the Department of Commerce. The largest amount was a $20 million order for two Lockheed L-100-20 transport planes, updated versions of the Hercules paratroop-carrier." George Black, *Garrison Guatemala*, New York: Monthly Review Press, 1984, p. 147.

30. Ibid., pp. 146-56.

31. Weisman, "Reagan Denounces Threats to Peace in Latin America," *New York Times*, Dec. 5, 1982.

32. See Herman, *Real Terror Network*, pp. 196-98.

33. In terms of the social and economic—basic needs—dimensions of human rights, the Cuban performance has been outstanding. But the U.S. analysts and media don't place any weight on this aspect of human rights or Cuban performance—they focus only on political and personal rights. On this level, Cuba, while seriously deficient, is better than Guatemala. See below, note 57.

34. For a great deal of evidence, see Herman and Chomsky, *Manufacturing Consent*, chap. 2; Herman, *Real Terror Network*, chap. 4. See also, Edward S. Herman, "Labor Abuses in El Salvador and Nicaragua: A Study of New York Times Coverage," *EXTRA!*, vol. 2, no. 7/8, Summer 1989, pp. 24-26.

35. These special circumstances of the Carter years are discussed in Lars Schoultz, *Human Rights and United States Policy toward Latin America*, Princeton University Press, 1981, pp. 358-79; the limits of the Carter era changes are discussed in Noam Chomsky, *Human Rights and American Foreign Policy*, Spokesmen, 1978, chap. 2. See also, above, note 29.

36. Reporter Lindsey Gruson stated in the *New York Times* that in Guatemala "the effort to improve the armed forces respect for human rights" is one of "two basic American policy goals" ("U.S. Pins Hopes on Guatemalan Army," July 5, 1990, p. A6). This official claim is taken as unqualified fact.

37. The apologetics included a vigorous effort to tie the Guatemalan rebels to Cuba, Nicaragua, and other external Red sources (see George Black, *Garrison Guatemala*, pp. 148-49). The serial lying consisted of apologizing for each successive military leader as devoted to protecting innocent civilians; then, after his ouster, acknowledging that he had been a distressingly bad man, even a mass murderer, in sharp contrast with the military leader now in power! This Orwellian retrospective admission of prior lying in the service of apologetics was never picked up in the mass media. See Americas Watch, *Guatemala Revised: How the Reagan Administration Finds 'Improvements' in Human Rights in Guatemala*, New York, 1985. For a summary of the Americas Watch account, and discussion of the media's handling of this story, see Herman and Chomsky, *Manufacturing Consent*, pp. 74-75.

38. Here again, the U.S. mass media watched this intimidation process in virtual silence. See Herman and Chomsky, *Manufacturing Consent*, pp. 78-79.

39. Ibid., pp. 59-71 for details and citations.

40. It referred to "the protective diplomacy of the U.S. Ambassador in El Salvador, William Walker." "Why Apologize for El Salvador?," *New York Times*, Editorial, Dec. 25, 1989, p. 30.
41. Lindsey Gruson, "Salvadoran Judge Seeks Help of U.S.," *New York Times*, Aug. 1, 1990, p. A7.
42. Chris Norton, "U.S. Ambassador tries to discredit Salvadoran witness in Jesuit murders," *In These Times*, Dec. 20, 1989-Jan. 9, 1990, p. 5.
43. See James Hamilton, "Witnesses 'Vanish', " *Lies Of Our Times*, August 1990, p. 16.
44. Martin Langfield, "Papers on priests' slaying withheld," *Philadelphia Inquirer*, Aug. 12, 1990, p. 4-A.
45. Amnesty International, *Report on Torture*, p. 81.
46. On this control mechanism, see Herman and Chomsky, *Manufacturing Consent*, pp. 26-31.
47. National Security Council 5419/1, in *Foreign Relations of the United States, 1952-54*, vol. IV, p. 1137.
48. In a very similar pattern, Nicaragua was accused by the Reaganites in the 1980s of having bragged about a "revolution without frontiers," and threatening to overrun Central America. This accusation was a fabrication, and like the earlier Guatemalan threat was an Orwellian inversion, as Nicaragua was under steady attack by the United States and its proxies from without and could not defend itself by attacking the sanctuaries of foreign aggressors without being accused of unreasonable and aggressive behavior. See Peter Kornbluh, *Nicaragua: The Price of Intervention*, Washington, DC: Institute for Policy Studies, 1987, pp. 170-73.
49. Schlesinger and Kinzer, *Bitter Fruit*, pp. 142-44.
50. Jim Morrell, "Contadora: The Treaty on Balance," *International Policy Report*, June 1985; Peadar Kirby, "Positions Shift On Contadora As Europe Backs Accord," *Latinamerica press*, Oct. 18, 1984; Council on Hemispheric Affairs, "Elliott Abrams Riding High as He Works to Thwart Contadora," *News and Analysis*, May 30, 1986.
51. U.S. and Western definitions of human rights stress political and personal freedoms and downgrade or entirely ignore economic and social rights. For vast numbers in the Third World, and large numbers elsewhere, however, the right to food, shelter, medical care, and employment are of first-order importance, and the right to subsistence is arguably a precondition to other rights being meaningful. These rights to basic human needs are not looked upon with favor by Western multinational corporations and political elites, and, as Henry Shue points out, liberal theory, which assumes the subsistence problem is already met, simply excludes from its orbit "no fewer than 1,000,000,000 people." (*Basic Rights*, Princeton, 1980, p. 183; see also his introduction and chap. 1.)
52. Political rights are less threatening to foreign investors than economic rights, as local political elites may be bargained with and made "reasonable." The political environment can most easily be favorably influenced if structural inequality is not upset and foreign intervention in electoral processes is not sharply limited. For many details on the extraordinary level and scope of U.S. intervention in the Nicaraguan election of 1990, see David McMichael and William Robinson, "NED Overt Action: Intervention in the Nicaraguan Election," *CovertAction Information Bulletin*, No. 33, Winter 1990; William Robinson, "U.S. Overt Intervention: Nicaraguan

'Electoral Coup'," *CovertAction Information Bulletin*, No. 34, Summer 1990; Holly Sklar, "Washington Wants To Buy Nicaragua's Elections Again," *Z Magazine*, Dec. 1989, pp. 49-64.

53. Latin American Studies Association, "The Electoral Processs in Nicaragua: Domestic and International Influences," Report of a Delegation Sent to Observe the Nicaraguan Election, Nov. 19, 1984.

54. Dianna Melrose, *The Threat of a Good Example?*, London: Oxfam, 1985, p. 14.

55. Inter-American Development Bank Report No. DES-13, *Nicaragua*, Jan. 1983, cited in ibid.

56. There were many others besides the alleged "revolution without frontiers" mentioned in note 48. See Kornbluh, above, note 48, chap. 4 and Morris Morley and James Petras, *The Reagan Administration and Nicaragua: How Washington Constructs Its Case For Counterrevolution in Central America*, New York: Institute for Media Analysis, 1987.

57. Amnesty International, *Guatemala: A Government Program of Political Murder*, London, 1981. While the Sandinista government did engage in brutalities against the Miskito Indians and contra supporters, at no time did they descend to the mass, and officially organized, slaughter of civilians engaged in by the Salvadoran and Guatemalan governments. Americas Watch was driven by Reaganite propaganda to state in 1987 that "the government of Nicaragua does not engage in a pattern of violations of the laws of warfare. Nor does it engage in systematic violations of the right to life or to physical integrity of detainees...". (*Human Rights in Nicaragua 1986*, Feb. 1987, p. 7). In the same document AW also notes that the U.S.-sponsored contras "still engage in selective but systematic killing of persons they perceive as representing the government, in indiscriminate attacks against civilians or in disregard for their safety, and in outrages against the personal dignity of prisoners" (p. 6). This point of systematic contra attacks on civilians was made repeatedly by AW and AI, and was confirmed by numerous independent observers.

58. Nicaragua under the Somozas provided a jumping off place for the 1954 U.S.-organized invasion of Guatemala and the 1959 Bay of Pigs invasion of Cuba, and it participated with Guatemala in a 1972 U.S.-sponsored invasion of El Salvador to prevent Jose Napoleeon Duarte from taking office following an election he won.

59. In fact, when the elder Somoza was shot by an assassin in 1956, the depth of U.S. official concern over his well-being was touching. As Bernard Diederich described it in his book *Somoza* (p. 48):

> The White House ordered a helicopter from the Canal Zone to move the wounded dictator from Leon to Managua, and then sent the commander of Washington's Walter Reed Army Hospital to Nicaragua to save him... Major General Dr. Leon D. Heaton, accompanied by two surgeons, left by midafternoon for the seventeen-and-a-half-hour flight to Managua. Meanwhile, a medical team headed by Colonel Charles O. Bruce had flown in early on September 22 from the Canal Zone to attend to Somoza's wounds. Bruce, the Canal Zone's health director, was accompanied by members of the staff of Gorgas Hospital, including the chiefs of surgery and orthopedics and an anesthetist. Tacho, as one eminent Nicaraguan doctor observed later, hadn't put his money into hospitals.

60. For a fuller discussion of the media's treatment of the Nicaraguan election, see Herman and Chomsky, *Manufacturing Consent*, pp. 116-32.
61. See David Shipler, "Nicaragua, Victory for U.S. Fair Play," *New York Times*, March 1, 1990 (Op Ed.).
62. For a discussion of this, stressing how much weight U.S. political analysts place on *small* changes in economic conditions as the most powerful influence on electoral outcomes, see Edward S. Herman, "The *Times* on the Nicaraguan Election," *Lies of Our Times*, April 1990.
63. For details on the "clearing the ground" for the 1982 Salvadoran election, see Edward S. Herman and Frank Brodhead, *Demonstration Elections*, pp. 119-26.
64. See Herman and Chomsky, *Manufacturing Consent*, chap. 3, and for a final comparison, pp. 140-42.
65. For evidence of its superiority in substance, and in the perceptions of independent observers, see Herman and Chomsky, *Manufacturing Consent*, pp. 120-40.
66. The U.S. administrations had refused to abide by the Tela accord of the Central American states, which called for disarming and disbanding all non-official forces as a first and essential step in a settlement. The U.S. failure to do this for the contras before the election made it evident that the end of military conflict was, at a minimum, not assured if the wrong party won the election. Furthermore, President Bush, in early November 1989, stated explicitly in a meeting with Violetta Chamorro in Washington, D.C. that the embargo would be lifted only if her UNO party won the election. (See Lauter, "Nicaragua's Opposition Candidate at White House," *Los Angeles Times*, Nov. 9, 1989, p. A19.) The U.S. media failed to note the interventionist and extortionist implications of this statement.
67. On this contrast, see Herman, *Real Terror Network*, pp. 208-10.

Notes to Chapter 19

1. The Western model, the institutional apparatus that prepares and disseminates it, and the extent to which the mainstream experts confine themselves to discussing Left and insurgent terror, are spelled out in detail in Edward S. Herman and Gerry O'Sullivan, *The "Terrorism" Industry*, New York: Pantheon, 1990.
2. This chapter is a book review of William D. Perdue, *Terrorism and the State: A Critique of Domination Through Fear*, New York: Praeger, 1989, originally published in *Monthly Review*, April 1991.

Notes to Chapter 21

1. Hyde Park in London is the most famous of these public places, where cranks and dissident speakers are free to get up on soap boxes and speak out.
2. Henry Cabot Lodge, *The Federalist*, London: G.P. Putnam's Sons, 1888, pp. 51-60.
3. In 1822, an older, perhaps more democratically inclined Madison wrote that "a popular government without popular information, or the means of acquiring it, is but a prologue to a farce or a tragedy, or perhaps both." Letter to W. T. Barry, August 4, 1822, in *Letters and Other Writings of James Madison*, New York: R. Worthington, 1844, vol. 3, p. 276.
4. A. J. Liebling, *The Press*, New York: Ballantine, 1964, p. 15.

5. The five factors to be discussed here are elements of the "propaganda model," spelled out in greater detail in Herman and Chomsky, *Manufacturing Consent: The Political Economy of the Mass Media*, New York: Pantheon, 1988.

6. Back in 1947, A. J. Liebling said that "I cannot believe that labor leaders are so stupid they will let the other side monopolize the press indefinitely." (*The Press*, p. 23). Liebling was not thought to have been an optimist, or to underestimate human stupidity. He may have underrated the economic costs of starting and maintaining a newspaper, however.

7. The median value of the wealth of the control groups of the largest media corporations in the mid-1980s, as measured by the value of stock they owned in the controlled mass media corporation alone, was approximately $450 million. See Herman and Chomsky, *Manufacturing Consent*, pp. 8-10.

8. Exponents of the neo-conservative view that the mass media have a liberal bias always avoid the question of ownership and control, implying that lower echelon personnel set their own agendas, without rules from above. The massive historic evidence that key owners like Henry Luce, DeWitt Wallace (*Reader's Digest*), Katherine Graham, Arthur Hays Sulzberger, Robert Sarnoff, and Rupert Murdoch have had definite policy agendas that they have enforced in their organizations is simply not discussed. The effects of profitability rules, and policies based on advertiser interests and sensitivity, are not discussed either. The neo-conservative analysts also don't do much in the way of analyzing actual news and opinion outputs. Their main focus is on whether the reporters and copy editors vote Republican or Democratic. For the neo-conservative view, see Michael Ledeen, *Grave New World*, New York: Oxford University Press, 1985, chap. 5, and Lichter, Rothman and Lichter, *The Media Elite*, Bethesda, MD: Adler & Adler, 1986. For critiques, see Herbert Gans, "Are U.S. Journalists Dangerously Liberal?," *Columbia Journalism Review*, Nov.-Dec., 1985; Herman and Chomsky, *Manufacturing Consent*, chap. 1.

9. See Barnouw's discussion of the evidence for this in Vietnam War coverage, *The Sponsor: Notes on a Modern Potentate*, New York: Oxford University Press, 1978, pp. 62-66.

10. On the huge impact of advertisers on the editorial content of women's magazines, see Gloria Steinem's account of her experiences with *Ms. Magazine* during the years in which it depended on advertising. "Sex, Lies and Advertising," *Ms. Magazine*, July-Aug. 1990, pp. 18-28.

11. See Barnouw, *The Sponsor*, pp. 79-121. The finding that advertisers don't very often actively intervene in programming misses the point: the main route for advertiser intervention lies in the nature of their demand and ability to choose.

12. For an examination of how this has been done on the subject of terrorism, see Edward Herman and Gerry O'Sullivan, *The "Terrorism" Industry: The Experts and Institutions That Shape Our View of Terror*, New York: Pantheon, 1990.

13. The largest of the dissident institutes, the Institute for Policy Studies, has a budget less than a fifth that of the Georgetown Center for Strategic and International Studies, the Hoover Institution, or the American Enterprise Institute.

14. Declaring that the Sandinista government of Nicaragua was "Marxist-Leninist" played an important role in obtaining mass media and Democratic

Party cooperation in the economic and military warfare carried out against Nicaragua in the years 1981-1989. As in the case of the overthrow of the democratically elected government of Guatemala by proxy invasion in 1954, both the press and Democrats accepted the false claim that the objective of the U.S. government in its actions was to bring about "democracy." See Peter Kornbluh, *Nicaragua: The Price of Intervention,* Washington, DC: Institute for Policy Studies, 1987, chap. 4; Herman and Chomsky, *Manufacturing Consent,* pp. xii-xiii.

15. See Herman and O'Sullivan, *The "Terrorism" Industry,* preface, chaps. 1-3, and 8.

16. These two cases are discussed at length in Chomsky and Herman, *The Washington Connection and Third World Fascism,* chap. 3.

17. Herman and Chomsky, *Manufacturing Consent,* chap. 5.

18. For details, see ibid., pp. xii-xiii and 116-42; Chomsky, *The Culture of Terrorism,* Boston: South End Press, 1988, pp. 39-61, 203-211; Jack Spence, "The U.S. Media: Covering (Over) Nicaragua," in Thomas Walker, ed., *Reagan Versus the Sandinistas,* Boulder, Colorado: Westview, 1987, pp. 182-201.

19. David Shipler, "Nicaragua, Victory for U.S. Fair Play," *New York Times,* Op. Ed., March 1, 1990; Anthony Lewis, "Out of This Nettle," *New York Times,* March 2, 1990.

20. At a press conference with Mrs. Chamorro in Washington, D.C., in early November 1989, President Bush stated explicitly that the U.S. embargo would be lifted only if her UNO party won the election. See Lauter, "Nicaragua's Opposition Candidate at White House," *Los Angeles Times,* Nov. 9, 1989, p. A15.

21. James Curran, "Advertising and the Press," in Curran, ed., *The British Press: A Manifesto,* London: Macmillan, 1978, pp. 252-55.

22. Sometimes these lies are corrected belatedly and in muted fashion in the mainstream press. The *New York Times* entitled an editorial of January 18, 1988, "The Lie that Was Not Shot Down," referring to the Reagan administration lie that the Soviet Union knowingly shot down a Korean civilian plane in September 1983. That lie *was* shot down, in the marginalized press; the mainstream press, including the *New York Times,* allowed it to survive and gave it intense coverage, based on maintaining a high gullibility quotient and refusing to investigate or question a lie convenient to ongoing state demands.

23. This was the basis of the distinction drawn in Herman and Chomsky between "worthy" and "unworthy" victims. See *Manufacturing Consent,* chap. 2. An important case of remarkable but system-supportive gullibility was the mainstream media's handling of the alleged Bulgarian-KGB connection to the 1981 shooting of Pope John Paul II. See ibid. chap. 4.

Notes to Chapter 22

1. See Philip Elliott, "Intellectuals, the 'information society' and the disappearance of the public sphere," *Media Culture & Society,* July 1982; Graham Murdoch and Peter Golding, "Information poverty and political inequality: Citizenship in the age of privatized communications," *Journal of Communication,* 1989; Erik Barnouw, *The Sponsor: Notes on a Modern Potentate,* New York: Oxford University Press, 1978, pp. 113-52, 179-82; P. Sepstrup, "Implications of Current Developments in West European Broadcasting,"

Media Culture & Society, 1989; P. Scannell, "Public Service Broadcasting and modern public life," *Media Culture & Society*, 1989. Scannell believes that the contribution of public broadcasting to the public sphere is more than modest.

2. Barnouw, *The Sponsor*, p. 95.
3. *Television in the Corporate Interest*, New York: Praeger, 1976, pp. 27-31.
4. Ibid., p. 97.
5. In the first half of the 1980s, NBC was taken over by General Electric Company, a huge multinational important in weapons and nuclear reactor manufacture; ABC was acquired by Capital Cities, a media conglomerate famous for its bottom-line orientation; and control of CBS was assumed by Lawrence Tisch of Loews, a large conglomerate in the cigarette, hotel and other businesses. A fourth network that has emerged in the 1980s and 1990s, Fox, is controlled by Rupert Murdoch, owner of a global media empire not known for its socially forward-looking policies.
6. *The Sponsor*, p. 138.
7. Jay Blumler et al, "Broadcasting Finance and Programme Quality: An International Review," *European Journal of Communication*, 1986, pp. 348-50.
8. A. Pragnell, *Television in Europe: Quality and Values in Time of Change*, Media Monograph No. 5, Manchester: European Institute for Media, 1987, p. 6.
9. Statement of Gabriel de Broglie, the departing head of the French national supervisory organization CNCL, in January 1989, quoted in G. Graham, "Never mind the quality," *Financial Times*, June 28, 1989.
10. Edward Palmer, *Television and America's Children: A Crisis of Neglect*, New York: Oxford, 1988.
11. George Gerbner and Nancy Signorielli, "Violence Profile 1967 through 1988-89: enduring patterns," mimeo, Jan. 1990.
12. This is an important reason for the surge in cross-border and vertical mergers in the communications business, as the value and importance to broadcasters of gaining access to old stocks of movies and TV series, and to the ongoing production of such programs, has risen sharply.
13. P. Sepstrup, above, note 1.
14. L. Huesmann and L. Efron, *Television and the Aggressive Child: A Cross-National Comparison*, Hillsdale, NJ: Erlbaum Associates, 1986.
15. Gerbner and Signorielli, above, note 11; Huesmann and Efron, ibid; Frank Mankiewicz and Joel Swerdlow, *Remote Control*, New York: Ballantine, 1979; G. Barlow and A. Hill, *Video Violence and Children*, New York: St. Martin's, 1985; National Institute of Mental Health, *Television and Behavior: Ten Years of Scientific Progress and Implications for the Eighties*, vol. 2: Technical Reviews. Washington: Department of Health and Public Services, 1982.
16. E. Krasnow, E. Longley and H. Terry, *The Politics of Broadcast Regulation*, New York: St. Martin's, 1982, pp. 194-96.

Notes to Chapter 23

1. Robin Andersen, "Visions of instability: U.S. television's law and order news of El Salvador," *Media, Culture & Society*, vol. 10 (1988), pp. 239-264; Raymond Bonner, *Weakness and Deceit*, New York: Times Books, 1984, chap. 7; Herman and Chomsky, *Manufacturing Consent*, pp. 49-53.

2. This is the language of a *New York Times* editorial of April 28, 1980.
3. See Herman and Brodhead, *Demonstration Elections*, chap. 5; Herman and Chomsky, *Manufacturing Consent*, chap. 3.
4. For a fuller treatment, Edward Herman, "Disinformation as News Fit to Print: LeMoyne and the Times on the Murder of Herbert Anaya," *CovertAction Information Bulletin*, Winter 1989.
5. Lindsey Gruson, "A Fingerhold for Dissent in El Salvador," *New York Times*, March 17, 1989.
6. For a discussion, Herman and Chomsky, *Manufacturing Consent*, pp. 64-69.
7. Lydia Chavez, "Defense Minister in Salvador Quits in Military Feud," *New York Times*, April 19, 1983.
8. "Elliott Abrams is Guilty," *New York Times*, Oct. 11, 1991 (editorial).
9. The *New York Times* still looked better than the McNeil-Lehrer News Hour, which was putting Abrams on and asking him open-ended questions even after the congressional Democrats were refusing to hear him as a witness because of his admitted earlier prevarications.
10. Juan de Onis, "U.S. Officials Concede Flaws in Salvador White Paper But Defend Its Conclusion," *New York Times*, June 10, 1981, p. A6.
11. See note 4 above; also Noam Chomsky, *Necessary Illusions*, Boston: South End Press, 1989, esp. pp. 223-236, 333-37.

Notes to Chapter 24

1. Eric Alterman, *Sound and Fury*, New York: Harper Perennial, 1992, p. 156.
2. This study is based on a reading and analysis of 136 Broder opinion columns in the *Washington Post* (WP) or *Philadelphia Inquirer* (PI) dating from 1980 through July 1994. The items from the *Post* were obtained by a Nexis search by topic area and key words covering some 45 major topics (example: EPA, S & L, Grenada, Angola, Iran-Contra, Guinier, Civil rights and William Bradford Reynolds). They supplement items from the author's personal collection of Broder Op Ed columns that appeared in the *Inquirer*. The author was assisted in this project by Adam Horowitz.
3. For a good account of the Reagan ploy, see Chomsky's *Necessary Illusions*, pp. 223-61.
4. Alterman has a good discussion of Broder's apologia for Reagan and the administration's Iran-Contra performance in *Sound and Fury*, pp. 154-155.
5. This chapter was published in abridged form in *EXTRA!*, Nov.-Dec. 1994; readers were invited to purchase this longer version from the publisher.

Notes to Chapter 25

1. On the pre-war appeasement of Saddam Hussein, see Murray Wass, "Who Lost Kuwait?," *Village Voice*, January 16-22, 1991, pp. 60ff.
2. Basic sources cited here are: Douglas Kellner, *The Persian Gulf TV War*, Boulder: Westview Press, 1992; Hamid Mowlana, George Gerbner and Herbert I. Schiller, eds., *Triumph of the Image: The Media's War in the Persian Gulf—A Global Perspective*, Boulder: Westview Press, 1992; John McArthur, *Second Front: Censorship and Propaganda in the Gulf War*, New York: Hill and Wang, 1992.
3. Kellner, *Persian Gulf TV War*, pp. 89-97 and throughout.
4. See Noam Chomsky, "The Media and the War: What War" in Mowlana et al., *Triumph of the Image*, pp. 60-61.

5. On earlier media apologetics for Noriega, see Chomsky, *Deterring Democracy*, London: Verso, 1991, pp. 150-58; on the earlier whitewash of Saddam Hussein, Scott Armstrong referred to him as "the man who charmed the pants off many American leaders and journalists in the 1970s," and Armstrong gives supportive citations from Evans and Novak, the *New York Times* and *Washington Post*, in "Sixty-Four Questions in Search of an Answer," *Columbia Journalism Review*, Nov. -Dec. 1990, pp. 23-24.
6. Kellner, *Persian Gulf TV War*, pp. 67-71.
7. Ibid., pp. 13-29; Pierre Salinger and Eric Laurent, *Secret Dossier: The Hidden Agenda Behind the Gulf War*, New York: Penguin, 1991, pp. 110-47.
8. See Kellner, *Persian Gulf TV War*, pp. 30-31; Salinger and Laurent, ibid, pp. 110-14.
9. Kellner, *Persian Gulf TV War*, pp. 31-37.
10. Ibid., pp. 37, 318-35.
11. Ibid.; and Thomas Friedman, "Pax Americana: What the United States Has Taken on in the Gulf, Besides a War," *New York Times*, Jan. 20, 1991. Friedman reported the urgency for the administration of avoiding diplomacy, as noted in the text above, then repeated later without qualification, in the Jan. 20 article, the administration claim that it had exhausted all diplomatic options—"Now that diplomacy has failed and it has come to war.."—a wonderful illustration of a reporter's doublethink capability.
12. This poll is discussed in Chomsky's chapter in Mowlana et al., eds., *Triumph of the Image*, pp. 58-59.
13. This opposition vigorously opposed the Bush war policy. The Bush administration, however, was not interested in and did not encourage or even talk with this opposition; and the media followed in line. Ibid., pp. 55-56.
14. The process of integration is well discussed in McArthur, *Second Front.*
15. Alex Jones, "War in the Gulf," *New York Times*, Feb. 15, 1991.
16. Kellner, *Persian Gulf TV War*, p. 421.
17. Ibid., chap. 3-5.
18. Ibid., pp. 203-6.
19. Ibid., chap. 9. After the War was over, it was also disclosed that the U.S. military had buried alive hundreds or even thousands of Iraqi soldiers by covering over their trenches with sand by bulldozer—in another episode of doubtful legality as well as morality. The U.S. mainstream media, which had failed to pick up this process as war news, gave it minimal attention and an apologetic twist when disclosure finally arrived in September 1991. See Nancy Watt Rosenfeld, "Buried Alive," *Lies of Our Times*, Oct. 1991, pp. 12-13.
20. Ibid., p. 381.
21. Ibid., pp. 399-404, 429-30.
22. See Patrick Tyler, "U.S. Officials Believe Iraq Will Take Years to Rebuild," *New York Times*, June 3, 1991, p. A1.
23. This chapter is a segment of an article "The Media's Role in U.S. Foreign Policy," *Journal of International Affairs*, Summer 1993.

Notes to Chapter 26

1. R. B. Du Boff, *Accumulation and Power*, Armonk, NY: M. E. Sharpe, 1989, p. 103.

2. This critical distinction is not made by "active audience" analysts, who assume that audiences with free choice alone, by mere savvy in selection and interpretation, can overcome any biases of media sovereigns. On the fallaciousness of this view, see Herbert Schiller, *Culture, Inc.: The Corporate Takeover of Public Expression*, New York: Oxford, 1989, chap. 7; William R. Seaman, "Active audience theory: pointless populism," *Media, Culture & Society*, vol. 14, 1992, pp. 301-311.
3. There is a wider array of choices on the fringe, but a large fraction of the population doesn't even know these fringe publications exist.
4. George Gerbner, "Science or Ritual Dance? A Revisionist View of Television Effects Research," *Journal of Communication*, Spring 1984, p. 170.
5. European Federation of Community Radios, *Final Report*, 3rd Congress, May 16-20, 1991, p. 5
6. In the North Italian province of Friuli, where two-thirds of the population speak Friulian, that language does not exist for the state-owned RAI. A community station, Radio Onde Furlane, has come into existence to service this 5 million person audience. See ibid.
7. "Factor in the prevalence of repeat callers, and it's clear that the caller pool [on radio talk shows] represents a statistically insignificant slice of the electorate." Jon Keller, " 'Hi, I'm Bill, a first-time caller'," *Boston Globe*, April 30, 1995.
8. A major spokesperson for this form of critique and analysis has been Karol Jakubowicz, an official in the General Secretariat of Polish Radio and Television. See his background paper, "Post-Communist Central and Eastern Europe: Promoting the Emergence of Open and Plural Media Systems," Third European Ministerial Conference on Mass Media Policy, Cyprus, Oct. 9-10, 1991. Similar views are common among members of European Federation of Community Radios. See text below and document cited in note 7, above.
9. See Chapter 22, pp. 174-178.
10. The right-wing victory of Gingrich and company in the national elections of 1994 was a setback for democratic broadcasting, among many other matters; Gingrich immediately began a campaign to defund PBS entirely. This has been a long-time aim of Reed Irvine of Accuracy in Media and the extreme Right in general, who are opposed to any independent broadcasting and prefer the air waves to be under the protective control of commercial interests.
11. The reality of this threat is illustrated by the fact that John Malone's Tele-communications Inc.(TCI), the largest cable network in the United States, has planned a new program lineup that includes the right-wing National Empowerment Television and The American Conservative Network, but excludes the only fulltime liberal TV network, The 90s Channel. The 90s Channel, carried on only seven of TCI's more than 1000 channels, was only retained on those by a court order, which expires on Oct. 31, 1995. Malone, an open admirer of Rush Limbaugh, also carries Pat Robertson's Family Channel, and owns part of it. (News Release of Denver Area Telecommunications Consortium, Jan. 30, 1995.)
12. A variant of the European system of allocation of time to citizens groups was proposed by Ralph Nader in espousing an "audience network." This would be a national membership institution of viewers and listeners, to be granted a congressional charter as a nonprofit corporation and be given

60 minutes of prime radio and TV time each day to air programs of its choice. Audience member contributions would be the prime source of funding; members would vote for a governing board, which would decide on programs. Apart from its extreme political unrealism, both at the level of legislative possibility and the potential of democratic organization and participation involving something as amorphous as an "audience," the proposal if implemented would not change the structure of the media—it would only insert an hour of noncommercial time in the midst of 23 hours of commercial programming. The proposal had not gotten off the ground by mid-1995. See Ralph Nader, "The Audience Network: Time for the People," (undated, provided by the Nader-related Audience Network Coalition); also, Ralph Nader and Claire Riley, "Oh Say Can You See: A Broadcast Network for the Audience," *Virginia Law Review,* Fall 1988.

13. See Herman and Chomsky, *Manufacturing Consent,* pp. 26-28.
14. See Chapter 22, pp. 178.
15. Many illustrations are to be found in Erik Barnouw, *The Sponsor: Notes on a Modern Potentate,* New York: Oxford University Press, 1978.
16. For history and analysis, see Ralph Engelman, *Public Radio and Television in America: A Political History,* (forthcoming, Sage, 1996); William Hoynes, *Public Television for Sale,* Boulder: Westview, 1994; "The Broken Promise of Public Television," *EXTRA!,* Sept.-Oct. 1993; "Tilting Right," *EXTRA!,* April-May 1993.
17. Robert H. Devine argues persuasively that without wide participation "the First Amendment is nothing more than a means for one class to gain consensus by distributing and circulating its ideas among members of subordinate classes." "Video, Access and Agency," paper given at the 1992 Convention of the National Federation of Local Cable Programmers, St. Paul, MN, July 17, 1992, p. 1.
18. They are, of course, lavish in funding right-wing journals and TV programs that propound market-friendly messages. See John Saloma III, *Ominous Politics: The New Conservative Labyrinth,* New York: Farrar, Straus and Giroux, 1984. In May 1995 it was announced that billionaire Rupert Murdoch had committed $3 million to help fund another right-wing journal, to be named *The Standard.*
19. David Barsamian, "Audio Combat," *Z Papers,* Oct.-Dec. 1993, p. 12.
20. Micropower station Free Radio Berkeley, which has fended off attempts at shutdown by the FCC thus far, claims that micropower stations are now able to broadcast to 60 countries via a shortwave radio station in Costa Rica. It reports that excerpts from broadcasts of microwave stations Anarchy Radio, Radio Free Detroit, San Francisco Liberation Radio and its own station have been relayed through Costa Rica. Free Radio Berkeley & the Free Communications Coalition put out a newsletter, "Reclaiming the Airwaves," available from Free Radio Berkeley, 1442 A Walnut Street #406, Berkeley, CA 94709 (510-464-3041).
21. Barsamian, above note 19, p. 11.
22. John Fuller and Sue Bomzer, "Friendly (and Not So Friendly) Competition in the PTV Overlapped Markets," PBS Meeting Presentation, PBS Research Department, June 19, 1990.
23. For details on this process, see Diana Agosta, et al., *The Participate Report: A Case Study of Public Access Cable Television in New York State,* New York: Participate/AMIC, 1990.

24. *Roar: The Paper Tiger Television Guide to Media Activism*, published in 1991 by Paper Tiger and the Wexner Center for Arts of Ohio State University, provides a short history of Paper Tiger plus other materials, including an excellent bibliography on the media and media activism.
25. See DeeDee Halleck, "Zapatistas On-Line," *NACLA Report on the Americas*, Sept.-Oct. 1994, pp. 30-32.
26. Ronfeldt's views are summarized in "Netwar Could Make Mexico Ungovernable," a Pacific News Service report dated March 20, 1995.
27. *Media Development*, Fall, 1991, pp. 6-8.
28. "Persian Gulf War: The Movie," in Mowlana et al., eds., *Triumph of the Image: The Media's War in the Persian Gulf—A Global Perspective*, Boulder: Westview Press, 1992, chap. 20.
29. LBBS, a community bulletin board system initiated by *Z Magazine*, began offering a "Left on Line School" in January 1995, with courses given by Barbara Ehrenreich, Holly Sklar, Noam Chomsky, and others.

Notes to Epilogue

1. See Chapter 15, at note 8.
2. On how the U.S. media and mainstream economists lauded this lock-in, entirely ignoring its violation of the Mexican people's democratic rights, see Edward S. Herman, "NAFTA, Mexican Meltdown, and the Propaganda System," *Z Magazine*, September 1995.
3. Cambridge: Cambridge University Press, 1960, p. 164.
4. "According to one U.S. oilman, 'Marcos says, 'We'll pass the laws you need—just tell us what you want.'" "Philippines: A government that needs U.S. business," *Business Week*, Nov. 4, 1972, p. 42.
5. A good discussion of this subordination is given in "The Bankers, The Businessmen, and the Lawyers," chap. 2 of Jonathan Kwitny, *Endless Enemies*, New York: Congdon & Weed, 1984.
6. See Herman, *The Real Terror Network*, pp. 110-37; also, Noam Chomsky, *Deterring Democracy*, London: Verso, 1991.
7. The great powers are free to ignore these rules at their discretion; lesser powers can do so only at peril and severe cost. Walden Bello, *Dark Victory: The United States, Structural Adjustment and Global Poverty*, London: Pluto, 1994; Susan George and Fabrizio Sabelli, *Faith & Credit: The World Bank's Secular Empire*, Boulder: Westview Press, 1994.
8. The U.S.-IMF-Zedillo plan for dealing with the Mexican collapse of December 1994 was first, to bail out the foreign and domestic investors, and second, to impose an austerity plan whose costs would, regretfully, fall on ordinary citizens who were still awaiting some gains from NAFTA and the other "reforms" that had given investors and the local elite huge windfalls. On the nature of the IMF rules, see above, pp. 113-6, 125-6.
9. "The government of an exclusive company of merchants is, perhaps, the worst of all governments for any country whatsoever." *The Wealth of Nations*, New York: Modern Library, 1937, p. 537. Smith's scepticism concerning the motives and activities of merchants and the threat of business power are omnipresent in this book.
10. In an article showing how the very profitable firm Intel had bargained down a New Mexican town with tax abatements that contributed to serious financial shortages for local schools, the *Wall Street Journal* quotes a U.S. Chamber of Commerce economist criticizing business's short-sightedness:

"They are not looking at it for the long term. They figure that the school system will take care of itself." An Intel official is also cited saying if Intel had to pay full property and sales taxes on its equipment it couldn't compete. "We take a look at what it costs to do business here, there, or somewhere else. That is all there is to it." This article shows that this is not all there is to it—that Intel bargains harshly to minimize its taxes and other costs. Robert Tomsho, "Growing Pains: Rio Rancho Wooed Industry and Got It, Plus Financial Woes," *Wall Street Journal*, April 11, 1995.

11. On May 17, 1995, Nobel Prize winning economist Milton Friedman proudly reprinted one of his earlier *Newsweek* columns in which he had called for the complete abolition of the Food and Drug Administration ("Woof! Woof! This Cat Just Won't Bark"). Friedman was proud to have anticipated the insights of those other great thinkers, Newt Gingrich and John Kasich, on the capabilities of the free market.

12. Daniel Faber, *Environment Under Fire: Imperialism and the Ecological Crisis in Central America*, New York: Monthly Review Press, 1993.

13. On business's aggressive funding of the Republicans when it appeared that they might be in a position to win big, see Ferguson, "G.O.P. $$$ Talked...," *Nation*, Dec. 26, 1994. A Forbes/Gallup poll of 338 CEOs found that 86 percent thought that the new Republican control of Congress would help "the country" and only 2 percent thought things would be worse; the summary statement in *Forbes* was an "almost too-good-to-be-true reaction to the election results." Howard Banks, "A Christmas List," Jan. 2, 1995, p. 121.

14. See "Backed by Business, G.O.P. Takes Steps To Overhaul Environmental Regulations," *New York Times*, Feb. 10, 1995, p. A22.

15. For a good account of new global organizing activity in communications, see "Local Community and Public Access TV," *Clips*, Sept. 1994. (This is a publication of Vidéazimut, An International Coalition for Audiovisuals for Development and Democracy, 3690 Jeanne-Mance, bur. 430, Montreal, Quebec, Canada H2X 2K5).

16. For a sketching out of some of the grassroots work being done internationally, see "Resistance is Global," chap. 6 in Jeremy Brecher and Tim Costello, *Global Village or Global Pillage: Economic Reconstruction From the Bottom Up*, Boston: South End Press, 1994. For an interesting illustration of the possibilities of local renovation based on grassroots participation, see Peter Medoff and Holly Sklar, *Streets of Hope: The Fall and Rise of an Urban Neighborhood*, Boston: South End Press, 1994.

17. Interview with Bishop Pedro Casadaliga, *Latinamerica Press*, April 6, 1995, p. 5.

Index

dren's programs, 8, 178, 180, 181; in Europe, 175, 177-78, 179, 216, 218-19, 221; loosened regulation of, 178, 180-81, 220; public, 20, 173-74, 176, 177, 218-22, 225; sex and violence in, 7, 178-79. *See also* radio; television

Broder, David, 189-205

Brookings Institution, 43, 192, 195

Brown, Jerry, 191, 193, 205

Brown, Ron, 76

Browne, Malcolm, 86, 87

Braeutigam, Ronald, 32

Bunce, Richard, 175

Burt, Sir Cyril, 87, 89

Bush, George, 16, 25, 197, 204, 257; coded racism of, 87, 91, 191.

Bush administration, 160, 207-12

C

Cambodia, 109, 127, 170

Camdessus, Michel, 55

Canada, 47, 112, 200, 252

capital flight, 24, 243

Capital Foundation, 170

Cárdenas, Cuauhtemoc, 47

Carter administration, 45-46, 117, 118, 143, 185, 202-3, 254

Casadaliga, Pedro, 237

Cassen, Bernard, 119

Cavanagh, John, 8

CBS, 101, 145, 260

Central America. *See* El Salvador; Guatemala; Nicaragua; Panama

Central Intelligence Agency (CIA), 81, 249

Chamorro, Violeta, 118, 134-35, 160

Chavez, Lydia, 187, 188

Cheney, Dick, 191, 207

Cheney, Lynne, 241

"Chicago boys," 35, 36, 57

Chicago School of Economics, 34-42, 232

children's television, 8, 178, 180, 181

Chile, 52, 58, 69, 232, 233; Chicago School of Economics and, 35, 36,

232; coup in, 82, 141, 232; economic "reform" in, 22-23, 54; state terror in, 35, 36, 54, 57, 118, 232.

China, 127, 231, 233

Chomsky, Noam, 19, 83, 162, 197, 205, 224, 225

Christian, Shirley, 188

Christianity, 132

Churchill, Ward, 105

cigarette industry, 4, 240

class warfare, viii-ix, 76

Clinton, Bill, 25, 28, 77, 112, 115, 247, 250, 251

Club of Rome, 45

Coase, Ronald, 41

Cobban, Richard, 106-7

Coelho, Tony, 74, 75-76

Cohen, Richard, 94

Cold War, 33, 57, 87, 233

"collateral damage," 98

Columbus, Christopher, 104

commodification, 3, 6-10

Commoner, Barry, 45

Communications Act of 1934, 173, 174

comparative advantage, theory of, 54-55

competition, 21, 48

Contadora agreement, 147

Cooper, Richard, 34

Corporation for Public Broadcasting, 221-22

Corradi, Juan, 184

corruption, 23, 75, 77, 80

CovertAction Quarterly, 223

crime, 9, 82, 201

Cuba, 60, 140, 143, 254

D

D'Aubuisson, Roberto, 186-87

death squads, 6, 65, 126, 240

Deaver, Michael, 210

Deep Dish Network, 226-27

de Leon Carpio, Ramiro, 116

I

India, 116, 161, 162
Indonesia, 162-3, 239; invasion of East Timor by, 103, 104, 170-71; U.S.-supported dictatorship in, 53, 56, 141-42.
"infant industries," 48
Ingersoll, Robert Green, 132
Inikori, J. E., 106
Institute for Policy Studies, 67, 258
Inter-American Development Bank (IADB), 51-52, 125, 148
international financial institutions (IFIs), 54, 58. *See also* Inter-American Development Fund; International Monetary Fund; World Bank
"internationalism," 28-29
International Monetary Fund (IMF), viii, 22, 51, 57-58, 60, 125, 265; power wielded by, 114, 116; U.S. domination of, 125.
International Public Affairs Consultants (IPAC), 92
Internet, 10, 227-28, 241
In These Times, 223
"investment theory" of politics, 75-76
Iran, 136, 207
Iran-Contra affair, 196, 200-201
Iraq, 127, 128, 135-36, 160. *See also* Persian Gulf War
Irvine, Reed, 188, 263
Israel, 93, 128, 143, 208
Italy, 6, 177, 240

J

Jackson, Brooks, 75-76
Jackson, Jesse, 76, 92
Jamaica, 112, 123-24
Japan, 5, 136; economic policies of, 27, 46, 48, 125; as trade rival of U.S., 28, 128, 136.
Jensen, Arthur, 87, 89-91
Jensen, Michael, 41
jobs, 25-30. *See also* unemployment

Johnson, Lyndon, 108, 176
"joint venture" model, 50-51
Judeo-Christian tradition, 131-32

K

Kahn, Herman, 97
KAL 007 episode, 183-84, 259
Kaldor, Nicholas, 41
Kamin, Leon, 89
Kantako, M'Banna, 224-25
Karnow, Stanley, 109
Keating, Charles, 39, 74
Kellner, Douglas, 210-11
Kelly, John, 208
Kennan, George, 252
Kennedy administration, 108
Keyes, William, 91, 92, 194
Khmer Rouge, 127, 170
Kirkpatrick, Jeane, 61, 240
Kitson, Sir Frank, 79-80
Knight, Frank, 34
Koning, Hans, 104
Kornbluh, Peter, 200, 205
Krauthammer, Charles, 189, 190, 196, 197
Kuwait, 212. *See also* Persian Gulf War

L

Latin America, 56, 118; bailouts in, 22-23; capital flight from, 24, 243; "denationalization" of elites in, 124-25; growing inequality in, 52-53, 56, 58-59; privatization in, 20, 22-24; U.S. support for state terrorism in, 50-51, 83, 118, 126, 139, 140, 141, 253. *See also* names of individual countries
Latin American Congress of Relatives of the Disappeared, 143-44
Latin American Studies Association, 148
law and order, 79-83
Ledeen, Michael, 45
Lehrer, Jim, 30

LeMoyne, James, 185, 188
less developed countries (LDCs), 48-49, 124-29. *See also* Third World
Lewis, Anthony, 100, 109, 189
Lewis, H. Gregg , 35
Lewontin, Richard, 89
libraries, 10
Libya, 156-57, 170, 192, 198
Lichter, S. Robert, 45
Liebling, A. J., 168, 258
Limbaugh, Rush, 87, 216-17
Lincoln Institute for Research and Education, 92
Lipstadt, Deborah, 107
Los Angeles Times, 180, 186
Luce, Henry, 68, 258

M

Maastricht agreement, 111, 114
MacEwan, Arthur, 59
Maddison, Angus, 46
Madison, James, 73, 167-68, 257
Magdoff, Harry, 53
Magenheim, Ellen, 41
Major, John, 119
Malone, John, 263
"managed" trade, 125
Manley, Michael, 123-24
maquiladoras, 47, 55
Marable, Manning, 94-95
Marcos, Ferdinand, 56, 126, 197, 233
Marenvich, Yurii, 24
"market," the, vii, 163, 164, 175, 232, 233-37; defined, vii; and democracy, vii-ix, 111-19, 232; expansion of, 3-11, 233-34; and slavery, 106; and U.S. politics, 73-77. *See also* "free trade"; transnational corporations
Marshall, Thurgood, 194
McNamara, Robert, 141-42
McNeil-Lehrer News Hour, 222, 261
media, 15, 79, 82-83, 101, 103, 112, 134, 154, 156-57, 169, 180, 203-4; access to, 168-72; alleged liberal bias of, 67-69, 189, 246, 258; alter-native, 6, 214-15, 222-27; coverage of Third World elections by, 73, 117, 127, 148, 150, 185, 186, 188; and government lies, 183-88, 259; and human rights, 143-44, 145, 184-88, 254; ownership of, 67-69, 76, 168-69, 175, 214, 258, 260; and the Persian Gulf War, 100-101, 135, 197, 199, 204, 207-12, 248-49; and race, 85-87, 89-90, 93-95; strategies for democratizing, 213-29, 263-64. *See also* radio; television
Medici, Emilio, 56
Meese, Edwin, 79
Meislin, Richard, 188
Menem, Carlos, 23, 50, 56
"mercantilism," 29-30, 50
"mere gook rule," 109-10, 132-133
mergers, 39-41
Mexico, 21, 47, 52, 105, 236, 251; bailout of, 22, 265; Chiapas rebellion in, 227, 236; media coverage of, 52, 117; and NAFTA, 28-29, 55-56, 57; poor labor conditions in, 28, 47, 50, 55-56; Salinas government in, 23, 50, 52, 57, 117.
military spending, 27-28, 199, 251
Milken, Michael, 40
Miller, Merton, 41, 42
Missing in Action (MIAs), 108, 110, 135
Mitchell, John, 79
Mobutu, President, 126, 233
Mondale, Walter, 75
monopolies, 34-35
Monthly Review, 223
Morgan, James, 125
Mother Jones, 223
movies, 7, 179, 240
Ms. Magazine, 223, 258
Mueller, Dennis, 41
Mulroney, Brian, 112
Murdoch, Rupert, 177, 258, 260, 264
Murray, Charles, 85, 86
Murrow, Edward R., 176

museums, 9
Mussolini, Benito, 82

N

Nader, Ralph, 205, 263-64
NAFTA. *See* North American Free Trade Agreement
Namibia, 195, 208
Nasar, Sylvia, 51-52
Nation, The, 107, 223
National Endowment for the Humanities, 241
"national security" considerations, 146-47, 150
National Security States (NSSs), 53-54, 56-57, 58, 74
Nazis, 97-98, 100, 216
neoliberalism, 235-37. *See also* "free trade"
"new-class" theory, 65, 66-67, 69
New Deal, 77
Newly Industrializing Countries (NICs), 51
Newsweek, 90, 99, 103
New World Information Order (NWIO), 156
New World Order (NWO), 26, 28, 51, 58, 60, 119, 123, 127, 204, 236
New York Times, 95, 103, 107, 135, 180, 184, 209, 246, 249, 251, 259; and economic issues, 30, 37, 45, 46-51; and human rights violations, 143-44, 145, 184-88, 254; and party politics, 75, 76, 247; and race, 87, 94.
Nicaragua, 118, 147, 256, 258-59; Chamorro government in, 118, 134-35, 160; contra war against, 6, 148, 171, 190, 256, 257; elections in, 117, 127, 149-50, 257; hypocritical denunciations of, 65, 148-49, 186, 255, 256; media coverage of, 171, 186, 190, 192, 197, 258-59; U.S. response to reforms in, 60, 112, 117, 126, 148-49; U.S.

support for Somoza dynasty in, 117, 140, 149, 256; World Court judgment won by, 127, 128, 160, 208, 251.
Nixon, Richard, 79, 80, 81, 110, 176
Nobel Prize in economics, 41-42, 54
Noriega, Manuel, 197
"normalization," 97-101
North, Oliver, 197, 200, 201
North American Free Trade Agreement (NAFTA), 25, 28-29, 50, 114, 232; benefits in, for transnational corporations, 21, 28; leading economists' support for, 54-57; media coverage of, 30, 112, 199-200; widespread public opposition to, 112, 192-93.
North American Indians, 104-5
Novak, Michael, 45, 61-69, 245, 246
nuclear terrorism, 155
Nunn, Frederic, 141
NWO. *See* New World Order

O

Olin Foundation, 33
Olympic Games, 6-7, 240
Orme, William, 200
Owen, Bruce, 32
Oxfam, 148

P

Pacifica, 224
Pakistan, 149
Palestinian Liberation Organization (PLO), 93
Panama, 134; U.S. invasion of, 127, 128, 133, 134, 191, 207, 208.
Paper Tiger TV, 226
Parker, Jay, 91-92, 194
Parry, Robert, 191, 200, 205
Passell, Peter, 44-51
PBS, 225, 263
Pearson, Drew, 189
Peattie, Lisa, 97-98
Peltzman, Sam, 38-39

PEMEX, 21
Pendleton, Clarence, 92, 93
People for the Ethical Treatment of Animals (PETA), 100
Perdue, William, 153-57
Perry, James, 91
Persian Gulf War, 25, 98, 127, 128, 133, 135, 157, 207-12, 248-49; media coverage of, 100-101, 135, 197, 199, 204, 207-12, 248-49; one-sided slaughter in, 133, 211, 248-49.
Peru, 47, 56, 105
Phelan, John M., 228
Philadelphia Inquirer (PI), 94, 101, 189
Philippines, 47, 50, 53, 54, 56, 233. *See also* Marcos, Ferdinand
Pinochet, Augusto, 23, 35, 126, 233
playgrounds, 9
Plotkin, Robert, 93
pluralism, 216
PM, 107
Poland, 150, 170
Political Action Committees (PACs), 74
"politically correct," 103-8, 164 defined, 248
Popieluszko, Jerzy, 187
popular culture, 8
Porter, General Robert, 141
prisons, 81-82, 247-48
privatization, 3, 9, 19-24, 114, 231
"product placement," 7
Progressive, The, 223
prostitution, 5-6
public enterprise, 19-24. *See also* broadcasting, public
Pyles, Craig, 186

Q

Qadaffi, Muammar el-, 156, 170, 198
Quayle, Dan, 202

R

racism, 85-91, 98-99, 132; in "mere gook rule," 109-10, 132-33.
radio; alternative, 6, 223-25; talk shows on, 87, 216-17. *See also* broadcasting
Radio Zinzine, 224
Rae, Bob, 112
Rayack, Elton, 36, 37
Reader's Digest, 223
Reagan, Ronald, 61, 79, 81, 111, 198, 200; business support for, 15, 75, 111; coded racism of, 87, 91; foreign policies of, 134, 143, 153, 191, 192, 198, 200; weakening of federal agencies by, 15, 80.
Reagan administration, 15-17, 28, 76, 183-84; corruption in, 35, 77, 80; and savings and loan industry, 15-17.
"recolonization" model, 50
Rees, Albert, 35
"reform," 19, 24, 56-57; altered meaning of, 51.
regulation, 13-20, 37-38
Rehnquist, William, 194
Reich, Robert, 29
reparations, 159-64
Republican Party, 76-77, 80, 87, 91, 93
"reverse discrimination," 163
revisionist history, 164
Ricardo, David, 31
Rios Montt, General, 143
Rio Sumpul massacre, 186
Robinson, Joan, 41, 54
Robinson, Ronald, 124, 125
Rogers, Joel, 75
Rogin, Leo, 31
Romero, Oscar, 186, 187
Ronfeldt, David, 227
Rose, Steven, 89
Rosenberg, Susan, 81-82
Rosenthal, A. M., 153
Ross, Leonard, 44-45
Rostow, Walt W., 233

116-18; and "free trade," 4, 48-49, 54, 57-60. *See also* Latin America, elections in; human rights; Latin America; less developed countries; state terrorism

Thomas, Clarence, 87, 91-92, 93, 194

Time, 90, 223

TNCs. *See* transnational corporations

Tobin, James, 27

Torres, Alejandrina, 81-82

torture, 56, 139, 245; condoning of, 36, 65, 118, 139.

transnational corporations (TNCs), 60, 234-35; and "free trade," 28, 48, 56; growing power of, 128-29, 234; and state-terrorist regimes, 57.

Tobin, James, 43-44

trickle-down theory, 43-46

Trilateral Commission, 227

Truman, Harry, 82

Tsongas, Paul, 193

Tsurumi, Yoshi, 30

Turkey, 150, 170

U

Ubico, Jorge, 142

unemployment, 26-28, 29-30, 55; "natural rate" of, 35-36.

Union of Concerned Scientists, 41

Union of Radical Political Economists, 34

unions, 30, 35, 113, 150, 170, 231, 232, 239

United Fruit Company, 142

United Nations, 49, 128, 160, 208

Uruguay, 22, 23, 118

U.S. Army School of the Americas, 140

U.S. Conference of Mayors, 26

V

Vietnam, 83, 104, 249; postwar, 127, 131, 135, 159-60, 162-63, 251.

Vietnam War, 43, 104, 108-10, 117, 132-33, 140, 162, 171, 176

Village Voice, 220, 222

von Hayek, Friedrich, 41, 42

Von Mises, Ludwig, 62

Vreeland, Diane, 9

W

Wade, Robert, 51

wages, 50, 56

Wallace, DeWitt, 68, 258

Wall Street Journal, viii, 4, 37, 91, 112, 116, 188, 246, 265-66

Washington Post, 30, 45, 94, 95, 144, 180, 189, 210

Watergate, 81

Watkins, Mel, 119

Watt, James, 77

welfare, 87, 91, 202

West, Cornel, 94-95

White, Robert, 188

Whitehead, Deborah Dafoe, 202

Whittle Communications, 8

Will, George, 189, 190

Williams, Eddie, 195

Williams, Walter, 94, 95

"wise use" movement, 235

World Anticommunist League, 92, 187

World Bank, 57-59, 59, 114, 125

World Court, 127, 128, 160, 208, 251

Wright, Jim, 74

Y

Yeltsin, Boris, 126

Z

Zaire, 233

Z Magazine, 223

ABOUT THE AUTHOR

Edward S. Herman is an economist and media analyst, Professor Emeritus of Finance at the Wharton School, University of Pennsylvania, a columnist for *Z Magazine,* and an active writer.

Other Books by Edward Herman

· The Great Society Dictionary (1968) ·

· Atrocities in Vietnam: Myths and Realities (1971) ·

· The Washington Connection and Third World Fascism*
(with Noam Chomsky, 1979) ·

· After the Cataclysm* (with Noam Chomsky, 1979) ·

· Corporate Control, Corporate Power (1981) ·

· The Real Terror Network:
Terrorism in Fact and Propaganda* (1982) ·

· Demonstration Elections* (with Frank Brodhead, 1984) ·

· Manufacturing Consent (with Noam Chomsky, 1988) ·

· Hope and Folly: The United States and UNESCO 1945-1985
(with William Preston, Jr. and Herbert I. Schiller, 1989) ·

· The "Terrorism" Industry: The Experts and Institutions That
Shape Our View of Terror (with Gerry O'Sullivan, 1990) ·

· Beyond Hypocrisy* (1992) ·

*Available from South End Press. To order with a Visa or MasterCard, please call 1-800-533-8478. Or write to South End Press for a complete catalog and order information.

ABOUT SOUTH END PRESS

South End Press is a nonprofit, collectively-run book publisher with over 180 titles in print. Since our founding in 1977, we have tried to meet the needs of readers who are exploring, or are already committed to the politics of radical social change.

Our goal is to publish books that encourage critical thinking and constructive action on the key political, cultural, social, economic and ecological issues shaping life in the United States and in the world. In this way, we hope to give expression to a wide diversity of democratic social movements and to provide an alternative to the products of corporate publishing.

Through the Institute for Social and Cultural Change, South End Press works with other political media projects—*Z Magazine*; Speak Out!, a speakers' bureau; and the Publishers' Support Project—to expand access to information and critical analysis.

For a free book catalog or information about our membership program—which offers two free books and a 40 percent discount on all titles—please write to South End Press, 116 Saint Botolph Street, Boston, MA 02115, or call 1-800-533-8478.